Latin American Politics

New Horizons in Comparative Politics

edited by Howard J. Wiarda

:W HORIZONS IN
PARATIVE POLITICS

Latin American Politics

A New World of Possibility

HOWARD J. WIARDA

Professor of Political Science
University of Massachusetts/Amherst

Professor of National Security Policy
National War College

Research Fellow, Center for Strategic
and International Studies
Washington, D.C.

Wadsworth Publishing Company

I⟨T⟩P™ **An International Thomson Publishing Company**

Belmont • Albany • Bonn • Boston • Cincinnati • Detroit • London • Madrid • Melbourne
Mexico City • New York • Paris • San Francisco • Singapore • Tokyo • Toronto • Washington

Editorial Assistant: Jennifer Dunning
Production Editor: Michelle Filippini
Print Buyer: Diana Spence
Permissions Editor: Jeanne Bosschart
Designer: Andrew Ogus
Cover Photograph: Sue Cunningham/Tony Stone Images
Compositor: Wadsworth Digital Productions
Printer: Malloy Lithography, Inc.

For more information, contact Wadsworth Publishing Company:

Wadsworth Publishing Company
10 Davis Drive
Belmont, California 94002, USA

International Thomson Editores
Campos Eliseos 385, Piso 7
Col. Polanco
11560 México D.F. México

International Thomson Publishing Europe
Berkshire House 168-173
High Holborn
London, WC1V 7AA, England

International Thomson Publishing GmbH
Königswinterer Strasse 418
53227 Bonn, Germany

Thomas Nelson Australia
102 Dodds Street
South Melbourne 3205
Victoria, Australia

International Thomson Publishing Asia
221 Henderson Road
#05-10 Henderson Building
Singapore 0315

Nelson Canada
1120 Birchmount Road
Scarborough, Ontario
Canada M1K 5G4

International Thomson Publishing Japan
Hirakawacho Kyowa Building, 3F
2-2-1 Hirakawacho
Chiyoda-ku, Tokyo 102, Japan

Library of Congress Cataloging-in-Publication Data

Wiarda, Howard J.
     Latin American politics : a new world of possibility / Howard J. Wiarda
        p.   cm. — (New horizons in comparative politics)
     Includes bibliographical references and index.
     ISBN 0-534-20988-2
        1. Latin America—Politics and government. I. Title. II. Series.
  JL952.W5   1994
  320.98—dc20   94-18453

Brief Contents

✦

Contents

✦

CHAPTER 6
....

Latin America's Changing Political Culture 84

CHAPTER 7

The Power Structure: Economics, Class Relations, and Interest Groups 102

CHAPTER 8

Political Parties and Elections 132

CHAPTER 9

Government, the State, and State-Society Relations   151

CHAPTER 12
....
Conclusion   208

Preface

✦

Latin America, as well as the world environment in which it now finds itself, has changed so greatly in the past few years that it seems like an entirely new and very different area. The changes are so vast and so rapid that persons who knew the area before, or thought they did, now find it all but unrecognizable. The vast transformations under way also mean that all the books about Latin America are sadly out of date.

The changes taking place include a new emphasis on efficiency and dynamism, a new spirit in favor of democracy and human rights, vast social changes that are altering the way Latin America looks, and a new emphasis on governmental modernization and economic reform. The despair that prevailed in Latin America in the 1980s—the so-called lost decade when Central America was in flames and economies were crumbling—is now giving way to renewed confidence and growth.

At the international level, meanwhile, the collapse of the Soviet Union and of communism there and in Eastern Europe has also had profound implications. The former Soviet Union has greatly reduced its presence in Latin America, there is no longer a rival to the United States for influence in the region, and the Cold War is (mostly) over in the Western Hemisphere; the discord, conflict, and repeated interventions provoked by the Cold War have largely ended. Hence, from Chile and Argentina at the tip of South America to the U.S.-Mexican border, Latin America is transforming itself—or is being transformed—both inwardly and outwardly as it races to catch up and to prepare for the world of the twenty-first century.

This book tries to capture both the old and the new in Latin America, and to fill in the void in our texts on the area that the profound transformations of recent decades have produced. The author is, by training, a political scientist, but one with a strong grounding in the history, literature, and sociology of Latin America. Hence, the approach is interdisciplinary, weaving together geographic, historical, cultural, social, economic, and political factors—and combining these with a focus on change, the making of decisions, and Latin America's place and role in the international environment.

The book is organized in a logical and coherent fashion, moving from the general to the specific, that helps encourage and facilitate learning. The Introduction discusses Latin America's rising importance and the changes that have made it significant to us. Emphasizing Latin America's multicultural background, Chapter 2 discusses the indigenous, Iberian (Spanish and Portuguese), and African roots of Latin American society. Chapter 3 deals with the encounter of Europeans with the New World, including sections on geography, race relations, and the colonial system. Chapter 4 covers the independence struggles of the nineteenth century, including the persistence of traditional, semifeudal forms into the modern era. Chapter 5 completes the historical overview by tracing how, beginning in the 1930s, the old oligarchic order began to give way to industrialization, rapid social change, and new political movements.

Chapter 6 focuses on the political culture of Latin America—the values and ideas of the area—and how this is changing, while Chapter 7 addresses economic, social structure, and the change process. Chapters 8–10 deal with political institutions and processes: interest groups and political parties, government institutions and how they function, and how Latin American policy- making works, in contrast with policy-making in the United States. Chapter 11 examines Latin America's foreign affairs and its place in the world arena. Finally, Chapter 12 assesses the current changes and how far Latin America has come toward democracy and economic development.

With twelve chapters, the book can be used as a semester-long text, with each chapter and subject area receiving approximately one week's attention. Or, since it is written in an easy, readable style and can be digested in a week or two, it can be used as one text among several others in a course focusing on Latin America or on broader themes of Comparative Politics, the Developing Nations, Social Change, or the Third World. The book is designed to stand alone or to be used in conjunction with a companion text, such as *Latin American Politics and Development* (Boulder, CO: Westview Press), which provides a detailed country-by-country analysis, or *Through Latin American Eyes*, (forthcoming), which offers Latin American perspectives on their own region.

The book is designed for a general reading audience, including college students, the general reading public, government officials, and advanced high school students enrolled in a social studies course on Latin America or a Spanish class. Anyone who wants a good, solid, readable, and even entertaining book on Latin America will find this volume a useful introduction to the area and especially to the recent changes there.

Many groups and individuals have assisted me in the preparation of this book. Institutional support was provided by Harvard University's Center for International Affairs, the University of Massachusetts/Amherst, the Center for Strategic and International Studies (CSIS) in Washington, D.C., and the

National Defense University. All these agencies have served as my professional "home" in recent years, and I am grateful for their assistance. The following individuals have read and commented on the whole or parts of the manuscript: Iêda Siqueira Wiarda, Library of Congress; Dael Chapman, Amherst Regional High School; Michael J. Kryzanek, Bridgewater State College; Daniel Hellinger, Webster University; David Dent, Towson State University; Harvey F. Kline, University of Alabama. Irina Schwerzmann and Elizabeth Wesley served as especially efficient and pleasant typists. However, in the end, the author himself is responsible for the views expressed.

HOWARD J. WIARDA
Hawling Brook Farm

About the Author

✦

Howard J. Wiarda is Professor of Political Science at the University of Massachusetts/Amherst, Professor of National Security Policy at the National War College, and Research Fellow at the Center for Strategic and International Studies in Washington, D.C. His career has encompassed university teaching and research, think tank policy advising, and government service in the departments of State and Defense. He is the author recently of *Politics in Iberia*, *An Introduction to Comparative Politics*, *Latin American Politics and Development*, and *American Foreign Policy*.

1
✦
Introduction

Latin America lies so close to us—right on our southern border—and yet, we know so little about it. In fact, Latin America is even closer to us than that, because of the large migration recently to the United States of persons of Latin American origins. It is said sometimes that, because of the large influx of Latin Americans into the United States, we are becoming, in part, a Latin American nation. And no longer is this Hispanic immigration limited just to California, the American Southwest, or southern Florida. Instead, the Hispanic community is being dispersed throughout the United States, and it is increasingly playing a more prominent role in culture, economics, and politics. At some point in the 1990s, Hispanics will become the largest minority in the United States.

Extending from Mexico through Central and South America, Latin America spans 8 million square miles and contains nearly 400 million people. It is twice as large as Europe and slightly smaller than North America, but with a population nearly twice that of the United States. It contains immense resources, spectacular geography, amazing flora and fauna, and vast frontiers and open spaces. It has the world's largest river system (the Amazon) and the second highest mountain range (the Andes).

The largest country in South America is Brazil, which ranks fifth in the world in size, sixth in population, and tenth in the volume of economic production. Mexico, one quarter the size of the United States, has one third the U.S. population. Argentina, along with the American Midwest, the central plain in Russia, and the Australian interior, has one of the world's richest agricultural areas, the *pampa*, which stretches for over a thousand miles from the Atlantic Ocean to the Andes Mountains. It is said that one can drive a plow the entire distance over the *pampa* and never hit a rock. Other important Latin American nations that are now making it into the ranks of significant economic and political powers are Chile, Colombia, and Venezuela.

Latin America no longer consists of wholly backward and traditional nations. Latin America is not nearly as poor and underdeveloped as many African or South and Southeast Asian nations. On the other hand, Latin America is not as modern and developed as Europe, Japan, or North America either. Instead, Latin America occupies an intermediary category, neither fully traditional nor yet completely modern, neither wholly underdeveloped nor completely developed. Latin America also has distinct features that make it hard to fit into any of these categories. Nevertheless, when we measure economic development or literacy or health care or the percentage of persons in cities (urbanization), Latin America comes out in the middle. Therefore, we need a new category to classify Latin America. We can call the area "transitional" or "in-between" because it is neither wholly traditional nor fully modern. The World Bank, an international lending agency located in Washington, D.C. that assesses and promotes economic development, calls these Latin American countries "Newly Industrialized Countries," or NICs. They occupy intermediary positions between the developed nations and the undeveloped ones.

Although we tend to lump all thirty-four nations in the region together and call them "Latin America," there are vast differences between them. Some are making it and some are not; some are large, viable nations, while others are so small, resource-poor, and impoverished that their future seems bleak. Not all of them are even "Latin." In the *geographic area* that we call Latin America can be found former or current Dutch colonies (Suriname, Curaçao, Bonaire, Aruba, Saint Maarten), French colonies (Haiti, French Guyana, Guadeloupe, Martinique), and British colonies (Jamaica, Guyana, Belize, Trinidad and Tobago, Bermuda, St. Kitts, St. Lucia, Dominica, Grenada, The Bahamas, Barbados, St. Vincent, St. Christopher and Nevis, Antigua), as well as a U.S.-linked commonwealth (Puerto Rico) and territories (the Virgin Islands).

However, when we use the term *Latin America* in this book, we mean really *Latin* America: those countries that constitute the overwhelming bulk of the land area and its peoples and that were colonized, settled, and shaped by Spanish and Portuguese influences. This is not to say these other areas are not important or interesting; rather, we can only do so much in one book, and so we choose to look at *Latin* America as distinct from the British, French, Dutch, or U.S. enclaves. In addition, because of the common cultural, social, political, economic, and colonial background of the former Spanish and Portuguese colonies, our discussion can have a unity and coherence that it would not have if we discussed all these countries.

If Latin America contains all this variety and all these resources, and if at least some of the countries are doing quite well, the questions become: Why has Latin America never lived up to its potential? Why does it lag so far behind the United States? Why is it so disorganized and chaotic? Why are there so many coups and revolutions? Why does it produce so many drugs? Why are its economies still underdeveloped? In short, why can't Latin America get its act together? These are the questions that most bother Americans about Latin America. They are also the questions and themes running through this book for which we try to provide some answers.

Images of Latin America

One of the reasons we know so little about Latin America is that our attitudes about the region are often shaped by prejudices and stereotypes. These stereotypes derive from magazine cartoons, television programs, and movies, as well as from deeper-rooted prejudices. Magazine cartoons often portray the area as governed by comical, mustachioed men on horseback who gallop in and out of the presidential palace with frequent regularity. Old movies picture it as a land of fumbling incompetents, or of sleepy peasants taking siestas under palm trees, or of women with bananas or pineapples on their heads dancing gaily in the streets. More recently, the stereotype of the "sleepy peasant" has been replaced by that of the guerrilla fighter dressed in green fatigues and carrying an M16 on his or her shoulder. None of these stereotypes is accurate, and they certainly do not present a complete picture of an ever-more-complex area.

The problem goes deeper than magazine cartoons and movie stereotypes, however. It stems from an attitude that refuses to take Latin America seriously, that often treats Latin America disdainfully and condescendingly. We in the United States tend to look at the area paternalistically and at its people as little more than children. We believe that we, with our advanced society, should *teach* the Latin Americans how they should run their government and economy. Never do we consider that we North Americans could ever learn anything from them, only that they should learn from us. And in the process of our teaching things *to* Latin Americans rather than genuinely engaging them in a dialogue, we seldom bother to learn about *their* culture, society, or politics. As James Reston, the *New York Times* columnist, once wrote, "The United States will do anything for Latin America [give it aid, Peace Corps,

Alliance for Progress] except read about it." And, we should add, not just read about it, but seek to understand it.

This condescending attitude has deep historical roots. And it is hardly confined to North Americans; Europeans often hold such prejudices as well. For example, the great nineteenth-century German philosopher Hegel referred to Latin America as having "no history," by which he meant it had no culture, no commerce, no ideas, no industry, and no development. In the same vein, former Secretary of State Henry Kissinger once said, "The axis of the world begins in Moscow, flows through Berlin, Paris, and London, proceeds through New York and Washington, and ends in Tokyo." Omitted from Kissinger's list of important centers, of course, is not only all of Latin America but all of Africa and the rest of the Third World as well. But it is not just Hegel and Kissinger; our history, our social studies, and our liberal arts tradition all focus on Europe and North America to the exclusion of Latin America.

These biases have such widespread and deep historical roots that they are very difficult to change. They go back hundreds of years to the founding of the colonies in North America by England and Holland and in South America by Spain and Portugal. North America was largely settled by Protestant, Anglo, and Northern European countries like England and Holland, while Latin America was settled by Catholic, Hispanic, and Southern European countries: Spain and Portugal. Hence, the prejudices that North Americans hold about Latin America are not just political and economic; they also have regional, religious, cultural, and even racial origins. Just as Northern Europeans have long tended to look down on the "Latins" of Southern Europe, so North Americans have tended to scorn Latin America. Such prejudices are rarely expressed publicly anymore, but they are still there in the lingering suspicion that, somehow, the Latins "just aren't up to it."

This book seeks to go beyond these historical prejudices by examining Latin America on its own terms and in its own context. It seeks not to condemn Latin America for its supposed failings, but to explain Latin America in terms comprehensible to North Americans. It seeks to grapple with the issue of why Latin America is the way it is, why its development lagged behind U.S. growth, and what Latin America is now doing to overcome its historic underdevelopment.

Why Study Latin America?

There are many reasons for studying Latin America. The simplest and most obvious is that it's an interesting area, endlessly fascinating. By this we mean that it's interesting for its own sake—for its culture, its society, its politics, and its change processes. Usually, however, we pay attention to Latin America solely because of its impact on *us* in terms of drugs, immigration, or foreign policy concerns such as in Cuba or Central America. Those foreign policy issues are also a good reason to be interested in Latin America, as we see in a moment. But even prior to that, Latin America is simply an intriguing area worth studying just for that reason alone: how it works, why it sometimes doesn't work, and most importantly, why it is the way it is.

A second reason is the rising Hispanic influence and presence in the United States. It should be noted, first of all, that long before the British colonists settled in Virginia and Massachusetts Bay, the Spanish had begun to explore and settle the American South and Southwest; the city of Santa Fe, New Mexico, for instance, is far older than any of the thirteen colonies along the Atlantic seaboard. The oldest settlement in North America is not Jamestown, Plymouth, or New York but St. Augustine, Florida, founded by Spain in 1565. And in the 1840s in the war with Mexico, let it not be forgotten, the United States took away fully one third of Mexico's national territory.

While Latin America was settled before North America and its settlements were initially larger and more prosperous, the United States industrialized first and became richer and more powerful. Latin America remained poor and was cast in a *dependency* position in its relations with Western Europe and North America. Often these stronger and richer nations—Spain and Portugal initially, then England and France, and eventually the United States—exploited Latin America's natural resources and its powerlessness for their own advantage. The considerable resources of Latin America were often drained away to these other nations while Latin America remained poor. The history of Latin America's relations with the outside world has often been one of victimization and forced subservience.

More recently, the United States and Mexico as well as the nations of Central America and the Caribbean have become far more *interdependent*. Our economies, our foreign policies, our societies, our drug problems, terrorism, trade, investment, and so on, all point to increased interdependence. Part of this new interdependence involves the massive influx of Latin American workers into the United States. This influx no longer just involves seasonal workers (mainly males) who work in the United States for a few months and then return home. Instead, it increasingly includes whole families, of all classes, whose intent is to stay for a long term or maybe permanently in the United States. While this large influx of Hispanics into the United States has contributed enormously to our economy and to a more diversified North American culture, it has also produced strains in school districts, law enforcement, and social welfare programs. These pressures have been particularly pronounced in the American Southwest, but they are by no means limited to that area anymore.

A third reason to study Latin America is to gain insight into another culture that we do not understand very well. When they think about culture, most people think of literature and art. But in this book, the term *culture*

refers not only to literature and art but also to political ideas and ways of be-
having, to what is called the culture of politics or of society or of economics.
Thus, we seek to understand why Latin Americans do things the way they
do, why they act the way they do, and how this is now all changing under the
impact of recent modernization.

Fourth, Latin America is interesting because it presents us with a case of
development that both parallels and differs from our own. On the one hand,
North and Latin America comprise two roughly equivalent parts of the
Western Hemisphere. Both contain wide open spaces, abundant minerals,
and rich land, and both were settled at about the same time by European
powers. On the other hand, even with these basic similarities, the history and
development of North America and Latin America have gone in fundamentally dissimilar directions. Why is that so? How could two areas that are so
similar in their backgrounds be so different in their paths of development?

A fifth reason for studying Latin America is that it has become increasingly important to us, both commercially and strategically. We now sell more
to Latin America than we ever did before, our imports (including such necessary and strategic elements as natural gas, aluminum, and oil) come increasingly from Latin America, and through immigration we are increasingly
importing our labor supply from Latin America. Mexico has become our second-largest trading partner, behind only Canada and ahead of Japan. Latin
America's emerging middle class has increasingly become a market for our
products; at the same time, many U.S. factories (for producing shirts, clothing, staples, cars, appliances, even major league baseballs!) have relocated to
Latin America to take advantage of less expensive labor. On all kinds of levels, the U.S. and the Latin American economies have become increasingly
interdependent.

At the strategic level, Latin America has also become important to us.
Ever since the Monroe Doctrine of 1823, the United States has tried to ex-
clude hostile foreign powers from gaining a foothold in the Western Hemisphere. In the nineteenth century, that meant actions directed against such
European powers as France, Spain, Great Britain, and Imperial (precommu-
nist) Russia. During World Wars I and II, it meant efforts to neutralize the
sizable German colonies in various Latin American countries and to repel
German political and military incursions into the area. After World War II,
during the era of the Cold War, it meant concern with Soviet influences in
Latin America and at times vigorous action to remove or eliminate governments and movements hostile to U.S. interests.

But now that the Soviet Union has collapsed and the Cold War has ended,
we shall have to rethink U.S. strategic interests in Latin America. Are they
drugs, immigration, human rights, democracy, the environment, or other interests? Posing the question in this way gives us a handle on the sixth major
reason to study Latin America. With the Cold War over, U.S. foreign policy
is moving away from an emphasis on strategic issues (the Soviet or Castro-

communist threat) and toward an emphasis on what are called the "new-agenda" items: drugs, immigration, trade, democracy, human rights, and the environment. These are precisely the issues that are surfacing in U.S.–Latin American relations. In fact, in Latin America more than any other area the new-agenda foreign policy issues are most strongly present: drugs in Mexico and Colombia, human rights in El Salvador, environmental damage in the Brazilian Amazon, massive immigration from the entire region, and so on. Latin America provides us with a wonderful "living laboratory" to study all the newer, post–Cold War foreign policy issues.

Latin America is a living laboratory in another sense, one that gives us a seventh reason for studying the area. Of the thirty-four countries in the region, twenty share a common Hispanic (Spanish or Portuguese) background. That means a common colonial background, a common religion (Catholicism), a common language (Spanish or Portuguese; the two are close), a common culture, and many common social and political institutions and practices. Within this common background, however, we have had a great variety of types of governments: numerous military as well as civilian regimes, regimes of the left as well as regimes of the right, liberal governments as well as authoritarian ones. Hence, within Latin America, we have a group of countries with common backgrounds but very different histories and political systems.

Given all the common features, what accounts for the distinct outcomes and the distinct character of each of the countries? Is it geography, is it the social or racial makeup of the different countries, is it economic resources, or is it the product of historical development? Almost like a chemistry lab, Latin America provides a well-defined area where we can see the common features of the several countries while also trying to explain systematically the differences between or among them—as well as the ways they differ from the United States. Explaining such similarities and differences is precisely what the political science field of comparative politics is all about, and for the reasons given there is no better area to do such a comparison than Latin America.

The final reason the study of Latin America is so interesting has to do with developing versus developed countries. We often divide the world into First World countries (advanced and capitalistic—the United States, Japan, Western Europe), Second World (communist states—now disintegrating or undergoing fundamental change), and Third World (underdeveloped countries). With the collapse of the Soviet Union as the leading communist state, all these categories require rethinking, but let us leave that issue aside for now. The fact still is that the U.S.-Mexican border is one of the few places on the globe where a First World country bumps directly up against a Third World country (to say nothing of the rest of Central America and the Caribbean). The flow of people, tourists, and investments, as well as drugs and a host of other goods and services, across this vast, often-unpoliced First World–Third World border gives rise to both immense conflicts and widespread cooperation. It also provides a marvelous vantage point for look-ing at the complex interrelations between the developed and the developing countries.

The above discussion indicates that Latin America is an interesting and fascinating area. There are many themes that are worth thinking and reading about, and analyzing. In the next section, however, we argue that not only is it a fascinating region, but that *it is also in our interest* to devote more atten-tion to the area.

Latin America in the Post–Cold War Era

The astounding events of 1989–91—the transformation of Eastern Europe and the collapse of the Moscow-centered defense arrangement of communist countries called the Warsaw Pact, the disintegration of the former Soviet Union, the fall of the Berlin Wall and the reunification of Germany, the fur-ther integration of the European Economic Community (EEC), and the emergence of Japan as a global economic power—force us not only to re-think our foreign policy in these areas of the globe but also to reorder our priorities among the world's regions. In this reconsideration, Latin America begins to look as if it will be a higher priority.

Latin America has not historically been thought of as among the United States' top foreign policy priorities. Rather, the Soviet Union has long occu-pied that position, followed by Europe, the Middle East, Japan, China, and Southeast Asia (Vietnam). Only after these higher regional priorities would Latin America be considered, vying at times with Africa for last place. Latin America was both secondary and derivative: When the Cold War rivalry with the Soviet Union extended to Latin America, then we also paid it attention; the rest of the time, we largely ignored it. We have not been very much in-terested in Latin America in itself, except when the Cold War forced us to turn our attention to the area.

U.S. foreign policy in Latin America traditionally has reflected these low priorities, alternating between indifference or "benign neglect" (which often proved to be not so benign) and dramatic, often military interventions. Never did the United States develop the mature, positive policy toward Latin America that has long been sorely needed. In recent years, now that the problems in Central America (specifically, El Salvador and Nicaragua) are off the front burner of policy issues, we are again reverting to a policy of benign neglect. Latin America is not only off the front burner, it may be off the stove altogether.

But the recent changes in the world force us to rethink our historical in-difference and condescension toward Latin America. The newer changes should lead us to elevate Latin America in importance rather than to dimin-ish it. This is not some mushy, romantic notion but one based on hard-headed realism. It is in the United States' *interest* to pay more attention to Latin America. Let us briefly review our other foreign policy priorities and see, by process of elimination, why this is so.

Our former enemy and superpower rival, the Soviet Union, has disintegrated. True, we still need to be concerned about the thousands of nuclear weapons in Russia, and we want Russia to develop into a democratic and prosperous country. However, the reality is that the formerly powerful Soviet Union has split up into fifteen feuding, chaotic, inefficient ministates, most of which have Third World–level economies and pose no real threat to us. We also want Eastern Europe to succeed, but that region will similarly be torn by ethnic, religious, political, nationalistic, and economic strife as far into the future as anyone can see; in any case, Eastern Europe will be mainly a Western European (chiefly German) project, and not so much ours.

The more strongly unified European Community (EC) is a major actor, a wealthy group with whom we have strong cultural ties, and a strategic ally. But it is becoming more independent from us and throwing up protectionist walls to keep out U.S.-made products. Similarly, in Asia: Japan has erected immense trade barriers that keep out American products and, at the same time, is putting together an Asian trading bloc similar to that of Europe that will also become harder to penetrate. China has more than a billion people, one fourth of humankind, but it is a very poor and disorganized country that has not proved as attractive as expected to American business investors. It is said of China that it "is the land of the future—and always will be."

In the Middle East, the United States has two fundamental interests: Israel and oil. However, the oil is ten thousand miles away in the midst of an often hostile region; moreover, substantial oil reserves exist in the Western Hemisphere—specifically, in Latin America. Meanwhile, the Arab-Israeli conflict is being negotiated and may be on the way to resolution; in any case, without a Soviet presence in the Middle East, the United States has less strategically to worry about. And while Africa is an interesting, rapidly changing area, and we have roots there, it remains geographically distant and politically unstable, and we have very little trade with the area.

That leaves Latin America as one of the few areas remaining for a *positive, cooperative, mutually beneficial* relationship. In the past, U.S. policy in Latin America has been negative and reactive, seeking to deny the area or any country in the region to the Soviets. "No second Cubas"—no revolutionary Marxist-Leninist regimes allied with the Soviet Union, sponsoring guerrilla activities in neighboring countries, and allowing their territory to be used as a base for Soviet activities or nuclear missiles—sums up the policy. But with the Russians no longer a threat or even much of a presence (currently reducing their presence in the area and even pulling out of Cuba), we now have a chance to put our relations with Latin America on a positive, proactive basis for the first time.

Instead of thinking of threats, therefore (for example, subversion, Castro-communists, the Soviet Union), let us begin to think of Latin America in terms of opportunities. Particularly as compared with other areas in this post–Cold War era, a positive and forward-looking U.S. policy in the hemisphere is now called for. Such a stronger Western Hemisphere orientation in terms of our overall foreign policy goals stands between the older U.S. role of global policeman, which we cannot afford and do not want, and a retreat into isolationism, which is unrealistic and self-defeating.

What are those positive ingredients that now recommend Latin America to us—especially given the problems inherent in other global areas?

1. **Democracy**. Latin America is now more democratic and can rightfully claim a better human rights situation than *ever* before. U.S. relations with the area can thus go forward based on a community of more or less *democratic* nations with common interests in representative government, human rights, and the rule of law, thus resolving many of the United States' hemispheric problems of the past in having to deal with either right-wing authoritarian or left-wing Marxist-Leninist regimes.

2. **Complementarity of interests**. The United States has heavy industry and manufacturing, advanced technology and know-how, abundant capital, and a highly educated population. Latin America has a wealth of natural resources, abundant labor supplies, and growing markets; moreover, it is close by. One would have to be blind not to see a future common market in these complementary factors—particularly as other regions shut the United States out, dry up, or otherwise prove less attractive.

3. **Oil**. Mexico, Venezuela, Colombia, Ecuador, and, we are now finding out, other areas in the hemisphere all have large and largely untapped oil deposits. It is much easier to ensure and defend petroleum supplies in these areas, as well as the trade routes across the Caribbean, than in Kuwait, Saudi Arabia, and the Persian Gulf.

4. **Interdependence**. What we earlier called the new-agenda issues—drugs, immigration, trade, debt, pollution, the environment—are all foreign policy *and* domestic issues. They are important in our international relations with other countries, but they also have a major impact internally on U.S. society. And all of these newer issues resonate most clearly and loudly in our relations with Latin America. Our borders have become porous borders, and in recent years millions of Latin Americans have migrated to the United States. Moreover, we are beginning to realize that we in the United States are directly affected by the poverty, malnutrition, and overpopulation of Latin America, in the form of massive immigration and the transfer of Latin

America's problems to our shores. In addition to the immorality of so much Latin American poverty next to so much North American wealth, we are starting to see that we help solve *our* domestic and foreign policy problems by helping Latin America to solve its problems. It is not only in Latin America's but also the United States' interest to have stable, democratic, prosperous, socially just nations in the region. In the American Southwest, California, and Florida, and increasingly in other areas, the interdependence of the United States and Latin America is recognized; it is now time to acknowledge these facts on a national level.

5. **Mexico**. Mexico is a special case. It lies right on our southern flank, it shares a 2,000-mile border with the United States, and we have long taken its stability for granted. But social, economic, and political pressures are pulling at Mexico. A destabilized Mexico would be disastrous, sending millions of Mexicans streaming north across the border and causing immense domestic and foreign policy problems for us. In this sense, with the collapse of the Soviet Union, Mexico (along with Japan) may be the most important country in the world to us. In terms of trade, tourism, investment, oil, natural gas, water supplies, pollution, labor supplies, and drugs, we are so interconnected with Mexico that, in effect, the North American Free Trade Agreement (NAFTA)—encompassing Canada, Mexico, and the United States— had already come into existence long before it was approved as a formal treaty. We therefore have an immense, even vital stake in a stable and prosperous Mexico—and by extension a stable and prosperous Central America, Caribbean, and South America—because an unstable and poverty-ridden Latin America will be a continuing problem for us as well as for them. Our interests and Latin American interests are now inexorably interlocked.

6. **Open markets**. Just about all the Latin American economies are presently undergoing major policy transformations, toward greater rationality, streamlining, efficiency, and privatization or open markets. Certainly, Latin America is now an easier and more buoyant market, especially for the United States, than the republics of the former Soviet Union, China, or Eastern Europe. Mexico has opened its markets *unilaterally* to U.S. investment; throughout the hemisphere, other countries are doing the same as they clamor to work out free trade agreements with the United States. Certainly, in Latin America (unlike Japan and East Asia), the United States will have a far more open-market system in which to operate.

These are not visionary or purely wishful notions. Rather, the considerations and recommendations offered here are based on new realities in both the United States and Latin America. It is time that we come to grips and deal positively with these new trends in the hemisphere. The logic of elevating in importance and dealing with Latin America on a positive, forward-looking, mutually beneficial basis seems compelling. With the Cold War over and other global areas sometimes hostile or shut off to us, the rationale for taking a new look at Latin America and for raising that area to a higher level on our list of priorities is powerful. When this list of hard-headed reasons for studying Latin America is added to our earlier list of more scholarly reasons, it makes a strong case indeed.

The year 1992 marked the 500th anniversary of Columbus's epic discovery of and encounter with the New World of the Western Hemisphere. As we continue to think about the meaning of these events, it is appropriate also, and potentially greatly advantageous, to revive the idea of a Western Hemispheric community of democratic nations, encompassing both North and South America, and to reassert a hemispheric policy that brings us closer together. Of course, we will also want to have good relations with other areas. But now is the time to put Latin America at or near the top of the list.

2
✦

The Indigenous, Iberian, and African Background

We usually think of Columbus "discovering" America in 1492. Columbus *did* discover the New World—for Europe! But at the time of Columbus's epic voyage, the importance of which should not be underestimated, the Americas were already populated by millions of persons. They did not think of themselves as being "discovered." Rather, they constituted the indigenous or native peoples of the Americas. They had migrated across the Bering Strait connecting Asia with Alaska thousands of years earlier. Gradually, they had dispersed and settled throughout North America, Middle America (the Caribbean islands, Mexico, and Central America), and all the way into South America. Long before the Europeans arrived, these native peoples had also "discovered" America.

Latin America consists of three major racial or ethnic strains: the indigenous peoples whom Columbus, thinking he was in Asia near India, mistakenly called "Indians"; the Iberians (Spanish and Portuguese colonists from Europe); and Africans who were brought in as slaves and servants. These three ethnic elements have mingled uneasily in Latin America ever since. Later, other groups (Chinese, Japanese, Middle Easterners, North Americans, other Europeans) were added to the Latin American "melting pot." Although these diverse groups have been assimilated and racially integrated to some extent, they also remain far apart in many ways. And yet, the pattern of race relations in Latin America differs markedly from that in the United States—at least as complex and maybe more interesting. It is worthwhile to understand Latin America's racial/ethnic makeup both as a contrast to our own and as an interesting subject in its own right. We examine each of the three major groups chronologically in the order of their arrival in the Americas.

The Indigenous Peoples

When Columbus and the Spanish explorers landed in the New World, the Americas were already inhabited by an estimated 30–35 million persons. Of these, only about 10 percent lived in North America; the rest lived in Latin America. In these numbers we discover one of the first clues to understanding the differences between the United States and Latin America: only a few million Indians in the former and over 30 million in the latter. Therefore, quite different issues of integration, assimilation, and race relations arose. These are differences not just of degree but of kind, and they strongly shaped the two distinct colonial experiences in the two parts of the Americas. Dealing with 30 million native peoples is a quite different task from dealing with 3 million.

Moreover, the Indians in Latin America were organized in a very different manner than were those in North America. In the United States, the early colonists found chiefly small, nomadic tribes of Indians that seldom numbered more than a few hundred. Latin America also had such small, nomadic groups. But in Latin America, the Aztec, Mayan, and Incan civilizations each numbered between 4 and 7 *million* persons, and each had sophisticated social, religious, and bureaucratic organization. The task of subduing small tribal units of a few hundred in North America was far easier than that of conquering these well-organized kingdoms of several million in Latin America. Furthermore, these differences in size had a major impact on how the Spaniards treated the Indians as compared with how the North American colonists did. It should be said that some parts of Latin America (Costa Rica, Chile, Argentina, Uruguay, Brazil, and Venezuela) had smaller numbers of Indians at the time of the conquest, and they were often organized in a more primitive way.

The larger Indian civilizations in Latin America, in addition, were quite advanced as compared to the North American tribes. In Latin America, these civilizations had developed philosophy, mathematics, religion, astrology, agriculture, and sports. They had elaborate trade and communications systems covering thousands of miles. They had quite sophisticated political systems, armies, divisions of labor, organizational structures, class systems, and ways of distinguishing between warriors, priests, and government officials.

They produced impressive art, crafts, designs, and construction—such as the pyramids and cities in Mexico and the road network and the mountaintop city of Machu Picchu in Peru. In all these areas, the indigenous peoples of Latin America were way ahead of the tribes of North America.

These three factors—overall numbers, size of the indigenous groups, and level of civilization—dictated also how the Spaniards dealt with native peoples, as compared with their North American counterparts. In the United States, we mainly dealt with our "Indian problem" by shooting the Indians, pushing them farther west, or eventually confining them to reservations. In Latin America, however, there were far too many Indians for them to be dealt with in this way. The Spaniards could not have killed all the Indians even if they had wanted to, and there were far too many (far outnumbering the Spaniards) for them to be herded onto reservations. So the Spanish tactic was to capture or kill the leadership (Montezuma in Mexico, Atahualpa in Peru) of these large Indian civilizations, substitute themselves for the Indian leaders, and continue to rule *through* the existing Indian structure. In other words, the Spaniards seldom completely defeated the Indians militarily; instead they took over the top of the pyramid of Indian government and society but largely left the pyramid itself intact—however, with themselves as the new *caciques* or chieftains.

There were deviations from this pattern. The smaller, often fierce, sometimes cannibalistic (the Spanish conqueror Verrazano, after whom a famous bridge in New York was named, was apparently eaten right in front of his own men as he waded ashore) tribes of the Caribbean were often wiped out not so much by the force of Spanish arms as by the diseases the Spaniards carried (smallpox, TB, influenza) for which the Indians had no immunity. In Chile and Argentina, the Indians were *conquered* rather than simply subdued—much as in the United States. In Brazil, too, the Portuguese *bandeirantes* (literally, carriers of their nation's flag) pursued and conquered that country's few Indians in ways comparable to the American Wild West. But the dominant pattern was to force the Indians to submit, as distinct from conquering or slaughtering them.

Once they had captured the pinnacles of indigenous power, the Spaniards functioned as overlords or feudal chiefs, with the Indians becoming a kind of "peasantry," owing loyalty and labor to the Spanish *conquistadores* (conquerors). The Spaniards were obliged to Christianize and "civilize" the Indians and to assume responsibility for their care, but these obligations were often neglected. Particularly as the Indian population declined drastically in the sixteenth and seventeenth centuries and labor became scarcer, the Spaniards sought not to eliminate the Indians but to preserve them. If the Spaniards wanted to continue to live like feudal lords in the New World, which required abundant labor supplies to work in the mines and on the sugar plantations and large estates, then they had to maintain the native peasantry, not kill it off.

A critical question faced by the Spaniards was whether the Indians had souls. To modern ears this sounds like a silly question, but in the sixteenth-century Spanish context where the religious orthodoxy of Roman Catholicism reigned supreme, this was a crucial issue. Recall that no European had ever seen an Indian before, and they were not sure if Indians were truly human or of some lower order. If they had souls, they were human and therefore had to be treated as such under Spanish law, which guaranteed certain God-given rights even to the lowest of human forms. But if they did not have souls, then they were not human, were not protected by Spanish law, and could be treated as beasts of labor just like horses or cattle. Obviously this was a crucial issue, both for the Indians and for the Spanish. The debate took years to decide, but was eventually resolved in favor of the conclusion that the Indians did indeed have souls and therefore did hold some inalienable rights under Spanish law and had to be treated humanely. In the meantime, however, before the issue was decided, the Indians were often terribly exploited. Later on, as we shall see, the Spaniards went through the same debate as to whether Africans had souls or not; and while that debate was being settled, Black slavery was introduced into several areas of the Americas.

The Spanish goal, unlike that of the European settlers in North America, was not to ghettoize the Indians or confine them to reservations, but slowly to assimilate them into Spanish society. The Spaniards took over the highest levels of the Indian social and political pyramid, but they ruled through the existing Indian structure. The Indians remained at the lowest rungs of Spanish society (as peasants); meanwhile, they were to be remade, paternalistically, as "little Spaniards." As might be expected, however, this process was uneven—and it remains so today. Some native peoples *were* assimilated. Others, such as the primitive peoples in the Amazon basin, were too far removed from the centers of Spanish and Portuguese civilization, and they remained isolated. Still others maintained only limited contact with the European colonial powers and largely retreated into isolation, maintaining their Indian beliefs and culture, resisting the message of Catholicism, speaking only their Indian dialects, and never joining the money economy or participating in the political process.

The dominant pattern, however, reflected a hodgepodge of indigenous and colonial influences. Some Indians formally converted to Catholicism but privately maintained loyalty to their native deities. Some participated in both a barter (native) and a money (Spanish) economy. Some spoke Spanish in the marketplace but their indigenous language at home. Some remained loyal to their tribe or community and had very little contact with the larger nation-state, of which they only had a vague understanding. In highland Peru or Bolivia, for example, one can still find Indians who ask, "Who won the war, General Bolivia or General Peru?"—thus personalizing what to them is a vague and abstract Western concept: the nation.

Just as there were levels and gradations of assimilation, so there were also levels and gradations of "Indianness." Here is another dimension on which the Latin American and the United States' patterns were different. In North America, the early British and Dutch colonists usually brought their families along. They came to colonize, farm, and settle. By contrast, the Spanish conquest of Latin America was primarily a *military* conquest; wives and children were not brought along. Right from the beginning, therefore, there was miscegenation (mixing of the races) between European conquerors and Indians. These *mestizos* (mixtures of Indian and White) often spoke both Spanish and Indian languages, knew both cultures, and served as middlemen between the two. The result of several generations of such racial intermingling was a variety of racial strains (for example, one-half or one-eighth Indian). As we shall see later in the chapter, each of these gradations had a separate place in the Spanish social hierarchy, with each level subject to different laws, often having separate courts, expected to behave in certain ways, and so on.

It helps us understand the distinct nations and societies that evolved in Latin America by indicating where the Indians were most heavily concentrated. In Middle America, Mexico and Guatemala have been thought of as "Indian nations" in the sense that 80–90 percent of their populations at the dawn of the twentieth century were Indian. Elsewhere in Central America, the numbers of Indians were smaller and the *mestizos* became the dominant element, whereas Costa Rica—farthest from the centers of Aztec and Mayan civilizations—had very few Indians at all and is considered (and considers itself) "European." In South America, Peru, Bolivia, Ecuador, and Paraguay are referred to as "Indian countries"; Colombia, Venezuela, and Chile (farther from the center of Inca civilization) are predominantly *mestizo* countries; and Argentina, Uruguay, and Brazil had relatively few Indians.

The fact of having Indians or "being Indian" came to be a central concern of national life in these countries. The Europeans who dominated these societies were often ashamed of their countries' Indianness and tried to hide or disguise it from outsiders. They preferred to be known as White, Western, Hispanic, Catholic, and European countries. Hence, they sought to encourage greater European immigration as a way of "lightening" their populations. They also tried to Christianize their Indians, not just for reasons of religious principles but also as a means of civilizing, pacifying, and Europeanizing them.

The problem was that, unlike in North America, in these Latin American countries the Indians were the great majority, not just a minority. Consider the difficulties the United States has had in fully integrating minorities constituting maybe 15–20 percent of the population into the national life. Then imagine if 80–90 percent of the population—as in Mexico, Guatemala, Peru, Bolivia, or Paraguay—had to be integrated. Moreover, suppose that vast majority was *so* unintegrated that it didn't speak the national language, share the national political beliefs, participate in a money/market economy, or even know that it was part of a nation-state called "Mexico" or "Guatemala." These countries' problems of integration make our own country's integration problem, however severe, pale by comparison. In fact, we can say that in the five hundred–year history of the Latin American countries, *no* government—colonial or independent, military or civilian, leftist or rightist—has ever made a major success of solving their integration problems. Many plans have been tried, but all have failed. Perhaps it is an insolvable problem. The problem of integration in Latin America is more akin to that of South Africa, where the Blacks are the overwhelming majority and the Whites a small minority, than it is to the United States. Now, however, under the continuing impact of racial intermingling and assimilation, these conditions are changing.

There has long been a great fear among the White Hispanic population in some countries of Latin America stemming from their minority position. The Spanish colonists traditionally were concentrated in cities such as Lima, Peru, where most of the national wealth, power, government, society, and military were located. However, only about 5 percent of the total Peruvian population lived in the capitol city, with the rest, mainly Indian (close to 20 million persons in contemporary Peru) inhabiting the Andean highlands. Hence, two societies relatively isolated from each other emerged—one White, Western, and urban; the other Indian, non-Western, and rural. For five hundred years, they have remained distinct and separated—not just socially and culturally but geographically as well. The fear of the Hispanic elements was that, *someday*, the Indians would mobilize, organize, and rise up—driving White, Western, Catholic civilization back into the Pacific Ocean from whence it came. So, over the centuries, the elites took great pains, as we will examine in more detail in later chapters, to keep the Indians in their place and to prevent that from happening. Nevertheless, currently, it *is* happening or threatening to happen: first, in the form of a violent, Indian-based (but *mestizo*-led) guerrilla movement called the *Sendero Luminoso* (Shining Path); and second, by more peaceful means, through massive Indian migration out of the mountains and into the capitol. Even now, Lima is changing into an Indian city. The *de facto* reconquest of Peru by its indigenous peoples may have begun.

The issue is more complicated, however. It is definitely not the case that *all* Indians want to drive White, Western civilization into the sea. Rather, most want to preserve and expand the national economy but also to secure a "bigger piece of the pie" for themselves. In addition, Peru is no longer populated solely by Indians or Whites—and the same is true of the other "Indian" countries as well. There are also *mestizos* who are at home in both Indian and Hispanic cultures, as well as every other gradation between White and Indian, plus sizable Chinese, Japanese, Black, and other ethnic communities. So it is not just a matter of Indian versus Hispanics. Nor should one underestimate the ability of the Hispanic elites to head off potentially catastrophic changes as they have often done in the past.

Racial prejudice against Indians exists in Latin America, but because of the many gradations between Indian and White the prejudice is softer and less blatant than racial prejudice in the United States. Furthermore, prejudice in Latin America is as much cultural as racial, which means it can be more readily overcome. When the author first went to Guatemala in 1963, for example, and had his shoes shined by a young boy in the central park, the author was surprised by the boy—obviously of Indian background—referring to his Indianness in the past tense. He would say, "When I *was* an Indian, I did…" But the author, brought up in a North American setting, thought, "He certainly *looks* Indian to me." The reality is, however, that this boy spoke Spanish, wore a cross that indicated he was Catholic, dressed in western pants and shirt as opposed to traditional Indian garb, and was involved in a money (shoeshining) economy. Thus, in his own eyes and that of his society, he was no longer "Indian"—even though racially he still *looked* Indian. Culturally, he had become *mestizo* (or *Ladino*—Latin and Indian—as they say in Guatemala). Throughout Latin America, in fact, education, clothes, job, and wealth—as well as color—define where one fits in society. This also means one can "change" one's color by acquiring more wealth, education, status, and so on. Because the racial lines are both blurred and fluid, racial prejudice is less overt in Latin America than in the United States.

The blurred, bridgeable nature of race also helps explain why there have been few Indian revolts or Indian power movements in Latin America. There, it is possible—as the author's shoeshine boy demonstrated—to transcend one's racial background and the prejudices it may engender, to leave these in the past. Almost all Latin Americans believe, pragmatically, that it is better to be Hispanic than Indian. Throughout Latin American history, there have been Indianist movements aimed at glorifying the Indian, raising the status of the Indian, even elevating the Indian to a position of national honor. But few of these have ever succeeded. Movements aimed at empowering Indians in Latin America have always run into the problem that, instead of taking pride in their Indian heritage, most of the Indians would rather be *mestizo* or Hispanic. Now, however, in Mexico, Guatemala, Ecuador, Peru, Bolivia, and elsewhere, real indigenous movements are springing up in which Indians take pride in their own cultures and are demanding political influence.

The issue in Latin America is not, for the most part, Indian power per se but how to raise the social and economic level of *all* groups and to achieve national development. Latin America has an often immense problem, as we have seen, of better integrating the Indians into national life, but few Latin Americans believe an Indian power movement would be the best way to do this—and most Indians do not accept that route either. The process has been going on for five hundred years already; not only is it glacially slow, but there are wide political differences on how best to accomplish it. In the meantime, we need to remind ourselves that the problem of integrating the Indians in Latin America is not only a far larger problem than the U.S. problem of integration, but its basic features are quite different from the U.S. situation as well.

The Iberians

The word *Iberians* refers to those peoples from the Iberian Peninsula, the southwesterly promontory of Europe that juts out into the Atlantic pointing toward America. Sometimes the term *Hispanic* is also used, but most often in reference only to persons of Spanish descent. Iberians includes the descendants of *both* Spanish and Portuguese.

In the same year that Columbus discovered the New World, 1492, Spain finally succeeded in driving out from the Iberian Peninsula the last of the Moorish forces that had occupied it for seven centuries. The Moors were a Semitic people from North Africa who had crossed the Strait of Gibraltar in A.D. 711 and, inspired by the militant missionary spirit of the Islamic faith, occupied almost the entire peninsula. The Spanish and Portuguese efforts to drive the Moors out of the Iberian Peninsula waxed and waned over hundreds of years. That struggle permanently affected the character and development of Iberia and made it different from other parts of Europe. Among other things, the centuries needed for this *Reconquest* of the peninsula made Spain more intolerant, gave its feudalism a special rigidity, retarded democracy and pluralism, and gave rise to institutions that in Spain and Portugal were quite different from those in Great Britain or Holland. The conquest of Latin America in many respects was a continuation of the earlier Spanish/Portuguese reconquest of their own peninsula from the Moors. Many of the same forms and institutions created in Spain and Portugal during this late medieval period were carried across the Atlantic. Therefore, to understand Latin America, we need to trace its social and institutional origins in Spain and Portugal.

The recorded history of Iberia begins with its conquest by Roman legions about two thousand years ago. Prior to that, Iberia had been a sparsely populated area of frequently warring tribes and clans. Rome gave Iberia its religion (Catholicism), a system of laws, a national road system, political unity, and a common language (Spanish and Portuguese are both derived from the earlier Latin). It is also worth noting that Rome *conquered* Iberia and considered it an integral part of that Roman empire; and when Spain and Portugal carved their own empires in Latin America some fifteen centuries later, they used as a model the system that they knew best: the imperial model of ancient Rome. It is said that Spain came to be "more Roman than Rome itself."

Catholicism became especially strong in Spain and Portugal. Just as Spain was more Roman than Rome, it was also "more Catholic than the pope."

Catholicism would become *the* national religion, both the official religion of the state and inseparable from it. Catholicism was not just a religion, therefore; it undergirded *all* behavior in the social, economic, political, educational, and intellectual spheres. Moreover, because of some unique features of Iberian history, Catholicism there was less tolerant of other religions than it was in other countries. Spanish and Portuguese Catholicism was most heavily influenced by Saint Augustine, who lived in the fifth century A.D., and by Saint Thomas Aquinas who lived in the twelfth century: it was hierarchical, highly structured, and authoritarian—just like the social and political systems.

Iberian Catholicism helped justify a social and political hierarchy based on rank, order, and unchanging social position. At the top was God, who was all-powerful, followed by angels, archangels, and cherubim and seraphim. Next were the powers, principalities, and kingdoms. Then came landowners, elites, and wealthy persons; next were artisans, craftsmen, merchants, and soldiers; finally, at the bottom, were workers, peasants, and the lower forms of life. See Figure 2.1.

Political power, wealth, land, and social standing all came from God, not from any notions of equal opportunity or "one person, one vote." It was everyone's duty, even the lowest peasant, to accept their situation in life and do their best in that position—not to question it, let alone rebel against it. Remember that all these positions, even poverty, came from God's "just" ordering of the universe; and in the context of the near-universal Catholicism then prevailing, God's will was immutable. Thus, one was born into a certain station in life, one married in that same station, and one's children grew up in the same social position—through generations and even centuries. The system was rigid and unyielding. Even today, in both Iberia and Latin America, children grow up with this powerful sense of place and position, not necessarily with the egalitarian assumptions that undergird American democracy.

Similar assumptions prevailed in the economic sphere. Like the social hierarchy, the total economic product was assumed to be fixed and immutable. Therefore, when one person gained, another one had to lose, and because that was immoral, no one could be allowed to move ahead. In this context, economic development and growth was—and is—not possible. The Catholic church also condemned charging interest as immoral usury and, until recently, was also very critical of capitalism. The result is that Spanish, Portuguese, and Latin American children do not grow up with the same Ben Franklin/Horatio Alger ethics as their U.S. counterparts: work hard, save your pennies, study hard, and get ahead. Instead, they are taught at an early age to be economically passive rather than ambitious, to wait for fate, God, or maybe the lottery to smile on them. Rather than exercising individual initiative or the kind of entrepreneurship that leads to economic growth, they learn early on to depend on the church or the state for handouts. These

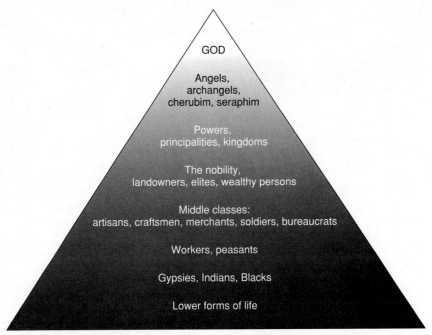

Figure 2 ✦ 1 The Spanish/Portuguese Social Hierarchy, c. 1500

fatalistic attitudes are now changing, but slowly, since they still have a strong basis in Latin America.

In the eighth century A.D., as we have seen, the Iberian Peninsula was again invaded and conquered, this time by Moors from North Africa. The Moorish invasion was part of an enormous Islamic expansion that swept through the Middle East and North Africa and into Southern Europe. The Moorish invasion did bring education and learning to Iberia, but it also gave rise to the inferior position of women in Latin society, an increased sense of militarism, and a reinforcement of the Spanish tradition of clannishness and tribalism. Islamic influences are still apparent in the language, diet, culture, and architecture of Spain and Portugal as well.

At least as important as the Moorish conquest of Iberia was the Spanish and Portuguese *Reconquest* of the peninsula that culminated, as we have seen, in the final defeat of the Moors in 1492. (The movie *El Cid* has been made about these events.)

No other European countries in their formative stages had anything comparable to the Reconquest; the Spanish and Portuguese experiences are unique. For one thing, the Reconquest emphasized military heroics and *machismo*, traits that would be carried over to Latin America. Second, since there was not a single unified Spanish or Portuguese army fighting the Moors but rather many local armies, the Reconquest emphasized localism and regionalism more than nationalism—a trait still found in both Iberia and Latin America. Third, because of the constant fighting, people came to live in walled enclave cities rather than on farms close to their crops. Fourth, the Reconquest was a religious crusade against the Islamic "infidel" as well as a military affair, so it was especially intolerant and violent. And fifth, the Reconquest meant that Spanish and Portuguese feudalism—unlike French or British feudalism, for example—was militaristic as well as economic. As the Reconquest, which began in the north, proceeded south, the conquerors inherited not only the land of the fleeing Moors but the right to both the labor *and* the military service of the people living in the reconquered area. In the all-important institution of the *hacienda*, or feudal estate, in Latin America, this unique combination of a feudalism that was at once social, economic, political, and military would also be present.

As the Moors were driven back and as distinguishable Spanish and Portuguese nation-states began to emerge in the period from the twelfth through the fifteenth centuries, some further distinguishing features began to emerge that would similarly be carried over to Latin America. Because of the almost continuous wars against the Moors, the emerging Spanish and Portuguese states placed great stress on unity and the authority of the state—as distinct from North American–style limited government and pluralism. With their kings claiming absolute authority, no independent legislature or judiciary ever emerged, unlike in the British and American systems. In addition, in both Spain and Portugal, such groups (known as "corporate" groups) as the Catholic church, the military orders (which formed the basis of the later national armies), and the independent towns had come into existence long before there was any overarching nation-state. Proud of this heritage, these groups often claimed that they were more important than the central state and independent from it. These factors help explain why in Latin America the church and the military often continued to act as if they were superior to the government and, in the case of the army, sometimes overturned it.

As the emerging Spanish and Portuguese regimes were further consolidated in the fifteenth century (just before the conquest of Latin America), they took on some additional special features. Politically, these regimes became more and more authoritarian and centralized. Not only did they drive the Moors out of the peninsula, but in that same epochal year of 1492, Spain expelled the Jews, who were their leading businessmen, intellectuals, and entrepreneurs. Seeking to snuff out all signs of pluralism, either religious or political, the Spanish monarchs also suppressed Protestant groups and all free-thinkers. In short, these governments became increasingly closed and authoritarian—traits that would be carried over to the New World.

Socially, these regimes also became hardened. Beneath the king, a small elite governed at the top, monopolizing land and power. The "middle class" (a few soldiers, merchants, and bureaucrats) was so small as to be almost nonexistent—in contrast to the North American colonies, which were largely settled by middle class people. A large peasantry did the manual labor and was excluded from political participation. Beneath that were gypsies and other "undesirables." In the Americas, of course, the Spaniards would find a home-grown "peasantry"—the Indians—whom they could also put to work. The church and the military occupied especially privileged positions.

Economically, Spain and Portugal were dominated by mercantilism, an economic philosophy that preceded capitalism. Under mercantilism, the king or the state (not individual entrepreneurs) took the lead in trying to stimulate the economy. The wealth of a nation was measured in its gold reserves, not in the productivity of its fields, factories, and labor force. To acquire such reserves, colonies were necessary—such as those in Latin America, which had abundant gold. Such colonies were to be exploited and milked dry solely for the benefit of the mother countries. Hence, the wealth of Latin America was used exclusively to benefit Spain and Portugal, not to stimulate Latin American economic development.

Intellectually and educationally, Spain, Portugal, and their colonies in the New World became similarly closed and authoritarian. There was no scientific experimentation, no empirical investigation, no intellectual examination of changing social conditions. Rather, the Spanish and Portuguese educational systems were based on the idea of *scholasticism*—rote memorization and the deductive method. One started with God's truth as found in the Bible and the writings of the church fathers (Augustine and Aquinas); from there, one *deduced* principles of behavior for everyday life. Knowledge was therefore fixed and immutable.

All these traits, institutions, and characteristics were carried by Spain and Portugal to Latin America. Their system, which they then implanted in Latin America, can be summarized as closed, authoritarian, absolutist, rigid, elitist, top-down, feudal, mercantilist, and scholastic—as basically medieval. This peculiar Spanish/Portuguese heritage helps explain why Latin America developed so differently from the United States and why for a long time it remained so backward.

Like the United States, Latin America is a product of both its indigenous peoples and Western civilization. But the indigenous element in Latin America, as we have seen, was far more numerous and influential than it was in North America. In addition, the fact that Latin America was colonized by Spain and Portugal, and not by England and Holland, resulted in significant differences in its institutions. Although Spain and Portugal were European nations, they represented a particular fragment or variant of the Western tradition that differed from that of the Northern European countries. Thus, the various colonies established in the Americas reflected the unique histories and traditions of these countries. In Chapter 3, we will see how these differences among the colonial powers actually worked out in the New World.

The African Americans

At the time of the discovery of America in 1492, Europe was already aware of Africa. Portugal had already explored the African coast by then, rounding the Cape of Good Hope and sailing north to the Indian Ocean while also establishing trading enclaves along the coast of West Africa. Several European courts had imported a handful of African slaves, and in some of the port cities of Europe, African workers could be found. Thus, Europe was acquainted with Africa—although only superficially.

Africans were brought to Latin America largely to replace the Indians as slaves and workers, because the Indians were dying off and were not regarded as reliable workers. As early as 1506—only fourteen years after Columbus's initial discovery—the first African slaves arrived at the Caribbean island of Hispaniola. As more and more Indians died, due to Spanish military incursions, hard labor in the mines and plantations, and the diseases that the Spaniards carried, more and more Africans were imported to replace them. By about 1570, the indigenous Indian population of the Caribbean—Cuba, Hispaniola (later divided into the countries of Haiti and the Dominican Republic), Puerto Rico, Jamaica, and the smaller islands—had been all but completely wiped out. Today, in the islands, almost no trace of the original Indian populations remains.

The Africans brought to Latin America, therefore, were seen chiefly as replacements for the disappearing Indian labor supply. Or, in the case of Brazil where there were very few Indians to begin with, African slaves were brought in to work on Portuguese plantations. Other Africans were imported to work in the port city and Gulf Coast plantations of Mexico, the coastal plantations of Peru, the trade routes across the Isthmus of Panama, and some coastal areas of Venezuela, Colombia, and Central America.

Because African Americans were distributed unevenly in Latin America, race and social relations differ considerably in different parts of the area. In the Caribbean islands and Brazil, race relations from the mid-sixteenth century onward were framed mainly in terms of the interrelations between Blacks and Whites, rather than between Indians and Whites, since the Indian element had already largely disappeared. In the mainland countries of Central and South America, race relations continued to focus chiefly on Indians and Whites, with Blacks constituting a very small minority: about 1–2 percent. In Chile, Argentina, Bolivia, Paraguay, and Uruguay (whose cooler climates were not appropriate for plantation systems), there were few or no Blacks at all.

The African Americans who were imported served as a supply of cheap labor to replace the Indians, as commodities to be bought and sold, not as persons. As with the indigenous peoples, Spain and Portugal long debated whether Blacks had souls or not. If they did have souls, then they had certain rights under the law; if they lacked souls, then they could be enslaved and treated as less than men. In fact, in the Caribbean islands and Brazil, a cruel, exploitive slave plantation system emerged that lasted in most countries until well into the nineteenth century—about the time that slavery was finally abolished in the United States. The main crop produced on these plantations was sugarcane—as compared with cotton in the United States. Slaves were needed primarily to cut the cane in harvest season, a hard and sometimes dangerous work. And, as in all slave societies, some masters were relatively kind to their slaves while others were cruel. Nevertheless, it is the *institution* of slavery that was itself so debilitating.

Recall that the original Spanish and Portuguese conquerors usually did not bring their wives and families along. Or, as in northeast Brazil, if they did bring their wives along, the Portuguese colonists often maintained two families: a White one in the plantation house and a Black one in the slave quarters. Right from the beginning, therefore, miscegenation occurred between Blacks and Whites as it had between Indians and Whites, and between Blacks and Indians. The result was that a sizable mulatto element (as well as other combinations) began to emerge in the Caribbean islands, Panama, and Brazil. By the nineteenth century, the mulattoes in Cuba, the Dominican Republic, Puerto Rico, Panama, and Brazil constituted a majority of the population. And in Haiti and the smaller islands of the Caribbean, Blacks were the majority, but mulattoes, comprising only 5–10 percent of the population, often constituted the elite.

With racial miscegenation in the islands (Black and White) and on the mainland (Indian and White) came new gradations in the Spanish/Portuguese social hierarchy. As long as there were just Blacks and Whites, Indians and Whites, and a few mulattoes and *mestizos*, the social hierarchy was relatively easy to figure out. But with the infinite gradations of racial mixing (for example, one-sixteenth Black or one sixty-fourth Indian), the issue became extremely complicated. The Spanish sought to designate each racial combination with distinct rules, laws, and sometimes even courts. Even today in social relations in Latin America, an elaborate set of terms is used to designate where people are located on the social-racial hierarchy. For example, the term *Indio* is used in some Caribbean islands to describe a person who is mulatto but has a reddish skin color, straight hair, and high cheekbones.

There are some fascinating exceptions to the general patterns we have been describing here. For example, in 1795 in Haiti, which in the eighteenth century was the richest and most intensive slave plantation society in the world, a slave revolt erupted that led early in the nineteenth century to Haiti being the first Black republic in the world—at a time when most countries still practiced slavery. In other Caribbean islands, groups of Black slaves (called *maroons*) escaped from their masters and established independent Black communities in isolated mountainous regions, some of which still exist today. In another unusual case, Great Britain, in the early nineteenth century, took Black slaves from its Caribbean islands and tried to set up a British kingdom on the so-called Mosquito coast (named for the Indians who inhab-ited the area, not for its flying insects) of Central America. Thus, today, along the hot, low-lying, tropical Caribbean coast of Costa Rica, Nicaragua, Hon-duras, and Guatemala, we have small communities of English-speaking, Protestant Blacks in what are predominantly Spanish-speaking, Catholic, and *mestizo* countries.

The Spanish/Portuguese social hierarchy was as rigid—at least in the-ory—in treating Blacks as it was in its dealings with Indians. The Spanish or Portuguese formed a small White elite. Blacks constituted a slave or servant class. Between were the mulattoes, who often served as middlemen. In other words, race and class were closely interrelated: Whites at the top, Blacks at the bottom, and mulattoes between.

Because of the extensive miscegenation, however, race relations in Latin America between Blacks and Whites, as between Indians and Whites, were always more muted and more relaxed than in the United States. Where one stood in the social hierarchy depended as much on cultural and social traits as on color. Moreover—and again unlike the United States—the lines were not so rigid, so it was possible to bridge them. For example, in the Caribbean and Brazil, a light-skinned mulatto who was well educated, dressed well, and held an important position would be considered "White," while a well-edu-cated, well-dressed Black who held an important position would be consid-ered "mulatto." In other words, one could "change" one's color—not literally but by social and cultural achievements. Education, dress, and official posi-tion were all means to achieve "Whiteness."

Racial prejudice exists in Brazil and the Caribbean, in that Whites are usually found at the upper end of the social scale and Blacks at the bottom. But the system has a fluidity lacking in the United States and a means by which people can rise in the sociopolitical scale. There is also prejudice in the notion that it is toward greater Whiteness that most people and coun-tries wish to gravitate. On the individual level, people may buy hair straight-eners and facial powders so that they appear "lighter"; on the national level, even the predominantly mulatto countries of the Caribbean try to encourage European immigration but not African immigration. Prejudice of a purely racial sort exists, but the cultural and social factors also influence how people are categorized and therefore make race relations more malleable and easy-going than in the United States.

The emphasis on assimilation and "Whitening" means that, until re-cently, there were few Black power movements in the Caribbean or Brazil. If people took pride in "Whiteness" rather than "Blackness" and tried to present themselves as Whites, and if their countries tried to encourage White-only immigration, there was little room for movements stressing Black pride. Now, however, this is changing, especially in some of the smaller islands of the Caribbean, such as Trinidad, where Blacks constitute the overwhelming majority. Nevertheless, the prevailing pattern in most countries remains the opposite one: trying to Whiten or lighten oneself or one's family through a variety of means.

Cuba is the one country in the area that long practiced U.S.-style racial discrimination. Cuba was so close to the United States and so dependent on it that even its racial attitudes in the form of "Jim Crow" laws were imported from the United States. Cuba had "Whites only" beaches, hotels, toilets, and dining rooms just like the American South before the civil rights movement. Fidel Castro's revolutionary regime abolished the Jim Crow laws, but in the higher echelons of the Cuban Communist Party, the armed forces, the universities, and the government, those with lighter skin continued to predominate.

In the era before the legal abolishment of racial discrimination in the United States, it was often difficult for these Black and mulatto countries of Latin America to function or to find acceptance. Imagine the reception accorded the first ambassadors of a Black Haiti in the early nineteenth century at a time when the United States and most other countries still practiced slavery and when many people still doubted that Blacks had souls. There were often crude, racist jokes about the Black and mulatto countries of the Caribbean and skepticism as to whether they could ever achieve democracy or develop economically. Time has proved these assumptions wrong; but even today our attitudes of superiority toward Latin America, its underdevelopment, its many revolutions, and its general inability to "get its act together" are still based in part on racial prejudice: the "Latins" (mulatto and *mestizo* countries) just aren't up to it.

Now, however, the Caribbean has attracted the attention of a sizable number of Americans who know it well and take a special interest in it. These include the considerable number of American academics, government officials, clerics, Peace Corps volunteers, students, and average citizens who have spent time in the Caribbean nations over the last thirty years. It also includes the *hundreds of thousands* of Dominicans, Cubans, Puerto Ricans, Jamaicans, and others who have settled in the United States recently—so many, in fact, that New York is now the second-largest Puerto Rican and Dominican city, and Miami the second-largest Cuban and Haitian city. It further includes the congressional "Black Caucus" and "Friends of the Caribbean," a group of about sixty congressmen and -women who have a special concern for Caribbean affairs. The Black Caucus was organized initially to pay special attention to the needs of Black Americans, but over the years it has also evolved a foreign policy interest focused on Africa and the Caribbean.

Other Groups

Beginning in 1492, as we have seen, three different ethnic groups came together in the formation of Latin America. These were the indigenous Indian groups whose presence in the Americas dated back thousands of years, the

White Iberians from Spain and Portugal, and the Blacks from Africa imported as slaves and laborers. These three groups interacted in complex and yet different patterns: mainly Indians and Whites on the mainland, and Blacks and Whites in the Caribbean islands and Brazil. Out of the racial miscegenation came two new racial types: the *mestizo* (Indian and White) on the mainland and the mulatto (Black and White) in the islands and Brazil.

In the nineteenth century, some other ethnic ingredients were added to the Latin American melting pot. For example, French colonists fleeing the slave revolt in Haiti migrated to Cuba and the Dominican Republic. And a few European as well as U.S. merchants and adventurers began to show up in Latin America.

But it was not until the last two decades of the nineteenth century, comparable to the period of renewed European immigration to the United States, that a new and sizable wave of immigrants came to Latin America—mostly Italian, Spanish, Portuguese, German, and Eastern European immigrants. They helped add to the sparse population of Latin America at that time, and went into agriculture and commerce. Many brought with them the entrepreneurial skills that they had learned in Europe; quite a few became wealthy and intermarried with the local Spanish or Portuguese elite families. Others became quite clannish and stuck with their fellow immigrants, forming small ethnic or nationality ghettos within the larger Latin American societies.

In the period between World Wars I and II, still other ingredients were added to the ethnic "stew." These included not only more Europeans but also Chinese, Japanese, Lebanese, Jewish, and other immigrants. Many of these groups also remained loyal to their own families and ethnic clans, integrating only incompletely into their new homelands.

Since World War II, the ethnic mix has become even more diverse: Germans, Americans, Arabs from a variety of countries (often grouped together and called *Turcos* or "Turks" in Latin America), Russians, Koreans, and others. Nevertheless, despite the diversity of the Latin American melting pot, some groups remain more important than others.

Dominant and Submerged Cultures

Three major ethnic elements—Indian, Iberian, and Black—were present in the early history of Latin America; and to these three have now been added a great variety of other ethnic influences. But not all of these ethnic elements have been equally important; some have been more powerful than others. Among the major ethnic groups, the Iberian (Spanish or Portuguese; often called Hispanic) has been dominant, while the other two—Indian and Black—have largely been submerged. These disparities in importance among the major ethnic groups derived from the fact that one was a powerful, conquering force that subordinated the continent to its power, while the indigenous population, considered inferior, was conquered, and the Blacks were brought over as slaves.

When we talk about Latin America, therefore, or at least its dominant institutions, it is largely the Iberian influence that we are referring to. The main religion of the area (Catholicism), the legal system (the Napoleonic codes), the governmental system (Spanish/Portuguese centralization and authoritarianism), the main intellectual tradition (scholasticism), the economy (mercantilist), and the social order (hierarchical, class-based) were all grounded in Hispanic traditions and practices. Often, the indigenous Indian institutions paralleled and were used to help reinforce the Hispanic institutions, but it was still the Hispanic institutions that dominated. As slaves, Blacks and their Africa-based institutions had little influence—at least among the dominant ruling groups.

Beneath the surface, however, was considerably greater diversity. The Indians became nominal Catholics, but underneath they often retained their Indian Gods and beliefs. Indian barter practices, dress, culture, social relations, and behavior often were less influenced by the Spanish/Portuguese conquests than was thought. The same can be said about the Blacks. The dominant institutions were often those of the Hispanic master, but below the surface Black music, dance, language, religion, and culture remained very much alive. It was *submerged* by the prevailing Hispanic culture but never completely snuffed out. Spain and Portugal dominated the pinnacles or prevailing heights of Latin America—religion, government, universities, the military, the social structure, the legal system, economics—but below those levels indigenous and Black cultures continually struggled to hang on and to preserve their own ways.

Now, both the indigenous and the Black cultures are reasserting themselves. The prevailing culture is still Hispanic, but indigenous and Black culture is being rediscovered and revived. Some Hispanic elements see this as a threat—and in some countries it may be so. In other countries, however, the survival of indigenous and Black art, culture, music, and numerous other traditions is seen as a healthy expression of a multicultural and pluralist society. As we proceed, let us keep in mind these notions of dominant and submerged cultures, which are presently undergoing redefinition and reassessment.

3
+

Encounter with the New World

When Columbus landed in the New World in 1492, it marked one of the great epochal events of world history. The discovery is comparable in importance to the formation of the Roman Empire, the Protestant Reformation, and the Industrial Revolution. The European encounter with America gave rise to the field of cross-cultural anthropology, as the friars who accompanied the Spanish *conquistadores* began to study the indigenous Indian civilizations. The discovery opened up vast new areas for exploration, trade, and also exploitation of native peoples. The gold and silver of the Americas flowing back to Spain and Portugal helped spark the Industrial Revolution in Europe. In addition, the discovery vastly expanded man's horizons, stimulated art and literature, proved to all that the world was round and, at the same time, that it was both larger (in terms of unexplored territories) and smaller (circumnavigable, as Magellan demonstrated) than had been imagined.

The discovery and colonization of the Americas, from 1492 to about 1570, also marked a turning point in world history: the beginning of *modern* world history. The Protestant Reformation, the start of capitalism, the Renaissance of ideas, the empirical method in science, the movement toward limited and representative government—all began during this period. These are all the trends and changes that we associate with the making of the modern world. The year 1500 is usually used to signal the break between the medieval and feudal world and the modern world. But recall that Spain and Portugal and their New World colonies remained locked in that pre-1500 medieval and feudal mold. It was the *rest* of Europe, and eventually their colonies in North America as well, that took the steps toward modernity. So Iberia and Latin America lagged behind while Northern Europe and North America forged ahead. We shall have more to say about these differences and their implications later in this chapter.

The Burden of Geography

The United States is blessed with numerous geographical advantages. We seldom consider these factors when we think about how and why some nations develop and others lag behind. But they are crucial in understanding the differences between the United States and Latin America.

The United States has moderate temperatures for the most part, a healthy climate, abundant rainfall, and in the midwestern heartland some of the best agricultural land in the world. The United States has a wide, fertile coastal escarpment on its eastern shores, which gave the early colonists prime territory on which to settle, farm, and build cities. It has a vast, natural, internal waterways system (the Hudson, Delaware, Ohio, Mississippi, Missouri rivers; the St. Lawrence Waterway; Chesapeake Bay; the Great Lakes) that is conducive to quick transportation and easy communications. Its mountain ranges are generally low and passable—until one hits the Rockies. It boasts abundant minerals and timber; most importantly, it has all the essential minerals needed to industrialize (coal, iron ore, petroleum), *and* it has them in juxtaposition—coal close to the iron ore so the former can be used in the smelting of the latter.

Latin America lacks all these advantages. Much of the area is hot, tropical, and close to sea level. Such debilitating diseases as malaria, cholera, tuberculosis, and intestinal infections thrive in such climates. The area has either too much rainfall, such as in the tropical jungles in the Amazon basin, or too little. Only Argentina has an area comparable to the American Midwest in terms of the richness of agricultural land; much of the rest of Latin America is arid or infertile or contains thin topsoils.

Latin America has, in most areas, a very narrow coastal escarpment. Rather, in much of the continent, the mountains come right down to the sea, making settlement, farming, and the founding of cities very difficult. And these are *real* mountains; the Andean chain, next to the Himalayas the second highest in the world at over 20,000 feet, makes penetration very difficult. Other mountain ranges in Brazil, Venezuela, Central America, and Mexico similarly retard colonization, transportation, and communications.

Latin America has vast river systems (the Paraná, Plata, Amazon, and Orinoco), but the rivers often flow the wrong way. By that we obviously do not mean that they flow uphill; instead, we mean that, unlike in the United States, they do not flow either through the major agricultural areas or by the major cities. Rather, they drain into what have until recently been considered empty and worthless areas, and they have not been boons to internal transportation and communications. In addition, the mountains and high, rugged plateaus render most of the rivers nonnavigable, and certainly closed to oceangoing vessels.

At the time of the conquest, Latin America had large quantities of gold and silver—most of which were shipped back to the mother countries of Spain and Portugal instead of being used for the internal development of Latin America. But most countries of the area lack those minerals—iron, coal, and petroleum—necessary for large-scale industrialization. Nor are the coal and iron readily available or in juxtaposition as in the United States. Venezuela and Brazil have major iron and other deposits of precious metals, and Chile has copper; but most Latin American countries are mineral-poor. Major oil finds in Mexico, Venezuela, Argentina, Peru, Ecuador, and Colombia have recently helped fuel these countries' development and offer promise for the future; but many countries of the area lack natural wealth and are mired in poverty. Internal disorganization, historically, has prevented the full development and utilization of the resources that do exist.

The high mountains and chopped-up terrain mean internal communications and transportation—prior to the arrival of modern air travel—were always difficult in Latin America. This is, in fact, one of the keys to understanding the area. Simply stated, geographic barriers prevented national integration. Because distances were great and the natural barriers almost insurmountable, people could seldom travel from one area to another, or to the capital city, let alone abroad. Only Costa Rica, Chile, and Uruguay, whose inhabitants live in a concentrated area, developed as closely integrated nations.

Given the geographic barriers, little sense of national identity could or did develop. People could identify with their own small valley or region, the *patria chica* or "little country," but not with a remote, inaccessible national center. Regionalism was strong, but nationalism was not. Similarly, political loyalty went to the regional *jefe* (chief or boss), *caudillo* (man-on-horseback), or *cacique* (chieftan), but not to the national government or president. Society, as we see in more detail later, was also organized around the local *hacienda* or feudal estate; loyalty went first to the local *patron* or godfather, and only later up the chain of command to the national palace. The only comparable situation in the United States was in the Old South, where rival elite families at the local and regional level jockeyed for control of the county courthouse and all the patronage, jobs, special favors, and political power that went with it.

Geography has in general hindered Latin American development rather than helping it as in the United States.

The Pattern of the Conquest

The Caribbean Islands

Latin America was "discovered" by Spain in 1492; the first area to be effectively settled and colonized was the island of Hispaniola (now divided into the countries of Haiti and the Dominican Republic) in the Caribbean. Hispaniola was the site of the first cathedral, the first monastery, the first hospital, and the first fortress and walled city in the Americas. It was also on Hispaniola that the first revolution in the New World took place, when Columbus's men rebelled against the Great Navigator's authoritarian and arbitrary ways. It was on Hispaniola, furthermore, that Spain's first social, economic, and political experiments, which later were institutionalized in other areas of the Americas, took place: the first slave-plantation system, separate laws and courts for the different racial and social groups, authoritarian political control, a rigid class and caste system, and the feudal system of the *hacienda*.

From Hispaniola, the Spaniards moved quickly to the other main islands of the Caribbean. The conquests of Cuba and Puerto Rico, for example, were launched from Hispaniola, which during these early years became the administrative center of Spain's empire in America, and not from Spain directly. The conquest of these islands was completed quickly, between 1500 and 1520. But none of them had the gold or silver in quantities that the *conquistadores* expected.

Mexico

Next came Mexico, one of the great conquests in history, for here the Spaniards faced not just small Indian tribes as on the islands, but the great Aztec civilization of 5 million persons. Hernán Cortés set sail from Cuba with but five ships, five hundred men, and sixteen horses—animals the Indians had never seen before. The Indians thought Cortés and his men were gods, and they believed that horse and rider were a single, overpowering creature. To the Indians, the mounted warrior was as innovative and devastating a weapon as the machine gun, the tank, or the nuclear bomb were in more modern times. That helps explain why the Spaniards, though outnumbered *ten thousand to one*, were able to conquer the Aztec empire so quickly. Tuberculosis also killed thousands of Indians as the Spaniards advanced. When Cortés captured the Aztec emperor, Montezuma, the entire empire, already beset by feuding and civil war, fell into his hands. By 1521, only two years after it began, the conquest of Mexico was essentially completed. Mexico was soon divided up by Cortés and his men into huge feudal estates—each one literally stretching from one mountain range to another mountain range on the distant horizon—just as had been done with the earlier conquests. This was the beginning of the system of huge landed estates in Latin America, as distinguished from the family farm system of the United States.

Central America

From Mexico, one of Cortés' lieutenants, Pedro de Alvarado, moved south and conquered Guatemala, center of the historic Mayan civilization, which stretched from the Yucatán in southern Mexico down through the isthmus of Central America. A few years earlier, in 1513, Balboa had crossed the isthmus at Panama and gazed out upon the Pacific Ocean. Soon Panama would become, as it is today, a major commercial center and trading post linking the Pacific with the Caribbean and the Atlantic. From Panama in the south and Mexico and Guatemala in the north, a pincer's movement was effected that quickly brought all of Central America under Spanish control. The American South and Southwest as well as coastal California were also explored and settled by Spain during this period.

South America

The settlement of Panama opened the way to new discoveries in South America. In 1530, Francisco Pizarro, his three half-brothers, and two hundred men sailed south from Panama down the Pacific and landed on the coast of present-day Ecuador. They meandered overland into Peru where they used the same technique to capture the Inca empire that Cortés had used in conquering the Aztecs in Mexico. Pizarro lured the trusting Inca leader to his camp, captured and killed him, and then established himself and his men as the feudal overlords of the Inca empire. This empire stretched from present-day Colombia and Ecuador, was centered in Peru, and reached through Bolivia and northern Chile; so when the Spaniards subjugated the Incas, they effectively ruled the entire west coast of South America.

The Atlantic or east coast of South America was settled and colonized after the west coast—even though the former was actually closer to Spain. The reason for this is that, whereas the west coast and its Inca empire had abundant gold and silver as well as vast Indian labor supplies to exploit, the east coast lacked precious metals and was populated by fierce, warring Indian tribes that were not easily vanquished. For example, Columbus as well as other early explorers had sailed the coast of Venezuela and the Guyanas in the early decades of the sixteenth century. However, they found little there to attract them (oil was hardly considered valuable then), so Venezuela was left largely unsettled. Indeed, this region was characterized by colonial neglect during most of the three centuries of Spanish colonial rule.

Similarly, in the Rio de la Plata region in the south (present-day Argentina, Paraguay, and Uruguay), there was little gold or silver to exploit, and the few Indians who lived there were especially warlike. The city of Buenos Aires was founded initially in 1536 by Pedro de Mendoza, but it was soon burned and abandoned. Only in the 1580s did the Spaniards "rediscover" and permanently settle Buenos Aires. Significantly, however, this second conquest was undertaken from the west, not from the Atlantic, by settlers spilling down the Paraná and La Plata rivers from the more valuable (to the Spanish Crown) mineral-rich colonies of Bolivia and Peru.

Southern Chile was the last area of South America to be conquered. Its high mountains made the terrain very difficult, it lacked gold and silver, and its indigenous Indians, the Araucanians, were especially fierce and resistant. Nevertheless, by the 1570s, Chile, too, had been largely conquered.

Brazil, as always, was a special story. It was discovered by the Portuguese explorer Pedro Alvares Cabral in 1500. Even before that, in 1494, in an effort to avoid future disputes between the then-major powers of Spain and Portugal, the pope in Rome had drawn a line down the continent of South America giving Portugal the eastern portion and Spain the western. For a long time, Portugal maintained only small enclaves along the Atlantic coast (Portugal was more interested in its lucrative trade with India and Asia), but Portuguese explorers eventually spilled over the coastal escarpment and settled the vast interior, eventually giving Brazil the approximate borders that it has today. From the beginning, Portuguese colonial administration was different from Spain's—"softer," less rigid, and less authoritarian.

By the 1570s–1580s, therefore, approximately eighty years after it had begun, the Spanish-Portuguese conquest of the Americas was virtually completed. It was a remarkable feat to accomplish in so short a time, particularly in an era before modern transportation and warfare. The Spanish and Portuguese achievements are all the more impressive if we consider that it took the English colonists in North America fully three centuries to conquer and settle their territory from east to west, whereas Spain and Portugal did it in less than one century and conquered a far larger and more difficult land area besides.

The next issue to discuss is how Spain and Portugal administered their vast new empires in the Americas and what kept them so stable for three centuries.

Colonial Administration

Spanish and Portuguese colonial administration in the Americas reflected the society of the two mother countries. It was authoritarian and top-down politically, mercantilist and feudal economically, rigid and stratified socially, absolutist and orthodox religiously, and scholastic and deductive intellectually and educationally. Actually, this structure and system of rule had been tried earlier, by the Portuguese in their enclaves in Africa and by the Spaniards in the Canary Islands (though, again, Portuguese colonial administration was generally less authoritarian and more humane than was the Spanish).

The Political Sphere

At the top of the colonial hierarchy was the king, or royal authority. Centered in Madrid and Lisbon, the king had absolute control over *all* aspects of the colonies. Land, minerals, Indians—all were part of the king's domain. Everything done in the colonies was always done in the name of the king— and *only* the king. Technically, the king permitted the *conquistadores* only *usage* of the land of the Americas and of Indian labor; land and Indians were supposedly not commodities that could be bought, sold, and converted to private property. But royal authority was thousands of miles away, communications between Iberia and the colonies required several months each way, and the royal will could not always be implemented in these isolated and distant lands. The reaction of the colonists to a royal edict that they found to be inconvenient was to try to obey in a strictly legal and technical sense and, meanwhile, to use their own judgment. The justly famous phrase of colonial officials when receiving a usually well-meaning but impossible-to-carry out edict from the king was "I obey but I do not implement."

The king ruled through the Council of the Indies. Located in Spain and appointed by the king, the Council was charged with setting overall policy and exercising everyday governance in the colonies. Such governance was exercised on behalf of the royal authority but not necessarily for the benefit of the colonies. The Council elaborated the laws that governed the colonies, held hearings on colonial matters, and resolved disputes—all in the name of the king. It had competence in all matters affecting the colonies: finance, military, religious, political, judicial, legislative. The Council oversaw the transplanting of the society and institutions of Spain to the New World.

Below the Council of the Indies in this hierarchical organization was the *Casa de contratación* or House of Trade. Located in the city of Seville in southwest Spain, through which all commerce with the colonies passed, the House of Trade was charged with overseeing and, in fact, monopolizing all trade with the "Indies." All-importantly, it was authorized to receive all the gold and silver coming from the Americas. Over three hundred years of colonial rule, the House of Trade was very careful and successful in centralizing trade, keeping non-Spanish merchants out of the Americas, and funneling revenues to the Spanish crown.

Spanish colonial administration in the Americas was also hierarchical, headed by a viceroy. The viceroy (which means literally vice-king), appointed by the crown, served as the king's personal agent in the colonies, and was responsible directly to him. The viceroy exercised power in the name of the king; his decisions carried the weight of royal decisions. The viceroys were always sent from the mother country to administer the colonies; never were persons born in the colonies, whose loyalties might be divided, appointed to these positions. The viceroy's main job was to execute and administer royal authority and decrees in the vast territories of the New World. Initially, there were only two such viceroys for all of Latin America, one located in Mexico City and the other in Lima, Peru. Eventually, Spain created two additional viceroyalties to help administer its Latin American empire, one in Buenos Aires in charge of the Rio de la Plata region (present-day Argentina, Paraguay, and Uruguay) and the other for Gran Colombia (present-day Venezuela, Ecuador, and Colombia).

Beneath the viceroy was the captain-general, who governed a smaller territory. For example, Guatemala was a *part* of the viceroyalty of New Spain administered from Mexico City, but it also had its own captain-general who governed this subterritory. In turn, beneath the captain-generals were governors, provincial or district administrators, and *alcaldes* (local mayors). Each of these officials, like the viceroys, was appointed by the Spanish crown, almost always came from Spain and not from the colonies, and acted as the royal agent of the king at his particular level. In reality, the closer one got to the grass-roots local level, the more likely it was that the official sometimes came not from Spain but from the colonies themselves. However, power was strictly centralized; local officials then as now had little independent authority.

Spain used additional institutions to administer its far-flung empire in the Americas. *Audiencias* (literally, hearings agencies) were the highest royal courts of appeal within each district, and they also served as a consultative council to the viceroy or captain-general. In this advisory capacity, the *audiencia* played a role comparable to that played by the Council of Indies to the king: they provided advice to the ruler and at the same time helped him administer colonial affairs.

The *residencia* was the official, judicial review of an official's (viceroy or captain-general) conduct at the end of his appointment. It held public officials to strict accountability for their activities while in office. The *visita* (visit) was an investigation carried out by a special agent dispatched by the king either to look into a specific grievance against a viceroy or other official, or to conduct a general investigation of conditions within the colony.

The *cabildo* (town council) represented the lowest level in Spain's administrative hierarchy. It was one of the few institutions in this vast and highly centralized, bureaucratic empire that retained some (usually small) measure of local autonomy. It was also about the only institution in which local, non-Spanish-born citizens could exercise any influence. However, the *cabildo* was limited by its lack of any independent revenue-generating authority, and it never evolved into an independent political body along the lines of the New England town meeting and assembly. The *cabildos*, limited to the local elites and landowners, were not the cradles of democracy that they are sometimes pictured to be.

The Spanish colonial system, as can be seen, was highly top-down, centralized, bureaucratic, and authoritarian. All power emanated from the crown or his designated agents. The system is considered to have been seldom intolerably bad, but never really good, either. It did succeed in administering Spain's vast territories in Latin America for over three centuries with a minimum of force and, at the same time, with very few protests or rebellions against Spanish rule. But it provided no training whatsoever in self-government or democracy, a shortcoming that would continue to plague Spain's former colonies down to the present day.

We have looked at the *political* structure of Spanish colonial administration; now we need to examine the economic and social base of the colonial system.

The Economic System

The conquest of the Americas was undertaken not just to attain military glory, or to expand the territorial domain of the Spanish and Portuguese crowns, or to extend the Roman Catholic faith to the indigenous peoples of the Americas. All these motives undoubtedly played a role in shaping the conquest, but they were not the only goals. Gold and greed also motivated the *conquistadores*. Indeed, selfless and selfish motives existed side by side, often even overlapping in individual colonists.

Recall that Columbus's voyage of discovery and *all* subsequent Spanish and Portuguese voyages were crown projects—that is, they all took place only with the official approval and licensing of the king. However, they were usually *privately* financed. Merchants, traders, or members of aristocratic families would put up the money to pay for the ship, the provisions, and the crew; but when the ship returned home, they expected to turn a profit from the sale of goods, gold, or perhaps slaves. Thus, while the conquest was at one level a feudal enterprise—in the arrangement of the landholding system and the use of native Indians as "peasants"—at another it was capitalistic—in the profit motive of the conquest's sponsors.

During the first decade after Columbus's discovery, the Spanish were mainly concerned with gathering up the gold that the Indians had or that could be readily mined. The islands (Hispaniola, Cuba, Puerto Rico), however, lacked an abundance of gold and the supplies were quickly exhausted. Hence, the next step in the *conquistadores'* search for wealth was the division of the land in the New World and the acquisition of an Indian labor force to work those lands. This was one of the most important—and lasting—institutions introduced by the Spaniards in Latin America.

The institution used by the Spanish to divide up the territories of the New World was called the *encomienda*. It is important to remember that the *encomienda* was not a grant of land per se. Rather, it reflected a feudal concept that grew out of the Reconquest of the Iberian Peninsula from the Moors and was carried over to the New World. In Iberia, the *encomienda* had been a *temporary* grant by the king, as a reward for their services, to the knights and military orders of manorial rights over the territories and peoples regained from the Moors. In the New World, *encomienda* meant the patronage conferred by royal favor to the *conquistadores* over the Indians, also as a reward for services rendered. Under the *encomienda*, the Spaniards were obliged to Christianize the Indians, educate and civilize them, and defend their persons and property—in return for obligatory tribute and labor. No grant of land was involved.

In practice, however, the obligations of the Spaniards toward the Indians frequently were overlooked. The Indians were assigned in lots to individual Spaniards to work on their farms or ranches or in their gold mines. The educating and Christianizing missions were often ignored or forgotten. The Indians were parceled out among the Spaniards to do with as they pleased. Thus, the natives were worked beyond their capacity, infant mortality climbed while the birth rate declined, and the system became one of de facto slave labor. At the same time, while the *encomienda* did not provide for a system of private or permanent property rights, the original territorial grants were passed on from generation to generation among the Spaniards, becoming both permanent and private. Moreover, these were *huge* territories—from mountain range to mountain range—often the size of a U.S. county or even state.

To correct the injustices of the *encomienda*, Spanish authorities introduced the *repartimiento*, which was a grant of wage labor. A Spaniard wishing a *repartimiento* had to file a petition with the viceroy stating that he had a farm or ranch and that he needed a specified number of Indians for a given period of time. In return, he promised to treat them well and pay them a wage. In practice, however, the *repartimiento*, like the *encomienda*, was subject to abuse. The system often degenerated into slave labor or peonage, the Indians were seldom paid, and the grant of labor frequently became permanent rather than temporary.

It is not hard to see how out of this system would grow the Spanish system of *haciendas* (*estancias* in Argentina, *fazendas* in Brazil)—one of *the* classic institutions of Latin American life. *Haciendas* were large, often huge, self-contained, quasi-feudal estates. Over time, the original grants of land for temporary use had became estates held in perpetuity. The owners of these estates were also the social, political, judicial, military, even religious authorities on them. All these powers were fused in a single person, the *patrón* or godfather, who ruled his estate like the king ruled his realm: absolutely and from the top down. On the estates, a two-class (and caste) system prevailed: owners and their family (white, Hispanic) at the top, and peons or slaves (Indians, and eventually Blacks in some areas) at the bottom. The *hacienda* system perpetuated itself into the nineteenth-century independence period, dominated all areas of life (social, economic, political), and, by its very strength and permanence, served to retard the growth of other, more modernizing economic activities such as commerce, trade, and industry.

The Roman Catholic church bolstered and usually reinforced the imperial system. Growing out of a medieval concept, church and state were thought to represent the "two swords" of God's power, religious and political. Unlike in the North American colonies, where church and state eventually were separated, in Latin America the two were fused into a single powerful authority. The church, in Christianizing the Indians, also assisted in subjecting them to Spain's political authority. Indians were obliged to accept Catholicism peacefully (the *requerimiento* or "requirement") or be subdued by the sword. In some areas of the Americas, such as Mexico and Paraguay, the church was also given vast lands and Indians to civilize and, thus, to subdue. Religious concepts such as authoritarianism and subjugation stemming from the Middle Ages (principally Saint Thomas and his sixteenth-century neoscholastic apostles in Spain: Suárez, Vitoria, Molina, Soto) undergirded the system of royal authority and empire; at the same time, the crown helped support and bolster the church and its institutions. Only a handful of priests defended Indian rights and insisted the Indians be treated as human beings.

The Social Structure

The social structure of the colonies was hierarchical, rigid, and two-class. The king was at the top of the pyramid of power, and all things had to be done under his authority and in his name, but he was far removed from the New World, and communication took a long time. In the colonies, the social structure and social life often revolved around the viceroy, the top-ranking official in the colony. The viceroy and his fellow *peninsulares* (officials sent out from the Iberian Peninsula, *not* native-born Latin Americans) had political power and often social influence, but they lacked economic power, which was exercised by the Creole or native-born Spanish landholders. So, while the Spanish system was rigidly hierarchical, at the top, *from the beginning*, the possibility existed for tension and, eventually, full-scale rivalry between these two groups.

The middle class in the colonies was small and never developed into a commercial middle class as happened in Holland, England, and the North American colonies. The middle class consisted of a few soldiers, some bureaucrats, and a few merchants, traders, and artisans. In other words, this was a traditional, feudal, medieval middle class, not a modernizing, risk-taking, entrepreneurial middle class. Even today, there are doubts as to whether Latin America has a strong enough middle class and social base like those of Western Europe or the United States for the permanent establishment of democracy and economic growth.

Below the Hispanic elite and middle class was a huge underclass of Indians and, later, Blacks. The ratio of Indians to Whites in the early decades of the colonial period was in the neighborhood of ten thousand to one. The social structure was based not just on wealth or social standing, therefore; it had ethnic and racial roots as well. Sociologists tell us that when a society is deeply divided along class lines, these are very difficult to overcome; but when a society is divided along both class and racial lines that mutually reinforce each other, these are almost impossible to overcome.

The Spaniards and Portuguese could not repeat in the New World the exact structure of society that existed in the Iberian Peninsula. The distances were too great for that, the land area too vast, and the social conditions quite distinct. In Iberia, Spanish and Portuguese society from the Middle Ages on had been based on a structure of "corporations" that included the military orders, the church, the cities and towns with their *fueros* (literally, "rights"—meaning, self-governing charters), the universities, and emerging artisan and craft guilds. In Latin America, however, there were no military orders; the church was not well institutionalized, particularly at first; towns and cities were few and far between and had no independent "rights"; universities and other groups were not well organized; and artisan and craft guilds were weak or nonexistent. These corporate groups—army, church, guilds—were organized in the main city centers but not throughout the colonies. Hence, instead of, or alongside, the few functional corporations that existed in Latin America, the Spaniards and Portuguese erected a system of social categories based largely on race, ethnicity, or *castas* (castes).

For example, one set of rules, laws, and obligations applied to pure-blooded Spanish *conquistadores* and their descendants, another to *mestizos* and mulattos, and still others to Indians and Blacks. Each rung in the social/racial hierarchy, including numerous in-between categories, had their own laws, courts, rights, and obligations. Rather than a corporatized society with numerous functional bodies as in Spain, Latin America was largely organized on the basis of class and caste. Later, during its independence period, Latin America would try to fill this organizational void with the corporate bodies and associations almost wholly lacking during the colonial era.

The treatment of the Indians by the Spaniards during the colonial era defies simplistic interpretation. Undoubtedly, many Indians died as a result of their enslavement by the Spaniards. On the other hand, most of the Indians died not as a result of Spanish arms or enslavement but because of the diseases the Spaniards passed on inadvertently for which the Indians had no immunity. The Indians may have gotten their revenge, however, in the form of syphilis. They passed this debilitating and sometimes deadly disease on to the Spaniards, who in turn carried it back to Europe, where it has been a scourge ever since.

Nor were the Indians entirely without their defenders in Spain. A Spanish friar, Bartolomé de Las Casas, who accompanied Columbus on one of his voyages and saw firsthand how the Indians had been enslaved and devastated, became their champion before the royal court in Spain. Las Casas was a vigorous pamphleteer on the Indians' behalf, helping to promote high-level discussion of the issue and a major national debate in Spain as to whether Indians had souls. As we have seen, for both Indians and Blacks, this was a crucial issue since it helped determine whether they were treated as slaves or as men with at least some rights.

In the New Laws promulgated by Spain in 1542, in the debates over whether Indians (and later Blacks) had souls, and in the hearings conducted at the royal court, the defenders of the Indians clearly were effective in advancing their case. Nevertheless, the colonies were so far away that royal decrees emanating from Madrid were only feebly implemented in the colonies. Moreover, the demand for menial labor was so powerful that the well-meaning laws meant to protect the Indians were often ignored. Finally, the crown itself, always in need of increased revenues and dependent on receiving regularly the "Royal Fifth" (20 percent of all commercial transactions with the colonies), failed to enforce vigorously its own laws. Hence, the Indians' situation was a mixed one: sometimes they were well treated, more often they were not. Their treatment varied depending on location, the particular viceroy or landowner in charge of their area, and the revenue needs of the crown. Many Indians were cruelly exploited, but others received the protection of the Catholic church and were organized into cooperatives on protected communes.

As a result of the conquest, large numbers of Indians went into what can only be called "culture shock." Culture shock occurs when people come into contact with another civilization so different from their own that they cannot cope with or adjust to it. In the Indians' case, their gods had failed them against the Spanish god, their empires had been defeated, their leaders were dead, and their civilizations had been broken or rendered ineffective. So, instead of either cooperating with the Spaniards or resisting them (both strategies were often futile), many Indians simply withdrew—into the mountains and into themselves. They often became inscrutable, inaccessible, and noncommunicative, having as little contact with Spanish civilization as possible. Today, many indigenous peoples in Latin America continue in that condition of limbo. Their own civilizations have been destroyed in large part, and yet they have not been assimilated into the Spanish or Western one. They remain withdrawn, frequently defying the efforts of all regimes, leftist or rightist, military or civilian, to integrate them into the national life. At present, some of these indigenous groups are trying to resurrect their ancient cultures.

The Spaniards and Portuguese were, in general, adept colonizers in the Americas, having earlier gained experience in Africa and the Atlantic islands of Madeira, the Canaries, and the Azores. The model they employed derived from the ancient Roman Empire under which Spain and Portugal had themselves been ruled 1,500 years earlier. What is interesting about the Spanish and Portuguese colonial systems is just how stable and long-lasting they were. Employing a minimum of force, these colonial empires lasted for over three hundred years. During this entire period, these empires only rarely had to deal with any protests, let alone rebellions, from their subjects. It is a measure of their success—coupled with the apathy and disorganization of their subjects—that these empires were able to control such vast territories for so long but with such an economy of force.

The Spanish and Portuguese empires were based on feudal and medieval concepts inherited from the mother countries that retarded their development and persisted up until the present day. In these respects, the Latin American colonies differed fundamentally from the North American colonies, which were rooted in more modern social, political, legal, and religious principles. In the eighteenth century, the Spanish and Portuguese sought also to update their empires. But it was precisely these efforts at reform that produced a backlash in the colonies that led, eventually, to rebellion and independence.

Change, Reform—and Rebellion

The Spanish and Portuguese colonial systems, while stable, were not entirely static for three centuries. Change occurred, but within carefully controlled bounds. Colonial administrators came and went, exhibiting varying skills and personalities. Spanish and Portuguese authority waxed and waned as Holland, England, and France sought to supplant them as imperial powers. Society and social relations in the colonies also changed over time, leading to greater resentments on the part of some groups.

The most dramatic social change was the precipitous drop in the Indian population in the seventeenth century. Because this decline occurred a full century after the initial conquest, it cannot be said to have been caused by the force of Spanish or Portuguese arms alone. Disease as well as hard labor undoubtedly had something to do with the declining indigenous population, but because the colonial powers had a need for Indian labor and because "peasants" were expensive, they wanted to preserve the Indian population, not destroy it. A major cause was the culture shock the Indians experienced when they saw their proud cultures and civilizations taken over and destroyed by the Spanish and Portuguese. One result was that millions of Indians went into depression and simply stopped reproducing. In addition, in some areas, there were mass Indian suicides. The demographic decline of seventeenth-century Latin America represented a very serious, but still quiet, form of protest against colonial rule.

The precipitous decline of the Indian population forced the Spanish and Portuguese to import larger numbers of Black slaves from Africa to serve as manual laborers. During this period, slave societies in areas around the Caribbean basin and in northeast Brazil came into prominence, as compared with the smaller-scale slave systems of the past. Blacks served as substitutes for the previously endless supply of Indian labor that was now declining. The nefarious slave trade intensified, and in the Caribbean (especially Haiti) and Brazil, more rigid and arbitrary plantation systems organized on exploitation and strict class/caste lines developed.

Another major social change was the growing split between Spanish officialdom sent over from the Iberian Peninsula (and thus referred to as *peninsulares*) and the Spaniards born in the New World (known as *criollos*). Under the Spanish system of maintaining loyalty to the crown, *all* officials in the Americas had to be *peninsulares*. But the *criollos* had lived in the Americas often for several generations, they had acquired wealth and social position, and they had begun to demand political power to go with their rising economic and social power. However, their ambitions were blocked by the *peninsulares* who served at the behest of the crown. Increasingly, the *criollos* came to see that their only means for achieving political and administrative power would be by substituting themselves for the *peninsulares*—which meant gaining independence.

A third change was the expanding economic and commercial life of the colonies. Under the colonial system, all the wealth and resources of the Americas existed only for the benefit of the crown, which had been milking the colonies dry of gold, silver, and other resources for hundreds of years. Increasingly, however, the *criollos* and the rising business and commercial classes in the colonies wanted the freedom to trade with other, more prosperous nations—such as Holland and England—and to break the Spanish/Portuguese trade monopoly. More and more, in fact, these other countries had been trading with Latin America in defiance of Spanish and Portuguese laws, but this had only whetted the appetite of local importers and exporters. No doubt, the desire on the part of Latin America commercial elements to open up the area to free trade was an important factor stimulating the desire for independence.

Meanwhile, important changes were occurring in the administration of the colonies. In the sixteenth and seventeenth centuries, Spain had been ruled by the Hapsburg monarchy. Initially hard-working and dedicated under the kings Charles V and his son Philip II, the later Hapsburg monarchy proved degenerate, imbecilic, and finally impotent. The Hapsburg royal line died off in 1700 having produced no heirs and was replaced by a branch of the Bourbon royal family, already ruling in France. Portugal did not undergo such a change of royal families as did Spain, but its colonial policies changed in ways parallel to Spain's when the Marques de Pombal served as prime minister from 1750 to 1777.

The Bourbons, and Pombal, were more modern and forward-looking than the Hapsburgs had been. They introduced street lighting, reforestation, new educational reforms, and French styles of dress and behavior in Iberia and Latin America. They centralized colonial administration and made it more efficient, and also expelled the Jesuits from Latin America.

These reforms do not appear to be very revolutionary. But in the isolated, still feudal and medieval colonies of Latin America, they had a profound impact. First, the deeply conservative Creole (native-born) colonists resented the effort to impose French styles and behavior on them. Second, the greater efficiency and centralization introduced by the Bourbon monarchs, while improving Spain's control over the colonies, was resented by the colonists themselves who, under the earlier, less-efficient system, had become used to operating on their own. Third, the deeply religious colonists strongly resented the expulsion in 1767 of the Jesuits, who had been responsible for virtually all education and social services in the colonies. Note also that the Bourbon monarchy (as well as Portugal's Pombal), while more efficient than the Hapsburgs, was no more democratic and may have been even more authoritarian. Thus, the Bourbon reforms, however progressive and well meaning, caused the colonists to consider, for the first time, that maybe they would be better off without the mother countries—that is, better off independent.

Other developments also began to push Latin America toward independence. One was the eighteenth-century Enlightenment and its ideas of rationalism, scientific inquiry, and individual initiative—all of which stood in conflict with historical Latin American Catholicism, scholasticism, and fatalism. Another was the revolutions in America in 1776 and in France in 1789, and the "heretical" ideas they exemplified such as liberty, equality, fraternity, and independence. A third factor was the efforts of the other great trading powers—England, France, and Holland—to break Spain's and Portugal's trade monopoly in the Americas, and the desire of the colonists to trade with these other powers. Finally, in the late eighteenth and early nineteenth centuries, several uprisings occurred in Latin America—rebellions that failed initially but that illustrated the discontent among all classes beginning to arise in the colonies.

These were the main *general* causes that helped create the *conditions* for independence sentiment to grow, but the major *precipitating cause* was events in Europe. In 1808, the French ruler Napoleon Bonaparte invaded Spain, deposed the Spanish king, and placed his brother Joseph on the throne. In Latin America, however, the colonists rejected Joseph Bonaparte and declared loyalty to the deposed Spanish king Ferdinand VII. In 1814, following widespread Spanish rebellion against French rule, Ferdinand VII was able to reascend to the Spanish throne, but only on the condition that he accept the liberal constitution drafted in 1812 that provided some limited freedom and put curbs on royal absolution. At first, the king repudiated these restrictions on his authority, but later he was obliged to accept them. When he did so, even these limited liberalizing changes were too much for the conservative Spanish Creoles in Latin America, who now moved defiantly toward independence. By 1824, all of Latin America had achieved independence from Spain except for Cuba and Puerto Rico, which remained as Spanish colonies until the Spanish-American War of 1898. These independence struggles are discussed in more detail in Chapter 4.

Brazil gained independence from Portugal in a slightly different fashion. When Napoleon's armies invaded Portugal, the royal family fled to Brazil— the first time a European monarch had ever set foot in the New World. After Napoleon's forces were driven out of Portugal, the king, Joao VI, returned to Portugal to reclaim his throne, but he left his son Pedro in charge in Brazil. When Joao died in 1821, Pedro was called back to assume the Portuguese throne; instead, he decided to stay in Brazil. In this way, Brazil became an independent monarchy, not an independent republic like the other countries.

Latin America on the Eve of Independence

In 1820, Latin America stood poised on the threshold of becoming an area of independent states. However, as a product of the highly centralized and authoritarian Spanish and Portuguese colonial systems, Latin America lacked any experience or training whatsoever in democracy or self-government, as the North American colonies had before achieving independence. In addition, Latin America was still locked into a feudal and medieval social and economic pattern (two-class, nonindustrial, noncapitalist, poor and backward) as compared with the modern or modernizing institutions of North America. Many of its resources had been exploited, and it lacked infrastructure. As a result, Latin America was destined to fall farther behind while the United States forged ahead. Moreover, in Latin America, the newly gained independence had little effect on basic social and economic institutions. Instead, Latin America remained essentially feudal and medieval.

4
✦
Independence and After

The Twilight of the Middle Ages

Most of Latin America became independent in the 1820s, approximately fifty years after the thirteen colonies in North America achieved their independence from England. That means the Latin American nations are younger by half a century than the United States and will celebrate various events of their bicentennials beginning in the early twenty-first century. But it also means that as nations, they are older, by more than a hundred years, than the "new nations" of Africa, the Middle East, and South and Southeast Asia, most of which are less than fifty years old. The Latin American nations also are more developed and institutionalized than most of the other emerging nations with whom they are often classified—a fact that leads to numerous errors in interpreting Latin America.

We generally think of revolutions as ushering in profound and liberating changes. That was certainly true of the British Revolution of 1688, the American Revolution of 1776, and the French Revolution of 1789. But in Latin America, the revolutions for independence were conservative events. They constituted *wars of separation* from Spain but not genuine social revolutions. They were aimed at restoring and bolstering the older regime, the *status quo ante* as represented by the Creole elite, not changing it. Independence in Latin America led not to social change, but to a strengthening and reinforcement of the church, the landholding class, and the newly created national armies. The sporadic efforts on the parts of Indians and Blacks to rise up and make these into social as well as political revolutions failed dismally and were brutally suppressed.

The feudal and medieval institutions and practices that characterized Latin America during the colonial period thus persisted into the independence period when, in somewhat altered form, they received a new lease on life. It was only around the turn of the twentieth century that the vast social, economic, and political changes began that would catapult Latin America into the modern world. We refer to this period of approximately 1890–1930 as the "twilight of the Middle Ages," when Latin America's historic feudal institutions began to break down and new, more modern structures began to emerge. Hence, in this chapter, we cover that hundred-year period from independence in the 1820s to the breakdown of the ancient system in the 1930s, when Latin America finally, tardily, began to enter the modern world.

Independence Struggles

Haiti, in 1804, became the first country in Latin America to achieve independence. But Haiti was a special case, and its example could not be repeated elsewhere. First, Haiti was a French colony, not a Spanish or Portuguese one. Second, Haiti's independence struggle began as a Black slave revolt and ended with the burning of the plantations, the driving out of the White French elite, and the destruction of the Western and European institutions established by the French. These clearly were not the outcomes that the White Hispanic Creoles about to wrest control from the *peninsulares* in the rest of Spanish America desired. Hence, the Haitian model was not followed elsewhere in the hemisphere; indeed, significant steps were taken by the Latin American Creoles to make sure that what happened in Haiti would *not* be repeated in their own territories.

As we saw in the last chapter, there were multiple causes—economic, intellectual, social, political, ideological—for the Latin American wars of independence. Furthermore, the movement for independence was not one single movement; rather, revolts against Spanish authority took place in the several different colonies at different times, often responding to distinct local conditions and producing different consequences. Immediately, the several colonies and colonial centers began to go their separate ways.

The first revolts in Spanish South America took place in Buenos Aires. The Viceroyalty of the Rio de la Plata (including present-day Paraguay and Uruguay, as well as Argentina) had become a very prosperous area, coveted by the British. When Britain sent an invasion force in 1806, the Spanish Creoles rose up to drive the British out—the first act of nationalism and of genuinely independent action in the history of the colony. Hence, a year or so later, when Napoleon's army invaded the Iberian Peninsula and dethroned the Spanish king, it was only natural that the Buenos Aires Creoles would try to "hold" the province for Spain. But that in itself was an act of independence, adding further fuel to the already glowing embers.

The first signs of revolt in Chile occurred in 1808 when Creoles moved to secure power for themselves in the wake of the death of the Spanish governor-general. Soon the Creoles in Buenos Aires and in Chile were cooperating, militarily and otherwise. The royalist forces (those loyal to Spain) in the Southern Cone (present-day Chile, Argentina, Paraguay, and Uruguay) steadily lost ground and were largely confined to the Banda Oriental (the "Eastern Bank" of the Rio de la Plata—present-day Uruguay). However, the main center of Spanish power in South America, the Viceroyalty of Peru, was still in royalist hands, and the viceroy there continued to threaten the patriots in Argentina and Chile with his army.

Napoleon's occupation of Spain also sparked independence sentiments in northern South America, then known as the Viceroyalty of New Granada (encompassing present-day Ecuador, Colombia, and Venezuela). New Granada was a hotbed of liberal and independence sentiment where French and North American ideas about the "rights of man" flowed freely. As early as 1809, a *junta* (council) had been formed in Ecuador to hold power for the deposed Spanish king, and others were formed in Colombia and Venezuela the following year; then, in 1811, a congress in Venezuela declared independence. As in the United States, however, where independence and Tory (pro-British) forces opposed each other for many years, so in South America the proindependence Creoles had to contend with powerful Spanish loyalists for nearly two decades.

In the Viceroyalty of New Spain (present-day Mexico and Central America), the revolt against Spanish authority took on the tones of social revolution. In 1810, a Spanish friar, Miguel Hidalgo, raised his *grito de Dolores* ("shout of Dolores," after the small parish where he served) and led the impoverished Indians in his area against Spanish authority. To the cry for independence was now added the shout of "death to the Spaniards"; and the murder of the owners and the destruction of the Spanish estates became major objectives of the Indian revolutionaries. This was not just independence sentiment being expressed but social revolution as well. However, Hidalgo only had a ragtag, unprofessional army (although numbering some 80,000), and his Indian revolt was eventually put down. But the lesson of this struggle was not lost on the White Mexican *criollos* as well as those in South America, who now took steps to ensure that independence would result from a conservative transfer of power and that social revolution would not rear its head again.

Over a fourteen-year period from 1810 to 1824, these several *separate* revolts in the Spanish colonies gradually coalesced. In the south, José de San Martín, a Creole from Buenos Aires who had had military experience in

Spain's wars against France, first drove the Spanish forces out of the Rio de la Plata region. Then, in 1817, his army crossed the Andes in an epochal march and drove the Spanish loyalists out of Chile. Meanwhile, in the north, "the Liberator," Simon Bolívar, had first freed Venezuela and then Colombia and Ecuador. That left Peru as the sole remaining Spanish stronghold on the South American continent.

San Martín and Bolívar now planned a pincer movement on Lima. San Martín's forces approached from the south, Bolivar's from the north; there was by this time also an army in Peru of proindependence forces. In the decisive battle of Ayacucho in 1824, the Spanish royalist forces were roundly defeated and the backbone of Spanish colonial rule broken. After a long struggle, Mexico had also achieved independence in 1821, but under more conservative auspices than the initial Hidalgo-led revolt.

Portuguese America (present-day Brazil) was a special case: a peaceful transfer to independence. As noted in Chapter 3, when Napoleon Bonaparte occupied Portugal in 1807, the Portuguese royal family fled to Brazil. Following Napoleon's defeat in 1821, however, Crown Prince Pedro chose to remain in Brazil. In the *grito de Ipiranga* (shout of Ipiranga), Pedro declared Brazil an independent state. However, it remained a monarchy for the next sixty-seven years, not a republic. By continuing as a monarchy, Brazil was spared the internal divisiveness, chaos, and instability that marked the Spanish colonies.

By 1824, then, all of Latin America except Cuba and Puerto Rico had achieved independence; Cuba and Puerto Rico remained Spanish colonies until the Spanish-American War of 1898. The long domination by Spain shaped eventually a virulent but frustrated nationalism in the two colonies that was even more intense than in the other Spanish colonies. Meanwhile, the other, now former, colonies were about to embark on a course of nationhood that would prove terribly disruptive and hinder development efforts for four decades.

Conservative Revolutions

It bears reemphasizing that the wars of independence in Latin America were not liberating revolutions except in the narrowest sense. They implied liberation in the form of independence from Spain and Portugal, but not political revolution in the sense of instituting equality or democracy, and certainly not social revolution in the sense of bringing Blacks or Indians into the social or political mainstream. Rather, these were conserving revolutions, designed to preserve and enhance the power and status of the White, Hispanic, Creole elite. In some quarters, the Latin American independence leaders borrowed the rhetoric (liberty, equality, fraternity) and even some of the institutions (separation of powers) of the American and French revolutions, but nowhere were these meant to reflect operative reality or to imply genuine democracy and equality for all groups.

Recall what happened to Hidalgo's Indian uprising in Mexico: it had been brutally suppressed, not just by Spanish royalists but by the Creole independence leaders as well. Haiti's slave revolt and the slaughter of the White ruling class also served in Latin America as a vivid and horrifying image of what happens when the lower classes revolt. Hence, in the newly independent republics, steps were taken to keep the lower classes in check: the franchise was severely limited, Indians and Blacks were denied the vote, slavery was continued, and repressive laws were introduced to maintain a quasi-feudal, two-class structure of elites and masses.

The power structure in the colonies thus remained largely the same after independence. In the Spanish and Portuguese colonial regimes, the main power centers were the church, the Hispanic or White elite, and, ultimately, the crown or royal authority. The church and the landowning class constituted the two main corporate pillars of the old regime in the colonies. With independence, little changed. The church remained just as powerful as ever—maybe even more powerful in some former colonies. The landed elites also retained or extended their power, the only change being the expulsion of the *peninsulares* and the greater societalwide influence wielded by the Creoles, who already had land, peasants, and economic power. Thus, the only substantive change in the power structure was at the very top: the severance of ties with the crown and the expulsion of royal authority.

Into the vacuum created by the withdrawal of the influence of the Spanish or Portuguese royal authority stepped the armies, which had led the struggle for independence. By the time of the Battle of Ayacucho in 1824, after waging an on-again, off-again fight against Spain for nearly twenty years, vast numbers of Creoles and their peasant retainers had acquired military experience, and many had achieved the rank (often self-appointed) of general. Hence, the army now took its place as the third corporate pillar (along with the church and the landed elites) of the system, replacing the crown as the ultimate arbiter of national affairs. Note again, however, that while the *cupola*, or top, of the Spanish colonial pyramid of power (royal authority) had been lopped off or repudiated, the basic social and political hierarchy remained intact.

This conservative, stand-pat, traditional power structure was reflected in the laws and constitutions adopted by the new Latin American nations. All these countries formally adopted constitutions modeled on the U.S. Constitution, with separation of powers, checks and balances, and so on; and they all contained lists of human and civil rights borrowed from the U.S. Bill of Rights and the French Declaration of the Rights of Man. But a closer examination of these new laws and constitutions reveals more a continuation of established practices than an emergent political and social consciousness.

Almost all of them gave the church and the Catholic religion a privileged place in society. All of them gave special protection to elites and landowners in the form of property and literacy requirements for voting, and therefore a highly limited franchise (1–2 percent of the population). In all of them, the executive had especially strong, even authoritarian power, enabling him to rule as a constitutional dictator (an extension or updating of the earlier authoritarian tradition), usually at the expense of an independent legislature or judiciary. Human rights could be, and frequently were, suspended by the simple presidential declaration of a state of siege or of emergency. And, in almost all of these constitutions or in subsequent organic laws (in Latin America, a notch below constitutional law but above legislative law), the army was elevated to a special place as almost a fourth branch of government, with the duty and even obligation to step into the political process when necessary to restore order, resolve conflicts, and establish domestic tranquility. Thus, subsequently, when the army seized power in Latin America, it often was doing so—contrary to most U.S. notions—not as an act of usurpation but as a legal and constitutional obligation. Of course, this power was also frequently abused by these selfsame armies, who sometimes took power on the slightest pretext and ruled arbitrarily.

Hence, the Latin American countries began their independent life with virtually all the institutions they had had as colonies, the main difference being the substitution of the army for the crown. In their efforts to retain the institutions of the past—an elitist, two-class social order, a mercantilist economy, a top-down political system, a feudal and medieval society—rather than usher in extensive social or political change, the wars of independence should be seen as conservative movements, not liberal or liberating ones. These were wars to separate from Spain, not social revolutions.

Problems of New Nationhood: 1820s–1850s

Immediately after independence, and for about thirty years thereafter, most of the Latin American nations fell into chaos. Their economies regressed to earlier, more primitive levels, and the commerce that had begun to develop in the eighteenth century was again curtailed. The clear, hierarchical social structure of the colonial era became more confused and chaotic. The political situation was very disorganized as rival armed bands, a legacy of the colonial struggles, vied for control of national power. Anarchy alternated with strong-arm rule, such as that by Juan Manuel de Rosas in Argentina and Antonio López de Santa Ana in Mexico. Only Brazil, which continued as a monarchy, and Chile, which quickly reestablished oligarchic rule, managed to avoid chaos and anarchy.

Eventually, however, some semblance of order began to reemerge. It's worth noting that the problems of nationhood that the new Latin American nations faced in the 1820s and 1830s were not altogether different from those faced by the new African and Asian states in the 1950s and 1960s. And just as these latter nations required some thirty years to begin to "get their acts together" and recover, so it took Latin America about three decades to begin to resolve its pressing problems.

National Boundaries

The first set of problems encountered by the new nations of Latin America was to define their national boundaries and, hence, to determine nationhood itself. Generally, the boundaries of the newly independent states followed the old viceroyalty boundaries; but as Latin America continued to fragment, the new nation-states got smaller and smaller. For example, Central America had been subordinate administratively to the Viceroyalty of New Spain (Mexico) but went its own way after independence in the form of a confederation. The confederation, in turn, split up in 1839 into the small, economically unviable, city-state-size countries found in Central America today.

The Viceroyalty of New Granada similarly split up into the nations of Venezuela, Colombia, and Ecuador—despite Bolívar's efforts to hold it together. In the Rio de la Plata viceroyalty, Paraguay separated from Argentina; and the Banda Oriental in 1829 was established as the separate buffer state of Uruguay between feuding giants Brazil and Argentina. Upper Peru (Bolivia) similarly became an independent nation, adding to the fragmentation.

On modern maps, the boundaries between these countries are usually shown in clear, purple colors. But high in the Andes, deep in the Amazon, and in the jungles of Central America, the lines are often far less clear. Even today, many borders in Latin America are subject to dispute, providing grounds for rival claims and the potential for future conflict. However, it seems doubtful that very many of these will produce full-scale border wars. Another problem is that these national boundaries usually have little to do with the original Indian kingdoms, and that has recently also become a subject of controversy in some countries.

Unitarism Versus Federalism

Even in those countries that did not fragment, immense centrifugal forces threatened to lead to disintegration. To prevent that from happening, several of the largest countries of Latin America—Argentina, Brazil, Mexico, and Venezuela—adopted federal-type systems. They sought to balance central authority with strong state or regional autonomy so as to forestall the disintegrative tendencies of neighboring countries. After independence, the power of local elites and of local *caudillos* (men on horseback) often increased at the expense of central government authority. Personal authority and charisma dominated over lagging and ineffective institutional structures.

The problem was that, unlike the North American colonies, Latin America had virtually no experience in or institutions of government at the regional or state level. Federalism had been put in place to prevent national fragmentation, but the reality throughout Latin America—even in the federal-type systems—was centralization. Here was the dilemma: Latin America had such weak institutions after independence that it required strict central control and direction to prevent chaos and complete fragmentation. Yet the authority, or authoritarianism, needed to hold the state and society together was so strong that it frequently verged on dictatorship. Indeed, these would be the mirror themes that would dominate Latin America in the early nineteenth century: anarchy on the one hand and authoritarianism on the other, with the countries of the area torn and frequently alternating between the two. In some countries, this dilemma has still not been resolved.

The Church Issue

The Roman Catholic church and the Catholic religion are more than simply *a* religion in Latin America; they are, historically, *the* church and *the* religion. Catholic teachings dominated not only in the religious sphere but in the economic, social, and political spheres as well. Moreover, the church was often the largest landowner as well, and in such countries as Paraguay and Mexico the church had special responsibilities not just to convert but to care for and govern the Indians.

The church-state issue flared and then gradually subsided in the nineteenth century. Initially, the newly independent Latin American states sought to inherit the right to appoint church officials, a power once given by the pope to the Spanish crown. Slowly, they moved toward a position of formal, constitutional separation of church and state, but even with that principle established constitutionally, the church in most countries remained powerful, and the line between church and state was often blurred. In Mexico, the church owned so much land—fully 60 percent of the national territory—that in the 1850s a reform movement was launched aimed at stripping the church of its power. Although the church issue waxed and waned and sometimes waxed again in various countries, the general trend by the mid-nineteenth century was toward a calming down and resolution of the divisive church-state issue.

Militarism

The military had not been a major force in colonial Latin America; in fact, it is surprising how few Spanish and Portuguese soldiers were needed to control these vast territories for over three hundred years. But with the withdrawal of royal authority, the newly created independence armies became the ultimate arbiters of national political affairs.

The military's role was enhanced by the chaos prevailing in these new countries. In the absence of functional institutions capable of providing efficient self-government, the armed forces were often obliged to step in to prevent a complete breakdown into anarchy. It is not that the military always or necessarily *wanted* to usurp power—although at times it did that, too—but that the chaotic conditions, as well as constitutional and legal requirements, often *obliged* the armed forces to intervene. Usually, these were not very professional armies at first, but their leaders were sometimes charismatic *caudillos* who used the ragtag military to seize power. Often, too, a single country would have several armies: a national army with some, usually small, degree of professional training, and then a number of unprofessional regional armies that vied for control of local customs houses as well as for national power.

Economic and Social Breakdown

In the first three decades following independence, Latin America suffered a severe economic and social breakdown. Economically, production plummeted, investment all but completely dried up, and agriculture often reverted to a more primitive, subsistence level. Trade declined, the amount of land under cultivation decreased, and the standard of living fell sharply.

Socially, a pattern of disorganization prevailed as well. With the authority of the Spanish crown now gone, the Spanish system of castes was also set aside, but nothing was created to replace it. Did the old system of hierarchy and elites still apply, or was it the new system of democracy and egalitarianism? Formally, these were democracies; but no one among the elites really believed that Blacks and Indians or mulattos and *mestizos* were equal. The absence of a significant middle class also meant that Latin America lacked a balancing social force between the extremes of wealth and poverty. The social order (or, better, disorder) was marked by uncertainty, chaos, confusion, and a general absence of new rules governing social relations to replace those set aside from the colonial era.

Ungovernability

The Latin American countries in the early nineteenth century had virtually no institutions, no base, on which to build a successful democracy. The end of the centralized, top-down Spanish system, under which all decisions were made in Madrid and which provided no training whatsoever in local self-government, left a political and institutional vacuum. Latin America had almost no associational life (neighborhood groups, community groups, charitable groups, and the like), as contrasted with the "web of associability" portrayed by Tocqueville in 1830's North America. It is not that Latin Americans were unable to govern themselves; instead, the problem was their countries had no infrastructure and no institutions and were therefore ungovernable.

In this context, an authoritarian "out" often looked very attractive. Liberal, representative, democratic rule was not a realistic option; rather, the choices were anarchy or Caesarism (that is, absolutism). Their constitutions proclaimed the new Latin American nations as republics, but the realities necessitated harder choices. One could see, in these conditions of constantly threatening chaos and disintegration, why an authoritarian solution would often seem attractive; or why the Latin Americans would frequently invent ingenious halfway houses—"democratic Caesarism," "tutelary democracy," or "guided democracy"—to help bridge the gap between their democratic aspirations and their anarchic realities.

The First Stages of Modernization: 1850s–1880s

Out of the chaos of the 1820s–1840s, a modicum of order began to emerge by the 1850s. Many of the earlier issues attendant on new nationhood were resolved or at least proved less troublesome. The economy experienced growth for the first time, and stability—or at least more stability than previously—was established. Latin America entered the first stages of modernization and began to establish what economist W. W. Rostow, employing an aeronautical metaphor, called the "preconditions for take-off."

In the economic sphere, by the 1850s in most areas, productivity began—after several decades of downturn—to rise again. New lands slowly came under cultivation. New stores, trading centers, and commercial establishments opened up. As capital began to flow, the first banks were chartered. The process was slow and uneven, to be sure, but throughout the area, an economic quickening occurred.

Fueling this economic growth was a wave of foreign investment. At first, Great Britain was by far the largest investor; later, in the 1880s and thereafter, the United States began to supplant Britain as the main foreign investor. It was British capital that built some of the first roads, dock facilities, and railroads in Latin America. British capital helped found the first banks, built the first telegraphs, and stimulated exports of coffee, bananas, beef, grain, and sugar. Significantly, the primitive Latin American economies now went from being overwhelmingly subsistence-based as they were during the first few decades of independence to being export-based, producing for a world economy. That meant that, for the first time, Latin America was involved in a capitalistic, global economy. Involvement in global markets provided economic stimulus, but it also subjected Latin America to the ups and downs of those markets—what later scholars would call *dependency*.

These changes in the economic sphere had profound implications for Latin American society. Cities began to grow in size and become cultural and social centers. Lighting, telephone and telegraph, and modern water and sanitation systems were introduced. Bicycles and eventually automobiles appeared. The population began to expand for the first time since independence, as better health care and sanitation practices were introduced. New areas of the countryside were opened up to cultivation and grazing as the rising population began to fill the vast empty spaces.

Immigration added to the rising population. The new immigrants were chiefly from Southern Europe (Italy, Spain), as well as Eastern Europe (Hungary, Czechoslovakia, and so on), although other nationalities or ethnic groups (Lebanese, Syrians, Chinese, Japanese, Jews) were also represented. This wave of immigration to Latin America paralleled the U.S. experience: immigrants came from most of the same sources and at the same time (1880s to World War I). Many of the immigrants brought with them entrepreneurial skills, and quite a number of them prospered as businessmen, traders, farmers, and importer-exporters.

The class changes provoked by Latin American economic modernization were similarly profound. A new business/commercial class began to grow in the cities and port areas, alongside the traditional landed elite, frequently intermarrying with it and eventually surpassing it in power. A small middle class—perhaps 5 percent of the population initially—also emerged, consisting of shop owners, businessmen, educated persons and professionals, and soldiers and government workers. The middle class gained political influence and eventually began to challenge the essentially two-class (lord and peasant) character of Latin American society. Similarly, a new urban working class began to develop alongside the traditional peasantry.

The changes in the political sphere were no less striking. First, national bureaucracies began to grow as governments were called upon to perform more functions, such as establishing foreign relations and building roads. Second, the level of popular participation increased, although ever so slowly because most persons were still illiterate and uninvolved in the national life. Third, the first political parties, interest groups, and associations were formed. Fourth, political authority became increasingly centralized as the regional *caudillos* were gradually deprived of their base of authority and as the central government and central armies became stronger. It is not certain whether there were fewer coups d'état during this period, but clearly the heretofore chaotic nations of Latin America began to settle down. Increased stability, of course, also had the effect of enabling the economy to grow even more and attracting additional investment.

One should not overdraw these changes. Latin America did take the first steps toward solving its historical vulnerabilities, principally its lack of organization and infrastructure. At the same time, throughout the 1860s, 1870s, and 1880s, the area continued to be plagued by instability, frequent palace revolutions, and internal chaos. Nevertheless, at least it was a start.

The Heyday of Oligarchic Rule: 1890s–1930s

By the 1890s, the pattern and *system* we have been describing had come fully into existence and was even consolidated and institutionalized in several of the largest countries. The "system" consisted of export-oriented agriculture (coffee, sugar, bananas, tobacco, rubber, beef) produced for a global capitalistic market, a social structure still based on elites but showing some adaptability to change, and a political regime characterized by top-down, centralized authority—albeit wrapped in "liberal" and "democratic" garb. This period from the early 1890s until the world depression of the 1930s was the heyday of oligarchic rule in Latin America.

This was a time of unprecedented economic growth during which all the trends identified in the previous section reached their culmination. Investment increased, more and more lands were opened to cultivation, exports rose, the population grew, and immigration continued. Some countries became very prosperous based on their export-fueled growth. As late as the 1920s, for example, Argentina's per capita income was higher than that of the United States (it later dropped sharply); in the decade surrounding World War I, to be "rich as an Argentine" was to be very rich indeed.

There were dark sides to this prosperity, however. As more and more lands came under production aimed at world markets, peasants and Indians were often stripped of their fertile lands and forced to settle in the infertile hillsides. In some regimes—Mexico, for instance—the social changes that accompanied economic development also engendered a stronger authoritarian apparatus to control them—and eventually full-scale revolution. Production for a world market, while increasing prosperity, also tied the Latin American economies to the vagaries of that market—including both its rising and falling—or to the quotas set by the large importers, now increasingly the United States. This implied greater dependency. During this same period, while general prosperity increased, the gap between the rich and the middle class on the one hand and the poor on the other increased.

Socially, a process of change also continued. The large landowners became even richer and more powerful, the business elites also gained power, the middle class continued to grow, and organized trade unions emerged for the first time. The business elites were fairly quickly absorbed by and became a part of the oligarchy. The middle class, however, resented its lack of political power in the form of the franchise and governmental positions commensurate with its rising economic importance. And, as in other countries at the same early stage of development, the rising, often politicized trade unions were looked on as at best a nuisance and at worst a threat that had to be dealt with through violence and repression.

Politically, this was an age of positivism. "Order and progress" were the main themes of the positivist philosophy, even emblazoned as a motto on the

Brazilian flag. Positivism in Latin America stemmed from the teachings of French political philosopher Auguste Comte, who argued that a well-ordered country, based on the principles of discipline, scientific organization, and the Darwinian notion of social hierarchy (with each person secure in his or her life station), was the best guarantor of progress. One can see why the Comtean ideas would be so welcome in Latin America: they promised order and stability in a continent not exactly known for these traits; they represented an updated, secularized version of the old Thomistic social hierarchy and therefore were acceptable to the elites; and they promised gradual, evolutionary, "scientific" change, not the destructive upheavals of the past.

In actual political practice, positivism and political development in Latin America took three forms. The first was oligarchic, elitist, "liberal" rule. In Argentina, Brazil, and Chile (the A, B, C countries of Latin America; also among the most developed), a conservative oligarchy consolidated its hold on power in the early 1890s and ruled more or less continuously until the 1930s. This oligarchy rotated the presidency among its members every five or six years, held regular elections (albeit without much competition), and generally ruled according to constitutional precepts—even while monopolizing power for itself. Paraguay, Peru, and Costa Rica are among the other countries that followed this pattern.

A second pattern was the "order-and-progress" dictator. The primary exemplar was Porfirio Diaz, who ruled Mexico from 1876 until 1910, although Ulises Heureaux in the Dominican Republic and Manuel Estrada Cabrera in Guatemala also fit the mold. These were strong-arm autocrats—*caudillos*, but *caudillos* in a more modern sense. They believed in authority and power, no longer just for its own sake but to establish "order" so as to achieve "progress." They brought in educated advisors, helped stimulate economic development, built national infrastructures (roads, bridges, docks), and achieved considerable modernization. Their strategy was not to rotate power among their members as the elites had done to give the illusion of democratic rule, but to maintain a monopoly and continuity of power for themselves. These men were among the longest-lived dictators in the history of Latin America, but they also brought significant progress to their countries and paved the way for even greater national unity and development in the future.

The third pattern was imposed from the outside, through U.S. Marine occupations. This pattern was particularly prevalent in the smaller, weaker, less institutionalized countries of the Caribbean and Central America. These countries had experienced little economic growth, they possessed few resources and meager internal markets, and they were plagued by chronic instability. Fearing that this very instability might invite hostile outside powers (Germany, France, Spain, Great Britain) to take advantage of the situation, a succession of U.S. presidents—McKinley, Roosevelt, Taft, and Wilson—repeatedly sent U.S. military forces to the Caribbean, expeditions that sometimes involved lengthy military occupations. The countries that U.S. forces

occupied were Cuba, the Dominican Republic, Haiti, Nicaragua, and Panama. The Marines usually built roads, port facilities, and bridges; installed some of the first telephone and telegraph systems; and imposed order and discipline on previously fractured societies. In all these respects, the U.S. occupiers carried out the same policies as the Latin American oligarchs or order-and-progress *caudillos*: to build the infrastructure to launch these poorer countries into new growth. However, the occupation forces often abused their authority and failed to develop the institutions that might sustain democracy after they left.

During this forty-year period of general Latin American stability (at least in the bigger countries) and prosperity, four major eruptions occurred that represent exceptions to the overall pattern. In Mexico, a violent and bloody revolution from 1910 to 1920 took place in the wake of Diaz's long rule and ushered in a new period of instability that was, however, followed by a capturing of power by the middle classes. In Uruguay, a middle class–led democratizing project in the early twentieth century ushered in Latin America's first social welfare state. Similarly, in Argentina in 1912, middle class pressure paved the way for a major extension of the franchise that had the long-term effect of wresting power from the oligarchy. In Chile, very nearly the same thing happened in the early 1920s: the middle sectors wrested political power away from the older elite groups. These middle class takeovers changed forever the structure of political power in these countries and served as examples of what would later happen in many of the less developed Latin American countries. The *patterns* by which these middle class takeovers occurred (out of the dust and chaos of the revolution in Mexico, through social welfarism in Uruguay, by means of the ballot box in Argentina and Chile) also shaped from that time forth the distinct social and political systems of these respective countries.

Collapse of the "System"

In 1929–30, all these regimes and the system of elitist-but-modernizing rule that they represented came crashing down. As the U.S. and European economies crashed in the world depression of that time, the demand for Latin American exports dried up, and their economies crashed as well. As the Latin American economies collapsed, so, too, did their still-fragile political systems.

Between 1930 and 1934, no fewer than fourteen Latin American countries experienced revolutions. The revolutions occurred in both the oligarchic-led regimes and those where authoritarian leaders held sway. During approximately the same time period, the U.S. Marine occupation forces were being withdrawn from several countries of the Caribbean and Central America, thus removing one further prop of stability from the region.

Note that these revolutions were not just the usual Latin American palace coups, "circulations" of elites, in which little changed except the personalities. Rather, these were often deeper and more profound revolutions signaling the decay, bankruptcy, and in some cases actual toppling of the older oligarchic order in Latin America. The revolutions of the early 1930s marked the transfer of power—albeit only partially in some countries—from the older Hispanic or Creole elites that had governed since independence to the new, rising middle classes—both civilian and military—often of more obscure social origins. With these changes at the top came also new social forces (middle and working class movements), new values and ideologies (Marxism, corporatism, Christian-democracy, social democracy), and new political institutions (mass-based political parties and interest groups). The upheavals that occurred during the tumultuous decade of the 1930s not only ushered in new social, political, and economic forces but also signaled—after some 450 years of the Hispanic system of hierarchy and authority—the twilight of the Middle Ages. Latin America would never be the same again.

5
✦
Entering the Modern World

In the 1930s, many of the structures associated with the medieval *ancien regime* in Latin America came tumbling down. Or, if they did not actually tumble, then new cracks appeared in their foundations—specifically, in the value system based on the assumption of a hierarchical, God-given station in life, the old two-class (lords and peasants) social structure, the influence of the *hacienda* as *the* socioeconomic base of national life, the power of the army and of the church, and the authoritarian and paternalistic political system. Of course, since the transition from more traditional to more modern structures and ways of doing things is seldom even or uninterrupted, many of Latin America's traditional pre-1930 practices and institutions continued to linger on; in some countries, they even staged a comeback for a time.

But now, added to these older ways were a variety of new social forces and political groups that either would have to be accommodated to the prevailing system or might seek to overthrow it. Change could be either evolutionary or revolutionary, but it was no longer possible—except temporarily—to uphold the status quo. Once the great motor forces of industrialization and modernization start turning, it is virtually impossible to hold them back, let alone revert to some preexisting system of order.

There were, actually, three separate yet in some respects interrelated processes at work here. The first, occurring in the last decade of the nineteenth century and the first decade of the twentieth, involved the incorporation of the newly wealthy men of business and commerce into the elite-directed system of Latin America. This process was not without its tensions since these new businessmen often lacked refinement and social standing. But they had money and often succeeded in marrying their children off to the children of the older landed elites. From about the turn of the century, old wealth and new wealth (including many immigrant families) in Latin America were quite closely wedded—often literally so.

The second process involved the middle class, or middle sectors, and was considerably less smooth than was the first process. In Mexico, it took a full-scale social revolution before the middle class was able to consolidate itself in power; in Uruguay, as we have seen, the middle class established a welfare state over the *strong* objections of the old elites; and in Argentina and Chile (and eventually in other countries), the middle class won the right to vote, but only after a strenuous and divisive campaign. The *way* in which these middle sectors were accommodated or won their rights in the various countries explains a great deal about social relations and the subsequent development of these countries.

The third process involved organized labor. This was a far more controversial process than the previous two, in part because the working class was organized around principles (Marxism, anarchism, socialism, syndicalism) not previously considered legitimate by the society. How the Latin American countries handled the rising presence, or threat, of the trade unions goes a long way toward explaining subsequent social policy and political development in the region. Labor could, alternatively, be accepted in the system, be rejected by it, or go through a long and difficult evolution. It is on the anvil of these relations between labor, employers, and the Latin American governments that much of the structure of modern Latin America was hammered out.

Two additional preliminary ideas require comment before we launch into the substance of this chapter. First, the Latin American nations clearly were becoming more varied in their modernization processes. Previously, it was possible to describe them in general terms that applied, approximately, to the continent as a whole because the history of these colonies and former colonies ran so parallel. Now, however, because the Latin American countries were following increasingly divergent development paths, we will have to treat them on more of an individual basis rather than as the products of a common pattern. The Latin American countries were, in short, becoming more unalike than alike, and our analysis needs to reflect that.

Second, we have implied that there is a *system*—a pattern to the way Latin America faced and contended with modernization. Given the chaotic conditions that prevailed in the early nineteenth century, as well as popular stereotypes about the area as disorganized and lacking structure, it may come as a bit of a surprise that Latin America has any system of society and politics at all. But, in fact, it does. That system may not always conform to the workings of U.S.-style democracy, but it is a *system* nonetheless, with its own dynamics, structures, and "rules of the game." Later in this chapter, we will begin to sort out what that system is, or was, and how it is changing.

Social and Political Change in Latin America

Since the 1930s (and even earlier in a handful of countries), Latin America has been undergoing profound social and political transformations. These are not just the stereotypical coups and barracks revolts that crop up in *New Yorker* and other cartoons, but more deep-rooted, societalwide *revolutions* that are changing forever the face of Latin America. These changes are not unlike the great revolutionary transformations that Europe, the United States, and a handful of other modern nations went through in earlier decades or even centuries. This is a revolution to usher in the modern age (democracy, industrialism, pluralism, and so on), and it affects *all* areas of Latin American national life: the value system or political culture, the economic system, the social structure, the political/governmental sphere, and the international environment.

Values and Political Culture

The first area of change is in the basic values, beliefs, ideologies, and understandings by which persons organize their lives. That is what we mean by *political culture*: those social values and cultural traits that specifically affect political behavior. Since the 1930s in Latin America, these basic values have been changing radically.

Prior to the 1930s, Latin American society reflected strongly authoritarian and nondemocratic values. I once heard a Latin American politician out on the stump say, "I need authority for my cattle, and I will need authority for my people." Instead of people cringing or dashing off an angry letter to the local newspaper, as would have surely occurred in the United States, the audience cheered. And not because they were coerced! Hierarchy, authority, discipline, a strong sense of place and rank—these values were at the heart of traditional Latin American political culture.

The political culture was also fatalistic. "*Si Dios quiere*" ("If God wishes"), something will happen; but not before. Such traditional North American values as taking individual initiative, lifting oneself by the bootstraps, and working hard to get ahead (the Ben Franklin/Horatio Alger ethic) had little resonance in Latin America. Life was hard and unchanging and in accord with God's will. One grew up in one's own *patria chica* (small country)—

usually an isolated region or valley—and married there, one's children grew up there, one died there, and so on, generation after generation.

Now this is all being changed, or at least challenged. The sources of the changes in the political culture are several. First, new ideologies—socialism, liberalism, Marxism, Christian democracy, and so on—are competing for the minds of Latin Americans. Second, new groups—political parties, interest groups, the Peace Corps—are fanning out into the countryside and planting the seeds of hope for a better life. Third, new grids of transportation and communications—road systems, markets, radio, television—are raising expectations and bringing new images and new values: democracy, social justice, consumerism, and the like. When the author first started going to Latin America, in the early 1960s, he noticed Indians in the infertile mountains eking out a meager subsistence by using a primitive pointed stick to jab between the rocks and plant one seed at a time. Now that Indian has probably migrated to the capital city to seek a better life; the ones who are left in the countryside or *campo* may still be using a pointed stick, but very likely they will have a cheap transistor radio glued to their ears.

It doesn't matter, in a sense, what this previously isolated peasant is listening to: Radio Havana, the Voice of America, the government station, a religious station, music, or, most likely, a baseball or *futbol* (soccer) game. *All* of them carry a vision of another world "out there" that is bigger, better, and more alluring than their own. Radio, television, highways, and farm-to-market roads are breaking down the traditional isolation and immobilism of the Latin American countryside as never before.

One can no longer convince Latin American peasants and Indians, as in the not-so-distant past, that they must be poor, live in substandard housing, and have diseased children with bloated bellies (a sign of malnutrition) because God or the church or the church fathers willed it that way, and that they must accept their station in life as immutable. The old ethos associated with the historical and traditional political culture just doesn't wash anymore. Instead, Latin America has come alive with diverse and competing ideas. The new ideas of democracy and social justice have seeped in, but often the old ideas continue to hang on. The result is a dynamic, vibrant, conflict-prone political culture in which the old values are fading but have not yet disappeared, while the new ideas are coming in but have not yet become institutionalized. The result is both excitement *and* possibilities for conflict. Whatever the outcome(s), the realm of values and political culture is one of the major areas in which change clearly is taking place.

The Economic Structure

A second area of change is in the economic sphere. First, in the last sixty years, Latin America has undergone major economic development. Despite the economic downturn of the 1980s (known in Latin America as the "lost decade"), the general long-term trend in virtually all countries has been one of growth. Since the 1930s in almost all countries, the gross national product has doubled, doubled again, and then doubled once more. The growth rates have not matched the miracle rates of Japan and Germany, but they have often been impressive nonetheless. There is still vast poverty in Latin America, but there has also been a general and overall economic quickening affecting all areas of national life.

Second, Latin America has urbanized and industrialized. Whereas thirty years ago two thirds of the Latin American population lived in rural areas, now two thirds live in cities, where the jobs and the future lie. Manufacturing and industry (petrochemicals, steel, automobiles, appliances, textiles, electronics, and a great variety of others) have grown at a furious pace. These are no longer "sleepy," rural, "banana republics" but increasingly industrialized nations. In many countries of the area, again contrary to popular stereotypes, manufactured items now account for a bigger share of export earnings than do primary products (minerals, foodstuffs, raw materials). Industry has changed the face, the economy, and the social relations of Latin America.

Third, much of this industrialization in Latin America since the 1930s was carried out under state auspices. Individual entrepreneurs were also influential in investing and stimulating production, but the largest industries were generally created, owned, and run by the state. The model used was called "import substitution industrialization" (ISI), which meant that goods that formerly were imported were now produced locally and protected by high tariffs. State-led industrialization also meant an enormous growth in the percentage of gross national product generated by the government (between 30 percent and 70 percent, depending on the country—far higher than in the United States) and in the percentage of the work force employed by the state. The form of the economy could thus be called statist, mercantilist, or perhaps state capitalism, as distinct from the laissez-faire (non-government-controlled) capitalism of the United States. It also meant that the highly statist Latin American economies were, over time, often inefficient, riddled with patronage appointments, and prone to corruption.

The industrialization and economic growth since the 1930s implied that Latin America was now caught up in world market forces that it could not control or exercise much leverage over, even more so than in its earlier period of economic takeoff. On the one hand, this meant vast new foreign investment and a major stimulus to the economy. On the other, it meant that Latin America was even more dependent on world market prices for its products, on changing consumer habits in the main U.S. markets (if we drink light beer or diet cola, it's great for our figures, but disastrous for sugar-producing countries in Latin America; if we drink decaf, it's good for our blood pressures, but bad for Latin American coffee growers), and on the quotas set by the big importers. Another by-product of foreign investment was that giant corporations like Kennecott Copper, the United Fruit Company, International

Petroleum, International Telephone and Telegraph, and General Motors could often mobilize more capital, more lawyers, and more influence than could an entire Latin American country. This put these countries at a disadvantage in dealing with the big companies and meant that their politics and destinies were often determined by these private concerns.

While economic growth in Latin America was generalized and often impressive during this sixty-year period, and while some of the new wealth did trickle down, not all groups benefited or benefited evenly. The rich got richer and the poor often stayed that way or got poorer. A more accurate way to portray these growth differentials is as follows: those who already had land and money profited greatly from the new economic opportunities; the middle class also did quite well but not as well as the elites; organized workers also saw their wages increase but not to the extent of the two previous groups; and the numerous peasant and marginal classes often saw their standard of living slip backward.

Implicit in this analysis is the fact that accelerated economic growth and industrialization in Latin America since the 1930s also gave rise to vast social and class changes. We turn to that subject next.

Social Change

The great motor forces of industrialization and economic growth in Latin America inevitably produced changes in the social structure as well. We look here at the changes development produced in the older groups in Latin American society, as well as the rise of newer groups, and finally how this produced more conflict-prone political systems.

Among the elite, economic growth has produced far greater diversity and pluralism than was present previously. There is no longer just a feudal landed class, but now a business elite, an industrial elite, a banking elite, an import-export elite, several ethnic or nationality elites, and so on. Frequently, these elite groups acted together or intermarried; other times, however, they competed among themselves for control of the government. In any case, within the elite there is now far greater differentiation among social groups and greater pluralism than ever before.

The Latin American armed forces also underwent great change. Prior to the 1930s, the officer corps had come mainly from the upper classes and could be counted on to side with the elites in almost all conflicts. Now, however, the officer corps comes chiefly from middle class ranks—usually mulatto or *mestizo*. It is better educated, more professional, and more experienced—including in the perils of trying to govern. It has its own institutional interests that it seeks to protect, and these are not always the same as the elites'. No longer can the armed forces be counted on to side automatically with the elites or to defend their interests. In fact, the armed forces are likely to be torn by all the same divisions found in the rest of society.

Much the same is true with regard to the Catholic church. No longer do its priests and administrators come exclusively from the upper classes. Rather, the church, like the army, now recruits its clerical personnel from the middle classes, from mulatto and *mestizo* ranks. Thus, parish priests can no longer be identified automatically with the interests of the elites. In addition, the church is so woefully understaffed in Latin America that it has turned to foreign-born clergy (Belgian, Italian, French, Spanish, Canadian, U.S.), who now often outnumber the native-born clergy in ratios of four or five to one. The foreign-born clergy naturally bring with them the values and ideologies of the societies in which they grew up, which usually are not in accord with historical Latin American hierarchical and elitist values. Moreover, under the impact of Pope John XXIII and his successors, Catholicism worldwide has become more modern and progressive. All these changes mean that the Catholic church can no longer be identified automatically with the status quo, either; it, too, is torn by dissent and internal conflict. The rise of various Protestant sects has offered a further challenge to the traditional church.

Among the newer groups, the middle class has emerged from comprising a mere 5–10 percent of the population in the 1930s to 20–40 percent today, depending on the level of economic development of the country. Argentina, Uruguay, Chile, Venezuela, Mexico, Costa Rica, and now Brazil and Colombia are among the countries where the middle class is larger; Peru, Bolivia, Ecuador, Paraguay, Guatemala, and Honduras have smaller middle classes. The middle class has become a powerful force in Latin America, dominating the military officer corps, the clergy, the bureaucracy, political parties, and various professional associations. However, the middle sectors are also deeply divided between members in the upper middle class and those in the lower middle class, and between those who take different political positions in the society. In addition, it is uncertain whether the emerging middle class will imitate traditional upper class ways (unwillingness to work with their hands, disdain for the lower classes) or, as the United States hopes, it will become a force for stability, moderation, and democracy. The middle sectors are clearly a rising influence in Latin America, but at present their ultimate political impact is unclear.

Organized labor has also become a major force in Latin America. Trade unions in Latin America date back to the turn of the century, but they wielded significant political influence only from the 1930s on. Industrialization, urbanization, economic growth, and foreign investment helped stimulate the rise of unionism, with many of the earliest and largest unions organized in firms owned by foreign companies. Only about 5–20 percent of the work force, depending again on the country's level of economic development, is organized into unions in Latin America, figures that do not differ all that much from the U.S. trade union situation, but are far lower than in Europe. The unions tend to be highly politicized but also internally divided (communist, socialist, Christian-democratic, U.S.-sponsored) in

Latin America, which hinders their capacity to influence politics; and they have also been the frequent target of repression. We shall have more to say on these and other groups' political strategies and activities in Chapter 7.

The unorganized poor, both urban and rural, are the largest group numerically in Latin America but the weakest politically. This group consists of both the *lumpenproletariat* of the cities (un- or underemployed slum dwellers prone to violence or receptive to radical appeals) and the rural peasantry (lacking regular employment and living in miserable conditions, with no future for themselves or their children). In recent decades, there have been various efforts to organize these two groups, by political parties, through peasant cooperatives, by religious movements, or through guerrilla movements. In addition, both urban and rural poor are becoming aware of their own interests—a reflection of the changing political culture discussed previously. Despite these changes, however, the urban and rural poor are still mainly inarticulate and unorganized, and therefore without much of a say politically in the issues that most directly affect them. Except for the possibility of voting at election time, democratization in Latin America has not yet reached very strongly down to this level. As a result, the urban and rural poor in Latin America have at times been resorting to direct action: land takeovers, demonstrations, looting, and food riots.

In sum, Latin America has become far more socially and politically pluralist since the 1930s, and also far more conflict-prone. Business groups, the middle class, and organized labor have all emerged to challenge or become major participants in the political process, taking their place alongside the traditional wielders of power: the landed class, the church, and the military, which are themselves changing. But three main problems remain with which we will have to wrestle at greater length later in the book:

1. Power in Latin America is still very unevenly distributed; some groups (economic elites, the military, the middle class) have *far* more money and influence than others.

2. Up to this point, the growing pluralism has given rise more to a conflict-prone and strife-torn society than to a consensual one.

3. Some groups (the urban poor, rural peasants, indigenous peoples) have been all but completely left out of the modernization process and are still mired in poverty and backwardness.

Political Change

The broad cultural, social, and economic changes surveyed here have also produced major political changes. These topics are discussed at greater length in subsequent chapters, but let us provide the general outlines here.

First—related to the changes in political culture—people in Latin America are more aware of political issues, even at the lowest levels of society. All those radios, televisions, movies, and new transportation grids have made the Latin American populace far more informed than previously. They are aware of their own interests (in contrast to the historical isolation), and they know if government is serving those interests. These are no longer "sleepy" and backward countries, but politically dynamic ones.

Second, reflecting the emerging social pluralism of Latin America, the number of interest organizations has increased dramatically. These include not only such well known groups as the church, the military, the oligarchy, professional associations, trade unions, and peasant leagues, but also new community groups, grass-roots associations, social movements (such as those advocating the rights of indigenous peoples), and local action committees. A great variety of such associations (although not yet comparable to the plethora of interest groups in the United States) have begun to organize at all levels of society, including for the first time among the poor. The organizational void that has always plagued Latin America and helps account for its political instability is now, finally, beginning to be filled.

Political parties are the third major area of change. Historically, the political parties in Latin America have been elitist associations of local notables organized for patronage purposes and for capturing the reins of government, but largely devoid of program, structure, or ideology. As such, they resembled the political parties in the old American South or the big-city machines in the North, which sought to capture the county courthouse or city hall, from which power and patronage flowed, but that lacked concrete programs or a sense of social responsibility. Now, however, as we will see in more detail in Chapter 8, the parties in Latin America are becoming better organized, presenting real programs or platforms, and reaching down deeper into society to include branches for women, youths, workers, and peasants.

A fourth change is in the structure of government or the state. Prior to the 1930s, government in Latin America was small, and its functions were limited (national defense, foreign affairs, limited public works). Now, however, governments have grown enormously, and their functions have multiplied. Most governments in Latin America now have between twelve and twenty cabinet ministries (as compared with four historically) as well as, often, hundreds of special agencies, offices, directorships, or government-run corporations. Accompanying industrialization and economic and social modernization, the size and scope of the public sector has vastly increased.

In part, this enormous increase in the size of governments in Latin America reflects the new demands for services. Governments are now expected to provide health care, electricity, water supplies, education, agrarian reform, housing, social welfare, jobs, environmental controls, and a *host* of other services—or else! The "else" means that governments had better provide those services or they will lose their electoral support and maybe even their power. This expectation of and demand for new and improved services is placing pressure on governments of the area as never before.

The International Context

The international environment has also changed a great deal since Latin America's "coming of age" in recent decades. Clearly, Latin America can no longer exist in its historical isolation; rather, it is a part of and *inevitably* caught up in world cultural and political, to say nothing of economic, currents.

First, the *world* political culture has come to Latin America. That means consumerism (the desire for appliances, television sets, and so on); it means Coca-Cola, rock music, designer jeans, and McDonald's; *and* it means the desire for democracy, human rights, and advanced social programs.

Second, the Cold War also came to Latin America. The Cold War struggle between the United States and the former Soviet Union was a two-edged sword: it meant that Latin America got more attention and dollars from Washington, such as via John F. Kennedy's Alliance for Progress, Ronald Reagan's Caribbean Basin Initiative, and George Bush's Enterprise Initiative for the Americas; but it also led to repeated U.S. meddling and sometimes intervention in Latin America's internal affairs. During the Cold War, the United States could be and often was both a force for constructive development in Latin America and a force for reaction and destruction—and, frequently, it was both at the same time. Now that the Cold War is over, the question is whether the United States will revert to its historical policy of benign neglect toward Latin America or whether the new agenda of issues—drugs, immigration, trade, environmental concerns, human rights—will keep U.S. attention focused on the region.

A third change in the international environment involves the variety of other nations (besides the United States) and agencies that have come to operate there. Germany, Spain, France, the Scandinavian countries, Japan, China, Israel, Canada, and others all have Latin America policies, or significant programs there, that are sometimes at odds with those of the United States. At the same time, such transnational actors as the Inter-American Development Bank, the United Nations, the World Bank, the International Monetary Fund, Americas Watch (a human rights group), the Organization of American States, and a host of other agencies both public and private are also operating extensively in Latin America. The presence of these newer actors on the Latin American scene has made the international context in which the countries of the area operate far more complex than it was previously.

Alternative Models of Development

The post-1930s political systems of Latin America began increasingly to go in different directions, to become more unalike than alike. More than that, out of the crisis of the 1930s came several alternative models or patterns of how the distinct Latin American regimes coped with the forces of change and modernization just described. These alternative coping methods, in turn, shaped the social and political arrangements in the several countries that persist to this day.

The 1930s were a "critical juncture" in Latin America.[1] There had been other critical junctures in Latin American historical sociology—for example, around the turn of the twentieth century when the rising commercial elements began to challenge the traditional landed elites, and in the 1910–29 period when the rising middle class clamored to be incorporated within the political system. But the 1930s represented a deeper, more profound critical juncture. It came in the midst of a severe economic as well as political crisis, it involved large masses of people for the first time, and it involved a group (organized labor) that was frequently oriented toward Marxian or anarcho-syndicalist principles that threatened to tear the system down if it was not accommodated to it. This was a more widespread, profound, and wrenching crisis than any Latin America had seen before.

The different Latin American countries coped or tried to deal with these rising social challenges in different ways, and the patterns that developed provide us with distinct models of the development process in Latin America. Moreover, the initial ways of recasting the political systems of the area to cope with accelerated change in the 1930s left both important *legacies* for the political systems and an important *heritage* in the several countries in terms of imparting some permanent characteristics to politics that persist today. Let us make the discussion more concrete by examining the several different models of change that emerged.

The Mexican Model

The Mexican case is unique, *sui generis*. In 1910, Mexico had a revolution. What began as an essentially middle class revolt to get rid of the dictator Díaz soon turned into a broad-based social revolution that involved the mobilization of the Indians as well. The period from 1910 to 1920 was violent and chaotic; in the 1920s, Mexico was still disorganized, but eventually some order and a reconstituted political system emerged out of the chaos.

The Mexican model consists of a single party–dominant system (the Party of Revolutionary Institutions or PRI) that has largely monopolized politics since the 1930s, a strong executive that helps hold the system together, a corporatist or sectoral system of interest representation that incorporates the new groups (labor, peasantry, popular) while excluding the traditional ones (the church and the oligarchy), and a mystique and mythos that centers around the Revolution. The system is top-down and authoritarian while also allowing for a considerable degree of freedom. Organized labor has been incorporated into the system, but it has been "domesticated" and is under the guidance and control of the state. That, essentially, is how the Mexican "model" has operated for the last sixty years. Now it is changing toward greater openness and competitiveness, but the basic structures of the old system are still largely in place.

Authoritarian Populism: Argentina and Brazil

Whereas Mexico experienced a social revolution early in the twentieth century, Argentina and Brazil did not. These two important South American countries also experienced upheavals in the 1930s, but their way of dealing with the forces of change was quite different from Mexico's. In both countries, a populist politician (Getulio Vargas in Brazil, 1930–1945 and 1950–1954; Juan Perón in Argentina, 1946–1955 and 1973–1974) emerged out of the tumult of the 1920s and 1930s who sought to deal with the rising importance of organized labor. Vargas's and Perón's strategy was neither to suppress organized labor, as other dictators were doing, nor to provoke a violent revolution as in Mexico. Rather, they chose to bring labor into the political system but under state direction and control. The model was one of authoritarian or top-down corporatism combined with the personalism and populism of their leaders.

However, authoritarianism is always destructive of the growth of democracy and viable political institutions. Perón ruined both agriculture and industry in resource-rich Argentina, and his personal style and populist politics evoked strong feelings both pro and con. Eventually, Argentina broke down into disintegrative politics characterized by swings between civilian and military regimes. Only gradually, in the 1980s, was the way opened toward democracy and renewal. Vargas, similarly, left Brazil an uncertain legacy, paving the way for ten years of disorganized democracy, followed by twenty years of military authoritarianism, and eventually—like Argentina—a return to democracy in the 1980s.

Incorporation Through Political Parties:
Chile, Colombia, Costa Rica, Uruguay, Venezuela

These five countries followed still another path: that of incorporating the labor movement more or less peacefully through the political party system. Strikingly, all five of these countries have become basically middle class societies—in all of them the extremes between wealth and poverty are not so great as in other Latin American countries, and in all of them a functioning political party system provided a key to labor incorporation and pluralism. Of course, these processes did not occur in exactly parallel fashion in all five countries; rather, the sequence ran roughly parallel to their level of development. That is, the most developed countries with the strongest middle classes, Chile and Uruguay, largely bridged the transition to a more participatory democracy (incorporating the organized working class) in the 1930s, Costa Rica managed the process in the 1940s and 1950s, and Colombia and Venezuela in the 1960s.

The successful integration of organized labor into a prevailing democratic regime in this early period was not always without conflict, however, nor was it necessarily permanent. These five countries, for example, are among the most politically sophisticated in Latin America; yet that did not prevent Chile and Uruguay from degenerating into brutal military dictatorships in the 1970s, or Colombia from being afflicted by repeated waves of violence, or Costa Rica and Venezuela from being torn recently by social and political conflict. Nevertheless, Colombia, Costa Rica, and Venezuela were the only countries in Latin America to avoid the wave of repressive coups that swept the region in the 1960s and 1970s and to maintain democratic continuity. Moreover, Chile and Uruguay's strong democratic traditions facilitated their return to and consolidation of democracy in the 1980s because they already had or could re-create democratic institutions.

Authoritarian Blockage: Paraguay, Central America, the Caribbean

A fourth way of dealing with the profound social and political forces unleashed in Latin America in the 1930s was to establish or reestablish an authoritarian regime that simply repressed the rising social movements. Whereas the previous three models had all tried, in one way or another, to accommodate and absorb the emerging labor movements, other political regimes sought to crush them. These included the dictatorships of General Alfredo Stroessner in Paraguay, Rafael Trujillo in the Dominican Republic, Jorge Ubico in Guatemala, Anastasio Somoza in Nicaragua, Fulgencio Batista in Cuba, and Papa Doc Duvalier in Haiti. To these regimes, the "problem of labor" was a problem for the police; when the workers started to get restless, government policy was to snuff them out. Some of these regimes were so brutal and so long in power that they verged on totalitarianism.

However, the lid can be held on a boiling pot only so long before an explosion occurs. Social and political change cannot be blocked and stymied indefinitely. When the inevitable eruption occurred, the only question remaining was whether it would be a communist revolution or could be channeled in more democratic directions. Cuba had a revolution that became Marxist-Leninist; Nicaragua also had a revolution that took a Marxist direction. The Dominican Republic and Guatemala had revolutions that were then aborted by U.S. military interventions. El Salvador during its civil war of the 1980s could perhaps fall in that category as well. Paraguay had a more or less peaceful transfer to a less repressive regime, and Haiti has yet to have a successful social and political breakthrough.

The countries in this category are all at the lower end of the scale of regional socioeconomic development. They therefore had only nascent trade union movements in the 1930s, which could be suppressed relatively easily. But as they industrialized and modernized in later decades, these countries, like their more developed Latin American neighbors, were obliged to deal with the rising social movements realistically rather than violently. However, their long-lasting authoritarian regimes had left an almost total void in these countries, which helps explain why the legacy in so many of them was social revolution and then intervention.

Modernization Under Military Auspices: Peru, El Salvador, Panama

Not all the military regimes that came to power in Latin America have been socially repressive (if nothing else, change had already proceeded so far that it was no longer possible to deal with it through brutal repression). Rather, some military regimes saw that it was in their interest to co-opt rather than crush the new social groups. We may call these "military modernizers" or "military populists"; the main examples come from Peru, Panama, and El Salvador.

In Peru in 1968, the military, faced with a deadlocked civilian political system, decided to seize power and rule in a *nationalist* and *progressive* fashion instead of the usually regressive one. In El Salvador in 1948, a centrist military government seized power from a repressive regime and guided the country for the next twenty years into mildly reformist and nondictatorial ways. In Panama, a military populist, Omar Torrijos, supplanted ineffective civilian governments and brought some social reforms to the country. The co-optation logic of this military-reform model was captured nicely by one Peruvian colonel who stated: "The bulls [meaning the people] are starting to stampede. When that happens you have three choices: you can turn and run, which is not very helpful; or you can kneel and pray, which also seems to produce limited results. The third option is for us, the Army, to lead the bulls onto higher ground."

But the option of military-led modernization, though more hopeful than the complete blockage scenario, did not work out very well either. In Peru, the reformist military regime gave way to a do-nothing military regime that was then superseded in the 1980s by a civilian democratic government. El Salvador's reformist colonels yielded to a repressive military that during the 1970s and 1980s helped produce revolution and civil war. Panama's military populists were eventually replaced by the thuggery of General Manuel Noriega. It is fair to say that neither the repressive authoritarians nor the more reformist military authoritarians were ever able to institutionalize their regimes sufficiently to allow for a continuation of their rule indefinitely into the future. These countries therefore remained explosive, and their political systems not well consolidated.

Muddling Through: Honduras, Ecuador

Several Latin American countries experienced none of the dramatic events described previously: no revolutions, no explosions, no headline-grabbing breakthroughs. Instead, they muddled through, or sometimes alternated between military and civilian regimes. The best examples are Ecuador and Honduras. Although both countries had periods of military rule, they were less repressive regimes than elsewhere. And although both of them also had periods of democratic rule, democracy was not well consolidated in either of them. Nor did they develop the effective party systems or the populist regimes that some countries did. Rather, these countries drifted from one kind of regime to another without ever conforming fully to any one model.

This mucking-along alternative may sound wishy-washy and ineffective, but one can think of far worse alternatives. Honduras and Ecuador never experienced dramatic democratic breakthroughs, but they also avoided both chaotic revolution on the one hand and very oppressive military regimes on the other. Change was handled gradually, through evolutionary and incremental methods, and not by dramatic lurches. One can make a strong case that such incrementalism not only is helpful to development but also is democratic. Considering the previously mentioned alternatives, there are far worse courses than mucking along.

The Latin American Political Process

With so many alternative routes to development, and with such seemingly disorganized politics, one may well wonder how it is possible to talk about a "system" or normal "processes" in Latin American politics. But, in fact, there are regularities and systemic aspects to the Latin American political process. The problem is that their system is different from our own and we lack knowledge or understanding of it.[2]

To better understand how the Latin American system works, let us start off with some propositions or "givens" about the area derived from our historical analysis. We will then move to an analysis of how Latin America confronted the change process that accelerated in the twentieth century, and what its *system* was for dealing with these changes.

Among the propositions we begin with are the following:

1. The political system has long been top-down, elitist, and authoritarian.
2. The state has long played a key role in national economic and political affairs.
3. The results of elections have not consistently been honored.

4. The military, along with the church and the oligarchy, has long played a key role in national politics.

5. Political institutions, associational life, and the infrastructure tend to be weak or not well consolidated.

This was the situation in Latin America throughout the nineteenth century—which we have characterized as a continuation of the Middle Ages. But what happens when such a top-down and elitist system begins to confront the pressures for change—as Latin America commenced to do toward the end of the nineteenth century?

The first group to which the prevailing elitist system needed to respond was the rising commercial or business class. That was relatively easy, as we have seen, because the new businessmen were few in number, they quickly absorbed the elitist values, and they intermarried with the old landed elite. In this way, the elitist system could go on largely as before, the only differences being that the number of persons in the elite increased slightly and the elite had to adjust to some new, capitalistic, entrepreneurial, *nouveau riche* values.

The next group that had to be absorbed was the rising middle class. That presented more problems than had been the case with the rising business class because the middle class was larger numerically and it did not always share the same values as the old elites. In countries such as Argentina and Chile, as we have seen, the middle class was brought into the political process through an extension of the franchise, but only after some wrenching political conflicts. The key words are "some" and "conflicts," however, not "revolution." For, over the course of several decades, from approximately the 1910s and 1920s in Argentina and Chile through the 1950s in the rest of Latin America, the middle class was gradually absorbed into the prevailing elitist system as well. In return for winning the right to vote, gaining access to the military officer corps, and getting good government jobs, the middle class also gradually took on the upper class virtues: disdain for manual labor, disdain for the lower classes, and so on. It is this "Faustian bargain" of becoming more like the elites in terms of political and social values in return for certain privileges and access that makes many analysts doubt if the Latin American middle class could become the bastion of democracy, moderation, and stability that it is, for the most part, in the United States and Western Europe.

Out of this experience of dealing with the emerging middle class came some characteristic features of the modern Latin American political process.

1. To be accepted by and accommodated to the system, a group like the middle class had to first demonstrate a power capability—that is, sufficient numbers of people and power to, actually or potentially, threaten the prevailing system. Such a power capability could be demonstrated

through electoral strength, street mobilizations, or close connections with the military officer corps.

2. Once such a power capability had been demonstrated, in order to be accepted into the system the group had to agree to moderate its aspirations and not seek by revolutionary means either to destroy the system or to co-opt the power of the traditional groups: church, army, and economic elites.

3. If it agreed to this bargain, the new group would qualify for the "perks" of the system: not just the right to vote but also good government jobs, patronage, and access to special favors and opportunities flowing from the state. In this way, the Latin American state sector had to be continuously expanded in order to provide employment for all these new middle class persons.

4. Since one could demonstrate a power capability in various ways, it followed that elections would not be the only route to power. Instead, mass demonstrations, popular mobilizations, and even military coups in which the middle class participated could also be used legitimately to demonstrate the group's power.

Several points should be emphasized. The first is that it was harder for the traditional Latin American systems to absorb the middle class than the new business elites, since its numbers were larger and it did not at first share all the aristocratic values; but over time the middle class was largely accommodated into the system under the conditions listed. The second point is that, as this process shows, the Latin American systems are more flexible than commonly acknowledged; the traditional system bent and accommodated to change but was not—except in a couple of instances—overwhelmed by it.

And that leads us to the third point: while some change occurred in the traditional Latin American system, consider what was left unchanged. This included the power of the elite groups, the hierarchical and top-down system, and the pyramidal structure of Latin American society. All of these elements were *compromised* slightly by the change process, but they were not destroyed, nor was their power or land or position taken away. Note that while the pyramid of power was expanded laterally to incorporate these new business and middle class groups, the system still remained pyramidal, with the historical wielders of power still in control. In addition, as part of the bargain that brought these groups in, they sacrificed their capacity to change society by revolutionary means. Latin America has had many "revolutions" as part of its political process that brought one or another military or military/civilian faction to power. But it is a profoundly *nonrevolutionary* area in the sense of having very few genuine *social* revolutions. That shows both how powerful yet flexible and how co-optive the traditional institutions have been.

The Latin American political process, as we have seen, worked quite well in absorbing first the business elites and then the middle class into the "system." But it worked less well with the next group: organized labor. Several factors contributed to the difficulties in co-opting labor into the system. First, considerably larger numbers of peoples—real *mass* organizations—were involved. Second, organized labor was often organized on a basis (Marxist, anarchistic, syndicalist) that was considered illegitimate by the traditional wielders of power. Third, the trade unions represented not just another potentially co-optive group but also a genuine threat to the established elites. The rise of the trade unions, in other words, raised the potential for real class warfare and revolution in ways that the previous groups did not.

The first response of the elite groups to the rise of trade unions early in the twentieth century was simply to repress them. But as industrialization went forward and the unions grew larger, and as organized labor demonstrated a genuine power capacity, that tactic became less and less feasible. Hence, during the 1930s and on into the post–World War II era, many Latin American regimes were attracted by the ideology and practice of *corporatism*. Corporatism had emerged in nineteenth-century Europe, chiefly in the Catholic countries of Southern Europe, as a way of responding to the "social problem" of rising labor movements. The question was, how to bring organized labor into the political process without provoking full-scale Marxist revolution. Corporatism was *one* of the answers provided; liberal pluralism as practiced in the United States was another. Under corporatism, labor would be brought in but it would be structured, controlled, and "tamed" by the state—which, of course, was still controlled by the elites. Both capital and labor would be subservient to the state and, so they would not get out of hand, be organized in official, government-sanctioned unions and employers' associations. The state, in consultation with labor and capital, would decide on such matters as wages and working conditions, adjudicate all workplace conflicts, bring social harmony to employer-employee relations, and thus avoid the harmful and potentially destabilizing effects of class conflict.

One can easily understand why corporatism, from the elite's perspective, was for so long—and is even today—such an attractive ideology and system of sociopolitical organization in Latin America. It enabled the elites to maintain control even while bringing into the system this new and potentially dangerous group: organized labor. It kept the basic top-down and hierarchical structures of society (also still elite-controlled) intact. It avoided Marxian revolution—also in the elites' and middle classes' interests. It was, however, in harmony with the way Latin America had previously handled change (through absorption and co-optation of rising social forces) and with its long Thomistic/Catholic tradition of a well-ordered, harmonious, integrated political system based on mutual obligation and government by the "best people."

Virtually every Latin American regime that came to power from the 1930s through the 1950s incorporated one or another aspect of corporatist ideology and organization: prohibitions on strikes, limits on labor activities in return for new social welfare programs, close supervision of internal labor union activities, incorporation of labor (and business) into state boards or the legislature or specialized agencies set up to help regulate and manage the economy. We should also remember that in the various countries corporatism could take different forms: a slightly leftist and socialist direction for a time under President Lázaro Cárdenas in Mexico, an almost fascist form under Juan Perón in Argentina, a more liberal form in Venezuela, and a Christian-democratic form in Chile, Brazil, and El Salvador.

At best, corporatism proved to be only a partial success. Recall how much corporatism with its co-optive strategies was in accord with Latin America's historical way of dealing with change. With organized labor, however, these strategies did not always work very well. In some countries, the co-optive tactics did work: labor leaders were often bought off, many were given comfortable government jobs or special access to avenues of enrichment, and they and their unions were incorporated into the prevailing social and political system. But in other countries, both labor and the government modified the corporatist approach in favor of a more pluralist, collective-bargaining (like the U.S.) model of labor relations. In still others, labor resisted the corporatist system and its presumed class harmony and took to the streets in protest. In some of these, real revolutionary potential began to build, particularly where lower class militias (often encompassing both workers and peasants) were also armed and mobilized. A class conflict potential began to build as contrasted with the presumed class harmony of corporatism. The specter of many more Cubas, of Castro-style revolutions pitting the lower classes against the elites, began to haunt Latin America.

As this threat from below grew in the 1960s, and as the historical co-optive methods appeared not to be working so well, the Latin American elites and middle classes began turning to their national armies for support. The military also felt threatened by armed lower class movements and thus was a willing ally. Hence, beginning in the early 1960s and continuing through the early 1970s, a wave of military coups swept over Latin America. Some of these were short-lived takeovers, but in many of them the armed forces and their civilian allies stayed in power for long periods, determined to completely restructure their historical systems of national politics. By 1977, twelve Latin American countries had military governments, and in five others, the military was so close to the surface of power as to make the distinction between civilian and military authority all but indistinguishable; in *all* of these countries, the traditional model of co-optation and assimilation ceased to apply. Instead, brutally repressive regimes not only violated human rights but also tried to snuff out and repudiate the historical process of gradual adaptation to change. These were often referred to as "bureaucratic-authoritarian" regimes; by the late 1970s, of the twenty countries in Latin America, only three—Colombia, Costa Rica, and Venezuela—still had democratic governments.

However, by the late 1970s and early 1980s, the march of the military authoritarians had largely run its course, for several reasons. The military had proved to be no more efficient in running their economies or governments than the civilians whom they replaced. Also, the leftist threat in most countries no longer (after Cuba's failures and Che Guevara's death in Bolivia) seemed so challenging, and the military was discredited for its widespread human rights abuses. In addition, international pressures for democracy began to grow, even as Latin America's own "civil society" (parties, unions, civic groups) began to reassert itself. Finally, the militaries themselves began to fear that their institutional position in society was being compromised by continuing in power. So, one after another, the Latin American countries returned to democracy over the course of the 1980s and gradually began to consolidate democratic institutions, leaving only Cuba, Haiti, and Suriname as nondemocratic.

So what has now happened to our model of the typical Latin American political process? Three points need to be made here; later in the book, we will return to these themes in greater detail. First, in most countries, the traditional co-optive model remains—although more tenuously—in place. That is, it is still often necessary for a new and rising group both to demonstrate a power capability and to agree to abide by the rules of the prevailing political game in order for it to be legitimated and accommodated to the system. We have seen how business, the middle class, and eventually many unions were co-opted in this manner. The state still offers guidance and direction to these groups, still must grant them recognition for them to be legally constituted, and still controls many of their activities. As emergent social groups—peasants, indigenous elements, women, the unemployed, domestic servants—begin to demand recognition and admission to the "system," they are still often treated in the same top-down, paternalistic, co-optive way as were the groups that went before.

Second, the decline and collapse of the other, alternative options helped enable the historic co-optive method to reassert itself. No one wants to be a "bureaucratic authoritarian" anymore. Nor, with the collapse and unraveling of the Soviet Union and the formerly communist countries of Eastern Europe, and Cuba's manifold problems, does anyone want to follow the Marxist-Leninist path anymore. Except for the advocacy of a rapidly dwindling number of persons, all of these alternative models have been completely discredited and abandoned.

A third theme relates to the overwhelming triumph of democracy—at least for now—in the area. An increasing number of countries—Costa Rica, Chile, Uruguay, Argentina, Venezuela, Colombia—are moving away from partial corporatism and the co-optive model and toward genuine democracy and pluralism, toward real independent interest groups and not just co-opted ones. In others—probably the majority, including some of those already listed—the newer liberal and the older elitist-driven co-optive models continue to exist side by side.

The result is a less clear picture of how the Latin American political systems actually work. Sometimes the co-optive methods are at work, sometimes genuinely liberal and pluralist ones operate, and often the two are intertwined in complex and sometimes confusing ways. In some countries, social-revolutionary movements also add to the pressure. These complex and overlapping processes make it harder to understand Latin American politics, but they also make these *systems* dynamic and capable of new combinations and new policy thrusts.

Notes

1. The term derives from Ruth Berins Collier and David Collier, *Shaping the Political Arena: Critical Junctures, the Labor Movement, and Regime Dynamics in Latin America* (Princeton, NJ: Princeton University Press, 1991); an earlier statement of many of these themes is Howard J. Wiarda, *The Corporative Origins of the Iberian and Latin American Labor Relations Systems* (Amherst, MA: Labor Relations and Research Center, University of Massachusetts, 1976), reprinted in a briefer version in *Studies in Comparative International Development, XIII* (Spring 1978), 3–37.

2. The model used here derives from Charles W. Anderson, *Politics and Economic Change in Latin America* (New York: Van Nostrand, 1967), as modified and updated by the author.

6
✦

Latin America's Changing Political Culture

Political culture is a useful concept, but it can also be an elusive and even dangerous one. Political culture refers to a nation's or society's basic or defining attitudes, beliefs, value systems, and behavior patterns. It suggests that politics is not defined solely by governmental institutions but also by the values and cultural attitudes that people bring to the political system and their expectations of it. People may be *passive* and apathetic about the political system; they can be *involved* or participatory in it; or they may be *subjects* of it.

In different countries, people will also have different expectations about what works in government and what doesn't, which institutions are appropriate for them and which not. The importance of political culture seems so obvious as not to be subject to argument: political culture sets the context and parameters within which the political process takes place. If one doesn't understand the role of traditional Catholic beliefs, of the historical experience of the mother countries Spain and Portugal, of Hispanic attitudes and practices, of beliefs, values, and traditional Latin American ways of doing things, then one cannot possibly understand the area very well.

However, the concept of political culture must be applied cautiously. For one thing, it provides insight into but hardly a complete explanation of why Latin America is the way it is; other factors (class structure, political institutions, the international environment) are also important. Second, political culture is often a vague concept subject to different interpretations, so we need to be careful and precise in describing it. Third, political culture is never fixed or permanent, so we need to recognize that over time the political culture will change. Fourth, even within a given country, there may be two or more political cultures operating: that of the elite and that of the lower classes or the indigenous elements, or those of distinct ethnic groups. Finally, while political culture is a useful concept for understanding distinct countries, it should not be used to imply ethnic stereotypes (all Germans are this, all Italians are that, all Latinos are such and such). Political culture therefore looks for *patterns* and dominant modes of beliefs and behaviors, but it does not presume that everyone in a given society shares all these beliefs all the time.

In short, information from art, music, behavior, religion, psychology, history, and sociology are all relevant in shaping—and therefore helping us understand—Latin American political culture. But these are also impressionistic materials that can, unless used carefully, lead to stereotypes and prejudice. So, where possible, we need to supplement these interpretive materials with hard data from serious, thorough, national public opinion surveys. With these cautionary notes in mind, let us look now at Latin American political culture.

Historical Latin American Political Culture

Latin America's historically dominant political culture is largely the political culture carried over to the Americas from Spain and Portugal during the period of conquest and colonization between 1492 and about 1570. That political culture was predominantly elitist, hierarchical, authoritarian, corporatist, and patrimonialist. It was definitely not a democratic and an egalitarian culture.

Roots of the Political Culture

It had not always been that way in Spain and Portugal. Spain, or at least some of its regions, had had a *cortes*, or parliament, even before the British parliament, which is usually considered the first such democratic institution. Distinct classes and social groups were represented in these early parliaments in the Iberian Peninsula. Indeed, the ideas of interest representation, of checks and balances, of human rights, and of countervailing power all were present in Spain and Portugal as far back as the twelfth century.

It is in this context that the distinctive Spanish and Portuguese concept of democracy developed, a theme that requires brief elaboration since we will return to this conception later in the discussion. The historical Iberian concept of democracy stressed group or corporate rights—of the church, military orders, towns and regions, universities, guilds, and so on—over individual rights. These groups often had been around for centuries and enjoyed a legally defined independence from the state or from arbitrary authority. Remember that while medieval Catholicism stressed the obligation of obedience to rightful authority, it also ascribed God-given natural rights that must be recognized, including the right to resist unjust tyranny. The relations of all these corporate groups to the emerging central state were spelled out in quite elaborate charters or organic laws that defined the rights and responsibilities of each. The independence of these groups from the state and the tension between their powers of self-governance versus the power of royal authority are what helped give rise in thirteenth- and fourteenth-century Spain and Portugal to the possibilities for further democratic development.

In the fifteenth and sixteenth centuries, however, the *corteses*, the independent groups, the local autonomy, were all eliminated. An authoritarian, centralized, and powerful state emerged that snuffed out these early stirrings of democracy. Under the Spanish monarchs Ferdinand and Isabella (1479–1516), and then continuing under the Hapsburg monarchy during the next two centuries, democratic autonomy was crushed and an absolutist, authoritarian, highly concentrated state, based on the principle of divinely sanctioned monarchy, triumphed overwhelmingly. It was this "Hapsburg model" of an authoritarian state that was transferred to Latin America and, once established, it continued indefinitely. The more open and pluralist democratic model was completely eclipsed for these centuries, to be revived only after Latin America achieved independence in the nineteenth century. However, democracy in Latin America, rooted as it was in these early Spanish corporatist or group practices, would also differ from the U.S. or Lockean-Madisonian forms.

Components of the Political Culture

In its political-cultural aspects, the Hapsburg model that Spain and Portugal carried to the New World was elitist, hierarchical, authoritarian, corporatist, and patrimonialist to its core. Each of these terms requires explanation as a way of helping us understand the historically dominant political culture of Latin America.

Elitism means not just that Latin America was ruled by its elites but that the idea and culture of elitism pervaded its entire society. If one is not of the elite, one aspires to live and act like the elites. Enlisted men want to be officers, colonels want to be generals, and generals often aspire to the presidency—not so much to perform public service as to enjoy the power, perks, and privileges of higher office. The lower classes want to appear middle class (so they frequently shun manual labor and carry their lunches in brief cases rather than lunch boxes), and the middle class wants to live like the upper class. Everyone wants to be a Spanish grandee—or at least the way they imagine a Spanish grandee to be: proud, aloof, aristocratic, and self-important; unconcerned with money, dignified yet disdainful of those lower in the social scale; a master of servants. This "aristocratic ethos" is conducive neither to democracy nor egalitarianism, and the disdain for manual labor and status preoccupations that go with it have not, historically, been conducive to capitalism and economic growth, either.

The notion of *hierarchy* is closely related to the phenomenon of elitism. Hierarchy means a careful rank-ordering of people from top (the elites) to bottom (in Latin America, Indians, Blacks, and peasants). One is born into a certain place or station in society, and one is expected to stay there, marry there, have children there, and die there—generation after generation and century after century. One learns to accept one's station in life and to act accordingly: haughty if one is an elite, and humble and deferential if one is lower class. Clothes, speech, family background, and demeanor are all determinants of where one fits in this social hierarchy, which, of course, had its origins in the medieval-Catholic conception of the rank-order of the heavens: God, angels, archangels, cherubim, seraphim, and so forth. Society becomes a "society of uniforms" all determining where one fits in the rank-ordering of people; society is also organized in terms of specific, almost typecast roles and functions—military, cleric, oligarch, student, worker—to which one's behavior is supposed to conform. Obviously, in a society organized on such a hierarchical basis, there will be few avenues of advancement, little social mobility, and a great deal of formality.

Authoritarianism is, of course, a political term referring to the top-down, nonparticipatory, nondemocratic nature of power in Latin America historically. Power is organized on an autocratic, often dictatorial basis, and not from the grass roots up. Popular sovereignty usually does not represent the final arbiter of national affairs, but rather reflects an authoritative decision made from on high. Or else, popular sovereignty will be rationalized as resting not among the public but in the hands of the ruler who "knows" their wishes. *Caesarism, Bonapartism*, and *dictatorship* are all terms associated with this authoritarian tradition.

But authoritarianism in Latin America stems not just from history and tradition but also from the very real conditions prevailing there. Historically, Latin America has been a vast and near-empty continent, and, especially in the early decades of postindependence, it lacked in organization, discipline, infrastructure, and associational life. In such a vacuum, Latin Americans have long feared that the forces of anarchism and barbarism would overwhelm them—hence the need for strong authority to forestall chaos.

Authoritarianism in Latin America is not limited to the top levels. Rather, it is a societywide phenomenon. Thus, the religious, educational, and legal establishments as well as government are infused with the requirements of top-down authority, and authoritarianism often prevails in trade unions, peasant associations, and other popular organizations as well. In short, every man from the lowest to the highest rank seeks to be in a position of authority over others. As one resident of the Dominican Republic told me after I had written a book about a particularly bloody despot in his country, "You have to remember, Howard, that every Dominican has a little of Trujillo in him."

Corporatism is a little more complicated—and less well known. Corporatism refers to the organization of society by sectors or functional groups (farmers, clerics, industrialists, armed forces, unions, universities, and so on) rather than on an individual basis (one man, one vote) as in U.S. society. Corporatism tends to stress group rights and responsibilities over individual or personal rights, meaning that one acquires the rights to organize and to participate politically only when one's group is recognized and granted legitimacy by the political authorities. Even representation in the parliament, on an advisory council of state, or on government boards and agencies may be organized on a group basis (seven seats or votes for the military, five for labor unions, and so on) rather than on the basis of democratically elected representatives. Latin society in the Mediterranean and the Americas has long had a history of such group representation.

Often, it is the state or government that structures, licenses, and thereby controls these corporate groups, which is why corporatism is often associated with authoritarianism. Corporatism implies a unified, organic, centralized system of political authority, with all the components closely tied together. Corporatism has deep roots in Hispanic society, tracing back to the very founding of the state and its relations with such early corporate groups as the towns, the military orders, and the church. Corporatism therefore has long been associated with Hispanic-American history, culture, and political organization, and often seems to Latin Americans almost the natural way to organize their social and political systems.

Patrimonialism is related to patronage, and all Latin American countries are organized to one degree or another on a patronage basis. It is a system of favors in return for favors, and patronage is the "grease" that smooths virtually all transactions. Patronage in the forms of jobs, gifts, money, or special access may be traded for votes; patronage may also occur in government programs, contracts, and licensing. If you've seen *The Godfather* or lived in a city with a political machine, then you probably understand the patronage basis of Latin American politics—except that there it operates on a national and not just a local level.

But in Latin America, just as every man wants to be a wealthy grandee, so everyone also wants to be a patron. That is how you control people and votes, and how you attach people to you. And as you move up the political ladder to become mayor, congressman, governor, or even president, you acquire an ever-larger patronage following. As you rise, they also rise; but if you fall, they similarly fall—and they may desert you in the process while latching onto another patron. The art of expanding one's patronage connections and networks in Latin America is a never-ending process that pervades almost all political transactions.

This general system of elitism, hierarchy, authoritarianism, corporatism, and patrimonialism served for a long time as the dominant political culture and organizational model of Latin America. It persisted through three centuries of colonial rule, survived independence in the nineteenth century largely intact, and has even continued into modern times, albeit in modified, updated form.

Four points should be made with respect to this traditional Latin American political culture. First, this model of an elitist-hierarchical-authoritarian-corporatist-patrimonialist society brought to the New World by Spain and Portugal corresponded in many particulars to the indigenous or Indian political culture, which was similarly organized on an elitist, corporatist, top-down basis; the two therefore reinforced each other and made authoritarianism even stronger. Second, this was a political culture of a particular time and place—Spain and Portugal circa 1500, after their earlier democratic institutions had been snuffed out—but it need not necessarily be a permanent set of features, as Latin America's recent movement toward genuine democracy attests. Third, and related, while this was the dominant political culture, other, subordinate political cultures existed alongside it, often based on more democratic precepts and hoping to rise to a majority position. Finally, we should keep in mind that political culture is not static (although the traditional political culture in Latin America was very stable for a long time and still has persistent features), but can and does change over time, along with shifting socioeconomic and political conditions. That is precisely what happened in Latin America.

The Emergence of Liberalism

In the late eighteenth century, the influence of French Enlightenment *philosophes* (philosophers and liberal intellectuals) began to be felt in Latin America, particularly by the young Creole intellectuals and political leaders who were beginning to flirt with independence ideas. Probably the strongest impact on these future leaders was the firebrand Frenchman, Jean-Jacques Rousseau.

Idealized Rousseauian "Democracy"

Rousseau is best known for his slim book *The Social Contract*, which was read widely in Latin America. The book, which is based on a presumed "state of nature" that bears a striking resemblance to Latin America, is a powerful argument in favor of liberty, equality, democracy, and participation. These goals, as well as Rousseau's passion in defending them, were very attractive to Latin American intellectuals. But while Rousseau's goals and vision were attractive, his means for achieving them were less so.

Rousseau emphasized the need for strong, centralized state authority and inspired leadership. He favored a tightly integrated and organic regime, not a pluralist one. He wanted a corporatist system in which each group was secure and fixed in place, but such a system generally precludes dynamism and change. He emphasized rights, but he said very little about responsibilities. Rousseau concentrated on the glorious ends to which the state should be dedicated, but he was not very careful about the means, such as democratic elections, to achieve his goals. Rousseau thus presented a wonderful vision for poets, romantics, and visionaries, but his neglect of means all too often paved the way to dictatorship and totalitarianism. For example, his focus on the "general will," which presumably was intuitively "known" by the "correct" leadership (without necessarily checking with the electorate!) has served as a formula for such varied—and failed—authoritarians as Trujillo, Somoza, and Castro. Rousseau gave us a pretty picture, but genuine democracy has to be built on more prosaic procedures like voting, diversity, competition, and civic responsibility.

The shortcomings of Rousseauian theory help explain why Latin American democracy has always represented a visionary but frequently unworkable system, whereas U.S. democracy, while less visionary, is more workable and practical. They also help illuminate why the United States and Latin America went in such different directions politically in the nineteenth century, why they remain different today, and why the Rousseauian form retains its popularity even now. For Rousseau's system promises that great goals can be achieved, even in the absence of an institutional infrastructure, through the ascension of a heroic leader who "knows" the general will and acts accordingly. Democracy, social justice, equality—all worthy goals—can be accomplished by inspired action or revolution even if the institutional underpinnings for achieving these goals are absent. Of course, in the real world that is not possible—democracy requires long and painstaking efforts; it cannot be created out of nothing. But in Latin America, the Rousseauian vision can be maintained as a great aspiration even when the harsh realities make it virtually impossible.

There are other reasons for Rousseau's popularity in Latin America, as contrasted with the dominance of the ideas of Locke, Madison, and Jefferson in the United States. Note that Rousseau's system of "democracy" is top-down, run by the elites, by intellectuals, by those who presume to know the general will. There is not much trust of the grass roots or real people here. Rousseau's tightly knit corporatist and organicist view of the state, as contrasted with the pluralist view, was also attractive to Latin Americans because it was, in a secular version, in accord with their Catholic-Thomistic traditions and because it enabled them to embrace liberty and democracy without actually changing their historically top-down institutions very much. Rousseau, in short, seemed to "fit" Latin America in ways that Locke or Madison did not; he offered a modern, "enlightened" view of the state that could be substituted for the older Hapsburgian model—but without fundamentally altering the existing sociopolitical structure of influence. That is why Rousseau was so popular in Latin America, and also why U.S. and Latin American "democracy" would go in such different directions.

The Legal/Constitutional Legacy

We are now in a position to understand why foreign observers so often misinterpreted Latin America in the nineteenth century—and why we continue to misunderstand the area even today. Observers look at the various Latin American laws and constitutions with their provisions for democracy, fundamental rights, separation of powers, and the like and, knowing that they have seldom effectively operated according to the constitutional provisions, pronounce Latin American democracy and history a "failure." That view of Latin America as a failure compared to the "successful" United States is widespread. We have assumed—based on our own political tradition—that because Latin America has not always conformed to legal/constitutional niceties, the area has not been successful.

But there is another and different view. If we look at the Latin American constitutions carefully—because constitutions provide one view of what the prevailing political culture is—we discover a different reality. First, there is no real separation of powers; as in the past, it is the executive that is overwhelmingly dominant. Second, these are not fully pluralist countries, but ones where power is still generally highly centralized and concentrated. Third, while there are long lists of human and civil rights in the Latin American constitutions, these can be circumscribed easily in case of "emergency." Fourth, such corporate groups as the army, the church, the elites, and, in the modern constitutions, the workers are afforded special privileges under the law. Fifth, the provisions for calling a "state of siege" or of "emergency," for proscribing (sending home!) the legislature, or for packing the courts are so broad that constitutional dictatorships are possible. All of these constitutional provisions are within the Hispanic or Rousseauian tradition of "democracy," although not the North American one. They show that if we judge Latin America not by our liberal standards of democracy but by their Hispanic-Rousseauian ones, the area has in fact conformed pretty well to its own criteria. These criteria may not have delivered all that much in terms of goods and services, but that again may be a U.S. criterion of good government and not so strongly a Latin American one. In recent decades, however, this attitude has begun to change as Latin Americans demand more and better services from their governments.

The Lockean/Madisonian Influence

While the Rousseauian formula has been, and may well still be, the dominant one in Latin America, new ideas and institutional forms have also
worked their way into the area. These include an emphasis on individual as
well as group rights, stronger and more independent parliaments, stronger
court systems, and the like. It would be convenient and make it easy to understand if we were able to say that Rousseau's system of "democracy" (centralized, top-down, organic) has now been definitely replaced by the
Lockean-Madisonian-U.S. type. But, in fact, despite immense U.S. pressures, this process of change is still only partial and incomplete. And because
a great deal of the change has come about due to U.S. pressure, it is difficult
to assess how much change has really been absorbed into the Latin American
psyche. After all, an authoritarian and nonpluralist political culture that has
now been in existence for more than five hundred years is not going to
change quickly or overnight—although it will change.

The fact is that Latin America reflects an often confused blend of both its
historic Hispanic and Rousseauian *and* its new North American–like democratic traditions. It has real political parties, competitive elections, checks and
balances, human rights observance, and the requirements of effective public
policy. But it also retains Rousseauian centralism, corporatism, organicism,
authoritarianism, and patrimonialism. These two traditions continue to exist
side by side, or they overlap, often in chaotic and inefficient ways. Latin
America has not repudiated its past or put its older institutions into moth-
balls, nor has it embraced entirely the principles of U.S.-style democracy.
Rather, it lives in a world of overlap where both exist, where neither is definitive, and hence where some fantastic compromises must still be reached.

The Electoral Process

Elections provide another way of assessing political culture in Latin America.
Historically, elections have provided *only one of several* legitimate routes to
power, with other means including a skillfully executed coup d'état, a heroic
guerrilla struggle, or a general strike or march on the national palace. In addition, most elections in Latin America in the past have been of the plebiscitary
type: that is, they were meant to ratify an existing government in power
through the option to vote "yes," rather than implying genuine choice. Further, the "political parties" in the region have historically been only a conces-
sion to a foreign "fad"; parties in Latin America have tended to be elite-directed
patronage machines devoid of programs, platforms, or ideology.

In recent decades, these historical practices have begun to change. Thanks
in part to foreign pressures and election observers, most elections in Latin
America have become genuinely competitive and genuinely democratic, with
real choices offered and ballots counted honestly. Moreover, again in part

due to foreign pressures, elections are increasingly viewed as the *only* legitimate means to power, while coups, revolutions, general strikes, and so on are viewed as illegitimate. Then, too, as Latin American society has become more modernized and mobilized, the political parties have begun to evolve (in some but by no means all cases) into genuine mass organizations that advance real programs and platforms and help to select candidates and to run elections.

Political Practice

Another measure of the changing political culture of Latin America is actual *political practice*. Historically, the military has often been the real power behind the throne in Latin America. Listen to the (not atypical) words of Colonel Byron Disraeli Lima of Guatemala, whose heroes are Napoleon, Hitler, and the Israelis—all "conquerors and warriors": "Latins take command from men in uniform [not from civilian politicians]. If a cabinet doesn't work, I prefer a *coup*." Colonel Lima made it clear that he had no use for human rights considerations and indicated he paid attention to them only because otherwise the United States would cut off aid to the Guatemalan army. He would never allow a military officer to be tried for past human rights abuses, and he suggested darkly that no civilian government should meddle in the internal affairs of the army or it would be quickly overthrown.[1]

These traditional military attitudes now are also beginning to change, so that Colonel Lima's views are widely considered to be those of a "Neanderthal." In most of the bigger countries—Mexico, Chile, Argentina, Brazil, Colombia, Venezuela—the armed forces have become quite professionalized and no longer hold such primitive views. In most countries, the military was thoroughly discredited and disillusioned by its previous experience in power in the 1970s—by its economic mismanagement and its inability to solve national problems. So, in the 1980s, the military in Latin America retreated to the barracks and is, for the most part, not eager to jump back into power again.

In the smaller countries of South America, Central America, and the Caribbean (Haiti, the Dominican Republic), one can still find expressions of the older and nastier attitudes personified by Colonel Lima. But *for the most part*, the armies of Latin America have learned their lessons, are more professional, and draw sharper distinctions between military and civilian roles. That is not to say coups are impossible in Latin America, but it is to suggest that, especially in the larger and more institutionalized countries, they have become less likely.

In all these ways—laws and constitutions, elections, actual political practice—Latin American political culture has been moving toward greater pluralism and democracy. However, the process is far from complete. It is part of the genius of Latin American politics and politicians that they are often able to bridge these chasms and govern more or less effectively despite the enormous gaps that continue to exist in attitudes, belief systems, and behavior. Let us now focus on Latin American public opinion regarding recent changes generally, and democracy specifically.

Latin American Public Opinion

Public opinion provides us with a more quantifiable, and therefore usually more accurate, reading on political culture in Latin America. The data we have, however, reveal more ambiguities about democracy in the area than democrats should feel comfortable with.

Numerous surveys in the mid-to-late-1980s by the United States Information Agency (USIA) as well as private scholars show that Latin Americans overwhelmingly prefer democratic, representative rule—fully 85–95 percent in country after country. Only about 5 percent favor Marxist-Leninist regimes, and an even smaller percentage favor authoritarian regimes. Furthermore, if we ask Latin Americans what specific kinds of institutions they prefer, once again, overwhelmingly, the answers are a free press, an independent legislature and judiciary, human rights, regular elections, and a nonabusive, nonviolent government and military. These responses lend support to the argument that democracy is not alien to Latin America, that Latin Americans are not "natural" authoritarians, and that the type of government they prefer is not much different from that of the United States.

However, when one probes more deeply, the responses become more mixed. For example, while Latin Americans prefer democracy, they also prefer strong leadership—the Rousseau principle—which can easily lead to Bonapartism or dictatorship. In situations of crisis, Latin Americans often seem to be willing to suspend human rights, limit press freedom, or send the congress home. When, for example, President Alberto Fujimori of Peru, faced with a severe challenge from the murderous *Sendero Luminoso* (Shining Path) guerrillas, suspended the constitution and dismissed the congress, his popular approval ratings soared to over 70 percent. The church also continues to enjoy special favors in most countries despite the constitutional separation of church and state. The military is still viewed widely as having a legitimate role in maintaining *internal* stability. Group rights and obligations are held in at least as high esteem as individual rights. All of these views are, potentially, destructive of democratic rule.

Another disturbing feature that emerges from these surveys is that while Latin Americans admire democracy in the United States and other countries, they are not sure that it works all that well for them. Latin Americans know their own history and recognize the absence of much experience with democracy. The "George Washington of Latin America," Simon Bolívar, for example, lamented this lack of democratic background. Latin Americans also are aware of the historical lack of associations, infrastructure, and organizations in their countries, which weakens democratic foundations and frequently gives rise to authoritarianism. Furthermore, they tend to be quite realistic about the venality of their own politicians, whom they feel need to be reined in by a tough leader. They are not sure their countries have the economic base to support stable democracy. And they recognize that in their past it has been strong leaders, if not dictators, who brought progress—Díaz in Mexico, Trujillo in the Dominican Republic, Gómez and Pérez Jiménez in Venezuela, Perón in Argentina, Pinochet in Chile—and not usually the democrats. Hence, while they admire democracy in the abstract, they are not entirely convinced it is right for them.

More recently, these traditional attitudes have begun to change. Latin America is more affluent than before and has a stronger economic base. It has begun to fill the void in its organizational space with associational life that makes the Latin Americans less fearful of democracy. The area is no longer threatened (except in a handful of countries—Peru, Guatemala, Colombia) by subversion and guerrilla extremists. Latin America is now more stable, benefits from better leadership, and feels more self-confident than previously. In addition, the armed forces have been discredited and, except in a few countries, are no longer viewed as such a severe threat. All these factors make democracy look like a better prospect than before.

Nonetheless, the best public opinion surveys available, even with the impressive democratization of the last decade, still provide quite a mixed picture. Let us look at two key countries initially to illustrate democracy's difficulties: Argentina and Venezuela. Both of these are highly literate countries, with a large middle class, among the richest in Latin America, and with strong political institutions. If democracy cannot survive in these two countries, it is unlikely to work anywhere in the region.

In Argentina, although 86 percent of the population support democracy as a system, only 36 percent of those surveyed had a favorable view of political parties—any party!—and less than 30 percent had favorable attitudes toward labor unions. Assuming that true democracy consists not just of representative institutions but also includes a pluralist group structure, then this lack of support for parties and unions is worrisome. Moreover, when asked what they mean by "democracy," 84 percent of Argentinians (almost as many as those indicating a preference for democracy itself) say "strong government." But strong government, again following Rousseau, can—and frequently has—led to dictatorship in Argentina. The troubling conclusion is that democracy in Argentina is more tenuous than is often thought, and that the "two forks in the trail" for Argentina—democracy and dictatorship—are often closer to each other than our usual categories suggest. More recent surveys indicate that the high figure in support of democracy in Argentina (86 percent) is also eroding.[2]

Venezuela is in an even more precarious position. Venezuela is the most economically developed nation in Latin America, with large cadres of able leaders, strong institutions, and widespread popular support for democracy and opposition to military coups. Yet, in 1992, Venezuelans were so unhappy with the leadership of democratically elected Carlos Andrés Pérez that his approval ratings had dipped below 10 percent—far lower than those even of George Bush! Because of widespread sentiment that these were centers of corruption, popular support for political parties, trade unions, and the bureaucracy had dipped almost to the vanishing point. *Half* of the electorate favored a socialist remodeling of the economy and society, but without specifying what form (democratic or Leninist) such socialism should take. The disillusionment was so widespread that several coups were launched against the government in 1992 that probably would have succeeded if the plotters had not bungled the attempt and if the United States had not provided money and support to bolster the government. And remember, this is the ***most developed*** country in Latin America with one of the longest traditions of uninterrupted democracy; if democracy cannot succeed in Venezuela, and in Argentina, it probably cannot succeed anywhere.

When we turn to the weaker and less well developed countries of Central America (as well as Ecuador, Bolivia, and Paraguay in South America), the prospects for democracy are even shakier. In Central America, for example, while the public overwhelmingly agrees (85–90 percent) with the notion that democracy is the best form of government, they are not sure it is right in their particular circumstances. These are small and weak countries that, in general, are less well institutionalized than the larger South American countries. Forty-seven percent of El Salvadorans and only *27 percent of Guatemalans* (where Colonel Lima holds forth) say they are best off when living under democratic rule. Throughout Central America, less than a majority believes that democracy is viable in that context. If the people themselves believe democracy will not or cannot work in their country, then democracy's prospects cannot be bright. Only in solidly democratic Costa Rica was there clear consensus (83 percent) in support of democracy.

When asked what they mean by "democracy," people gave some rather strained answers that had little to do with classic democracy, which usually includes regular elections, genuine competition and pluralism, and human rights and freedom. For example, Uruguayans equate democracy with social welfare—reflecting Uruguay's long tradition of cradle-to-grave social programs. Argentinians refer to a strong, patronage-oriented state that carries out social programs for the workers. Brazilians cite economic equality; they also identify democracy with getting favors from public officials—a traditional Brazilian practice but one that has no relationship to any previous definition of democracy. However, it should further be noted that in Argentina and Uruguay only 30 percent of the respondents could provide *any* definition of democracy, as compared to 50 percent in Brazil. Clearly, these still are countries with little knowledge of or experience with democracy.

It is not just democracy, however, that is viewed as a foreign and often strange implant; *all* institutions in some of the most important Latin American countries rank very low in popularity and legitimacy. In the fall of 1985, an important survey conducted in Argentina, Brazil, and Uruguay showed dangerously low support for most national institutions, with Brazil registering the lowest scores of the three. People were asked to rank their confidence in the main national institutions on a scale of 0 (representing no confidence) to 5 (representing high confidence). The responses were then totaled and compared for the three countries. A cumulative score of 300 indicated a high degree of confidence (about 80 percent) in the institution, 250–300 meant substantial majorities (two thirds to three quarters) support it, 200–250 indicated majority support, 150–200 meant a plurality (less than half) of support, 100–250 indicated little confidence in the institution, and under 100 meant virtually no support at all. The results are given in Table 6.1.

Several features are striking about these numbers. The first is the low level of confidence in *any* institution in *any* of the countries: no institution inspires high or even substantial confidence, and *only* the educational system in Argentina and Uruguay has majority support. In fact, relatively few institutions have even plurality support. Most inspire little public confidence, and for quite a few there is no support at all.

Brazil's figures are considerably lower than those of the other two countries, indicating very low confidence in all institutions. Note that after the educational system and the church, the armed forces rank third in terms of confidence level, which indicates the military may well be a major force in Brazil's future. We have already seen that in such countries as Argentina, Venezuela, and Uruguay (to say nothing of such even wobblier countries as Peru, Colombia, Ecuador, Bolivia, and Paraguay), support for democracy and its undergirding institutions is quite thin; but in Brazil, the figures are truly alarming. None of these figures augur well for the future of democracy in Latin America.

This same survey asked other questions that provide further insight into Latin American attitudes and political culture. For example, when asked if democracy was suitable in a country that is underdeveloped economically, 56 percent of the respondents in Argentina and Uruguay said democracy was possible even with economic underdevelopment. In Brazil, however, the figure was exactly reversed: 56 percent said economic development should come *before* democracy. When asked about the prospects of democracy versus authoritarianism, 65 percent of respondents in Argentina said democracy would be strengthened and only 20 percent thought authoritarianism would return. In Brazil, however, only 40 percent had confidence in democracy's future while an almost equal percentage (35 percent) thought authoritarianism

Table 6 ✦ 1 Confidence in Main National Institutions—Argentina, Brazil, Uruguay

	Country		
Institution	Argentina	Brazil	Uruguay
Presidency	184	84	151
Congress	184	136	160
Judiciary	179	102	166
Political parties	151	60	143
Educational system	204	170	205
Civil service	125	101	115
Police	160	83	126
Armed forces	118	141	61
Labor unions	123	108	146
Press	151	121	138
Private industry	133	90	80
Catholic church	175	170	95
Neighborhood organizations	164	135	95

Source: United States Information Agency.

would return; in Uruguay, 45 percent predicted democracy's continuance while an equal number predicted authoritarianism in the future. When asked if military takeovers might be justified in times of crisis, 65 percent of the Argentines said no, while in Brazil and Uruguay 45 percent said yes.

These data are stunning. They indicate that even in the relatively developed countries of Latin America—Argentina, Brazil, Uruguay, Venezuela—democracy is not particularly well established. Democracy in the abstract is admired, but Latin Americans express strong doubts, given their chaotic histories and often underinstitutionalized political systems, whether democracy works in *their* countries. And there is meager political support for democracy's essential underpinnings such as labor unions, interest groups, and political parties. In sum, in all the countries, there are strong doubts about the viability and permanence of democracy, very few democratic institutions that inspire confidence, and very few accepted and internalized rules that would restrain non- or antidemocratic actions.

None of this public opinion data is very encouraging for the cause of democracy in Latin America. A country that we thought was solidly democratic—Venezuela—with strong democratic institutions for the last thirty-five years, has been shown to be not overly supportive of democracy; and in 1992, Venezuela's elected government was twice almost toppled by military coups. Countries such as Argentina and Uruguay, which rank high in Latin America by all measures of socioeconomic development, have also been shown to be very tenuous democracies. In just about *all* the other countries, democracy is still at risk—more so in Peru, Bolivia, Ecuador, and Central America and less so in Chile and Costa Rica. The data help explain the continuing attraction of Rousseauian, organic and top-down forms of democracy, and even of the authoritarian alternative if democracy proves chaotic or unworkable.

Disillusionment with Democracy?

The 1980s were the high point of prodemocracy sentiment—and even euphoria—in Latin America. People were confident and optimistic about democracy's future in the hemisphere. The long-time authoritarian regimes in many countries had been or were in the process of being ousted from power, and people thought democracy would solve all their problems. But since those heady years, a great deal of disillusionment, despair, or maybe just realism has set in.

The causes of this changing mood are many and complex, but there is no doubting the widespread frustration with and disappointment in democracy. Although support for democracy as an abstract system remains strong throughout Latin America, the popular sentiment is that the new democracies are not being run well and that the benefits of democracy that everyone expected have not materialized. Democracy has so far not delivered much in the way of social programs and economic growth. Corruption has become a serious issue in almost all the countries. There is a lingering popular fear of repression but at the same time an overall disenchantment with politics, including democratic politics. Few of the necessary reforms or structural changes have materialized. The democratic leadership has often proved incompetent, indecisive, or corrupt, and support for the area's current presidents and institutions has dwindled. The new democratic regimes are often proving to be as susceptible to graft and patronage pressures as their military predecessors—maybe more so since elected governments feel they owe a payback to their constituents for their support. The signs of discontent are widespread, the mood is often gloomy, and democracy could prove to be among the casualties.

The armed forces, while reluctant to intervene, are among those most unhappy with the deteriorating conditions and with democracy's inefficiencies and incapacities. But at the street level, in letters to the editor, and in popular demonstrations, new calls for order and discipline (which usually translates into military rule) are being heard. Terrorism helps fuel these demands, as do corruption, drug trafficking, and the excesses and flamboyant policies of some democratic leaders. The political parties have not provided the trained and capable cadres to manage public administration efficiently. Stagnant economies in many countries of the area have contributed further to the broad discouragement. And the lack of much help from abroad, from any source, has largely left Latin America to struggle through on its own.

All these fears and disillusionments with democracy have been measured at the public opinion level for some time, but now they are being felt at the level of practical politics, too. In Haiti, which is not necessarily a representative case, the elected government of Jean Bertrand Aristide was overthrown by the military in 1991; and no amount of U.S. pressure and sanctions has so far succeeded in restoring much real democracy to that country. In Peru, embattled President Alberto Fujimori invoked emergency laws, sent the congress home, and began ruling by decree. Brazil voted to impeach its president, which, while not a coup d'état, was not exactly a sign that democracy is healthy in Latin America's largest country. In Venezuela, Latin America's richest country, after two serious coup attempts and numerous smaller ones, democracy hangs on by the slenderest of threads. Virtually everywhere else, democracy is very precarious, often held up by handfuls of heroic leaders and, sometimes, generous infusions of U.S. support, but not by much else.

The disillusionment with democracy may not mean a new wave of military takeovers—Latin America shudders at the thought of a renewed era of authoritarianism. Military regimes may regain power in several of the less institutionalized countries of the area, but a hemisphericwide turn to dictatorship as occurred in the 1960s and 1970s is unlikely. Also, in some countries, democracy is being deepened, participation in expanding, and the reform of economic and political institutions is going forward. These are healthy signs for democracy, but democracy clearly is still on trial: it cannot be taken for granted, it requires continuous nurturing, and it may even be upset in various countries.

Political Culture and the Future

Democracy has made great—even amazing—progress in Latin America in the last two decades, but substantial obstacles to democracy's successful consolidation remain. The political culture of the area has turned significantly toward democracy, pluralism, and more open economic as well as political processes. But the elements of the traditional political culture—hierarchy, authoritarianism, elitism, organicism and corporatism, and patrimonialism— still often overlap in confusing ways with the newer, more democratic attitudes. This mix gives Latin America its dynamism, but it also provides the possibilities for instability.

Meanwhile, although democracy is still shaky in many countries of the area, other aspects of the historical political culture are changing. Many countries, for example, are making a new and serious commitment to liberal, open markets and to economic reform, recognizing that in the modern world and for a modern economy, the traditional statism and mercantilism will no longer work. And in Mexico and some other countries, there is widespread recognition that if they wish to become fully developed, a better education system, a more efficient and streamlined economy, and a smaller and less patronage-dominated state system are all absolutely necessary. To the extent that these ideas sink in and become more widespread, Latin America's future looks more hopeful.

Notes

1. See the report of this interview in *Wall Street Journal* (October 30, 1985), pp. 1ff.
2. Additional data and more information about the public opinion surveys may be found in Howard J. Wiarda, *The Democratic Revolution in Latin America: History, Politics, and U.S. Policy* (New York: A Twentieth Century Fund Book, Holmes and Meier, 1990).

7

✦

The Power Structure

Economics, Class Relations, and Interest Groups

Latin America is often indiscriminately lumped together with other Third World countries or developing areas. True, Latin America has abysmal poverty, high illiteracy rates, widespread malnutrition and malnutrition-related diseases, and other characteristic signs of underdevelopment. But Latin America, with the exception of Nicaragua and Haiti, is nowhere as poor as sub-Saharan Africa, South and Southeast Asia, and parts of the Middle East and Oceania. At the same time, Latin America is nowhere as affluent as the United States, Western Europe, or Japan. Rather, Latin America occupies an intermediary position, neither very rich nor—any more—very poor, either. We therefore need a new set of explanatory tools and terminology to deal with Latin America and to reflect these realities: the terms *transitional* and *middle income* help us get at the point we are making, that Latin America lies somewhere between the developed and the underdeveloped worlds.

Another popular image of Latin America is that it is two-class system dominated by the oligarchy. Clearly, a power structure or power elite exists in Latin America, and in the past the region *was* dominated by the landed oligarchy. But the term *oligarchy*, which usually conveys strong overtones of disapproval, is much too simple to describe the current power system in most Latin American countries. In all these countries, the historical landed oligarchy has now gone into other pursuits (banking, industry, commerce, insurance); at the same time, a variety of new elites—businessmen, importer-exporters, financiers, industrialists, persons from diverse ethnic communities—have risen up to contest for power with or supplant the old landed oligarchies. In addition, with the rise of the middle class and of an organized working class, it is no longer possible to describe Latin America in simple, two-class (lord and peasant) terms; the emergence of a variety of elites similarly makes our identification of a single "power structure" more complicated.

One further note of caution is necessary before we plunge into the discussion. Clearly, in recent decades, Latin American politics and society have become more pluralist than before. But Latin American pluralism is not quite like the pluralism of the interest group struggle in the United States, where literally thousands of interest groups are represented in Washington, D.C. In Latin America, the number of such groups is far more limited (often fewer than ten); the groups are often organized under the state (one of the hallmarks of corporatism) instead of independent of it as in the United States; and there is little real interest group *lobbying* in Latin America comparable to that which occurs in the U.S. Congress. In addition, some of these groups, such as the armed forces and the business community, are very powerful in Latin America but are often *integrated into* and an integral part of the state or government, as compared with their *separation from* the state in the U.S. system. In some cases, these groups are even more powerful than the government itself.

These features add intriguing complexities to our efforts to understand Latin America. They indicate once again how Latin America differs from both other Third World areas and such already developed nations as the United States. In the discussion that follows, we attempt to clarify these issues and to wend our way through the thickets of misunderstanding about the area.

The Socioeconomic Situation

Latin America is a land of extremes as well as of all points in between. It has great wealth—and great poverty. It has some of the most sophisticated, most cultured, and best-educated people in the world—and some of its most primitive. It has some of the world's largest industrial firms coexisting alongside some of the most primitive agricultural practices. It has many very calm, peaceful social institutions (the extended family, close interpersonal connections, religion) together with some ofttimes violent politics. It has long alternated between sometimes brutal dictatorships on the one hand and near-libertine democracies on the other. But now, abundant signs indicate not only that Latin America is leaving its extremes of wealth and poverty behind, but that its political system has began to settle down as well and become more moderate.

Geographical Factors

A number of indicators give clues to the overall socioeconomic situation. First, let us look at extremities of size (see Table 7.1). Brazil is a huge nation, fifth largest in the world (behind only Russia, China, Canada, and the United States) and almost a whole continent in itself. Argentina is the second largest nation in Latin America, followed by Mexico. Bolivia, Colombia, Peru, and Venezuela are also sizable nations, comparable to the major countries of Europe. At the same time, the nations of Central America (El Salvador, Guatemala, Honduras, Nicaragua, Costa Rica, Panama), of the Caribbean (Haiti, the Dominican Republic, Cuba), and elsewhere in South America (Ecuador, Paraguay, Uruguay) are much smaller nations—really "city-states," with, typically, a single large city and a surrounding countryside, and often lacking in resources and development potential.

In general, the larger states in Latin America (Bolivia and Peru are the major exceptions) tend both to be more developed economically and to have a firmer institutional infrastructure. The smaller states (Costa Rica and Uruguay are the exceptions) have smaller markets and are less well off economically, have a weaker political infrastructure, and, because they are so small, have questionable viability as nation-states.

Population Distribution

Next, let us compare populations (see Table 7.2). Again, what we see are great extremes. Not only is Brazil a giant among nations in terms of size, but with its population of nearly 150 million it is by far the most populous nation in Latin America, and eighth in the world. Mexico is next with approximately 90 million persons. Argentina and Colombia both have over 30 million, while Peru and Venezuela both have about 20 million. At the other end of the spectrum, Costa Rica and Panama have less than 3 million each, while quite a number of countries are clustered in the 3–10 million range. Not only are these smaller nations resource-poor, but they lack the population base to support large-scale industry and manufacturing, and therefore they may always be consigned to economic underdevelopment. Note also the rates of population growth in these countries: they have generally been declining since the 1960s, but in some countries are still proceeding faster than economic growth, which results in a net *decline* of per capita income.

Table 7 ✦ 1 Extremities of Size

Country	Area in Square Miles
Argentina	1,078,266
Bolivia	412,777
Brazil	3,286,170
Chile	286,396
Colombia	439,828
Costa Rica	19,238
Cuba	42,857
Dominican Republic	19,129
Ecuador	115,000
El Salvador	8,060
Guatemala	45,452
Haiti	10,714
Honduras	45,000
Mexico	760,373
Nicaragua	57,143
Panama	28,575
Paraguay	150,518
Peru	513,000
Uruguay	72,172
Venezuela	352,143

Social Indicators

Next, let us examine social indicators: life expectancy, illiteracy, and infant mortality (see Table 7.3). As regards life expectancy, note that Argentina, Chile, Costa Rica, Panama, Uruguay, and Venezuela have all crossed the 70-year life expectancy threshold that separates the developing from the developed world. Most European nations, the United States, and Japan are all in the 75-year range; in Latin America, the country with the highest life expectancy, Costa Rica, is already at that standard and five other nations are very close to it. Note also the *overall improvements* since the 1960s.

Next, let us look at illiteracy rates. Note that Argentina, Chile, Costa Rica, Mexico, and Uruguay are all below the level of 10 percent illiteracy. In other words, they rank with the United States and many other developed countries with over 90 percent literacy rates. Moreover, Colombia, Ecuador, Nicaragua, Panama, Paraguay, Peru, and Venezuela are all within a few percentage points of getting their illiteracy rate below 10 percent. The countries with the highest rates of illiteracy are Haiti, Guatemala, and Honduras, which also are among the poorest countries in Latin America. But note again, in all countries, the significant improvements since the 1960s.

Table 7✦2 Total Population (thousands of persons)

Country	1980	1981	1982	1983	1984	1985
Argentina	28,237	28,663	29,086	29,505	29,921	30,331
Bolivia	5,570	5,720	5,875	6,034	6,200	6,371
Brazil	121,286	124,068	126,898	129,776	132,658	135,564
Chile	11,145	11,327	11,519	11,717	11,919	12,122
Colombia	24,794	25,356	26,931	27,518	28,113	28,714
Costa Rica	2,284	2,351	2,421	2,493	2,566	2,642
Dominican Republic	5,697	5,836	5,978	6,123	6,269	6,416
Ecuador	8,123	8,361	8,606	8,857	9,115	9,317
El Salvador	4,525	4,583	4,625	4,663	4,707	4,768
Guatemala	6,917	7,113	7,315	7,524	7,740	7,963
Haiti	5,413	5,510	5,609	5,711	5,815	5,922
Honduras	3,662	3,797	3,939	4,085	4,234	4,383
Mexico	70,416	72,123	73,872	75,663	77,497	79,376
Nicaragua	2,771	2,861	2,957	3,058	3,163	3,272
Panama*	1,956	1,999	2,043	2,088	2,134	2,180
Paraguay	3,147	3,250	3,358	3,468	3,580	3,693
Peru	17,295	17,755	18,226	18,707	19,198	19,698
Uruguay	2,914	2,932	2,951	2,970	2,989	3,008
Venezuela	15,024	15,485	15,940	16,394	16,851	17,317
Total	346,983	354,934	363,034	371,284	379,650	388,086

*Population for former Canal Zone included from 1980,
which slightly raises the growth rates for 1971–80.
Source: Latin American Demographic Center, Santiago, Chile.

The final social indicator used here is the rate of infant mortality. This is usually measured in terms of the number of deaths per one thousand live births, and is thought of as among the best indicators of health and nutrition standards. Note that our usual leaders are again at the top—that is, with the lowest infant mortality: Argentina, Chile, Costa Rica, Panama, and Uruguay. All of the countries, thanks to better health, nutrition, and education, have been significantly reducing infant mortality since the 1960s. However, Haiti, Bolivia, and Peru still have very high infant mortality rates—comparable to those of the poorer Third World countries.

Gross Domestic Product

Now let us turn to measures of gross domestic product, or the total amount of goods and services produced by the economy on a yearly basis, as mea-

				Average Annual Growth Rates (%)		
1986	**1987**	**1988**	**1989**	**1961–70**	**1971–80**	**1981–89**
30,737	31,137	31,534	31,929	1.4	1.7	1.4
6,548	6,730	6,918	7,113	2.4	2.6	2.3
138,493	141,452	144,428	147,404	2.3	2.4	2.2
12,327	12,536	12,748	12,961	2.3	1.5	1.7
29,323	29,942	30,568	31,195	3.0	2.2	2.1
2,716	2,791	2,866	2,941	3.4	2.8	2.8
6,565	6,716	6,867	7,019	3.2	2.6	2.3
9,565	9,816	10,070	10,327	3.2	3.0	2.7
4,846	4,934	5,032	5,138	3.4	2.3	1.4
8,195	8,434	8,681	8,935	2.8	2.8	2.9
6,033	6,147	6,253	6,382	2.0	1.9	1.8
4,531	4,679	4,829	4,982	3.1	3.4	3.5
81,201	83,039	84,886	86,740	3.3	2.9	2.3
3,384	3,501	3,622	3,745	3.2	3.0	3.4
2,227	2,274	2,322	2,370	3.0	2.8	2.2
3,807	3,922	4,039	4,158	2.9	3.0	3.1
20,208	20,727	21,256	21,791	2.9	2.7	2.6
3,025	3,042	3,060	3,077	1.0	0.4	0.5
17,792	18,272	18,757	19,246	3.5	3.5	2.8
396,603	405,224	413,932	422,596	2.8	2.5	2.2

sured in millions of dollars (see Table 7.4). Note that Brazil, with its size and resources, is by far the largest producer in Latin America; in fact, Brazil ranks tenth in the world. Next comes Mexico, but with only about half the production of the Brazilian economy. Argentina and Venezuela—both rich in resources and with sizable populations—come next, followed in turn by Colombia, Peru, and Chile. After that the figures drop off sharply as we get to the smaller, resource-poor countries.

Of special interest in this table are the last three columns, which list trends as measured by decades. Almost all the Latin American countries showed strong rates of economic growth during the decades of the 1960s and 1970s. In several countries, perhaps surprisingly, the rates of growth were right up there with Japan, West Germany, and other "miracle growers"; and *almost everyone did well* during these two decades. But look at the figures for the 1980s. In almost every country, reflecting the debt crisis and the grave economic recession

Table 7 ◆ 3 Social Indicators

Country	Life Expectancy (years)			Illiteracy Rates (% age 15 +)			Infant Mortality Rates (per 1000 live births)		
	1960	1970	1989*	1960	1970	1989*	1960	1970	1989*
Argentina	65.8	68.1	70.6	8.6	7.4	4.5	57.6	44.2	32.0
Bolivia	44.4	47.9	53.1	61.2	36.8	25.8	159.8	143.2	110.0
Brazil	57.1	61.0	64.9	39.7	33.8	22.3	103.6	83.8	63.0
Chile	59.6	65.7	71.5	16.4	11.0	5.6	101.4	55.6	20.0
Colombia	56.3	61.0	65.7	27.1	19.2	11.9	96.0	66.1	46.0
Costa Rica	64.6	69.0	73.7	15.6	11.6	6.4	71.8	37.8	18.0
Dominican Republic	55.7	61.2	66.0	35.5	33.0	22.7	109.8	88.0	65.0
Ecuador	55.9	60.4	65.5	32.5	25.8	17.6	111.8	87.2	63.0
El Salvador	54.5	57.9	62.2	51.0	42.9	27.9	59.0	88.0	59.0
Guatemala	48.9	55.4	62.0	62.2	54.0	45.0	112.4	87.2	59.0
Haiti	45.2	49.8	54.7	85.5	78.7	62.4	178.4	145.4	117.0
Honduras	49.7	56.2	64.0	55.0	43.1	40.5	128.2	101.0	69.0
Mexico	59.6	64.3	68.6	34.5	25.8	9.7	81.8	63.6	47.0
Nicaragua	50.4	55.7	63.3	50.4	42.5	13.0	121.4	95.8	62.0
Panama	63.4	68.1	72.1	23.2	18.7	11.8	56.4	36.4	23.0
Paraguay	64.7	65.8	66.9	25.5	19.9	11.8	72.6	50.6	42.0
Peru	50.6	56.4	61.4	38.9	27.5	13.0	130.0	107.0	88.0
Uruguay	68.1	69.3	71.1	9.5	6.1	4.6	48.0	45.2	27.0
Venezuela	62.6	67.1	70.1	37.3	23.5	13.1	65.2	45.4	36.0

*Most recent estimate—around 1988–89.
Sources: World Bank, Social Indicators of Development, 1989; ECLAC, Statistical Yearbook for Latin America and the Caribbean, 1989.

of that period, growth ceased. Note in the main chart the year-by-year decline in the 1980s for most countries. However, since then, there has been a dramatic recovery: in 1990, 1991, and 1992, almost every country in the region showed significant improvements.

Our final indicator is gross domestic product *per capita* (see Table 7.5). This is a simple calculation: we take the gross domestic product, divide it by the number of persons in the country, and arrive at a figure that enables us to rank the countries on a wealth-per-person basis. The range *globally* is a per capita income between about $18,000 per year in the highly developed countries and less than $300 per year in the true "basket cases." In Latin America, Argentina and Mexico, at over $3000 per year each, are the two wealthiest countries on a per capita basis; but note that the per person income of even these more successful Latin American nations is only about one sixth that of the highly developed countries. Nevertheless, the standard of living in Argentina and Mexico is close to the levels of the poorer European countries, such as Romania or Bulgaria, or of Russia.

Uruguay is almost at the $3000 mark, followed by Venezuela—in the past, the wealthiest country in the area—where the standard of living has been declining and which is now facing severe social and political problems. Brazil and Chile are both at $2300 per person per year, Panama is over $2000, and Costa Rica is at $1900. Most of the other countries are over $1000, which used to be the cutoff point (always an arbitrary number) between genuinely developing nations and underdeveloped ones. The Dominican Republic and Peru are also very close to the magical $1000 figure. That leaves only, in descending order, Bolivia, Haiti, and Nicaragua as the truly impoverished areas in Latin America, comparable to the poorest nations of the world.

It is important to emphasize how many Latin American nations have dramatically improved their per capita income since the 1960s, how many of them are truly "making it" in the modern world. Of the twenty nations listed, fifteen are over the $1000-per-person-per-year level, two others are very close to that threshhold, and only three are still in the "poor" range. The World Bank calls these successful modernizers "Newly Industrialized Countries," or NICs, a designation that is meant to apply chiefly to the larger, more industrialized nations: Argentina, Brazil, Chile, Colombia, Mexico, and Venezuela. Clearly, however, quite a number of other countries, even though not without their economic, social, and political problems, are also doing quite well.

The trouble with these per capita figures, however, is that they tell us little about how income is *distributed* in Latin America. They represent *average* income but they do not indicate who got what share of the pie. The reality is that income and power are more unevenly distributed in Latin American than in just about any area of the globe—a phenomenon we will examine in more detail later in the chapter in the context of the organization and operation of

Table 7 ✦ 4 Gross Domestic Product (in 1988 $ million)

Country	1980	1981	1982	1983	1984	1985
Argentina	102,140	94,124	88,157	90,405	91,710	87,049
Bolivia	5,861	5,908	5,628	5,179	5,188	5,187
Brazil	277,919	269,388	273,015	266,114	280,398	303,627
Chile	24,650	25,976	22,378	22,251	23,664	24,178
Colombia	32,829	33,577	33,958	34,580	35,859	37,144
Costa Rica	4,017	3,925	3,643	3,739	4,032	4,064
Dominican Republic	4,334	4,506	4,574	4,798	4,808	4,681
Ecuador	10,966	11,400	11,550	11,087	11,481	11,950
El Salvador	5,998	5,392	4,990	5,045	5,143	5,228
Guatemala	7,504	7,554	7,286	7,100	7,134	7,092
Haiti	2,334	2,267	2,190	2,206	2,213	2,219
Honduras	3,716	3,767	3,685	3,671	3,769	3,908
Mexico	151,919	165,147	163,385	155,738	161,376	165,920
Nicaragua	3,040	3,216	3,188	3,308	3,211	3,059
Panama	4,473	4,663	4,892	4,879	4,872	5,099
Paraguay	4,710	5,119	5,065	4,912	5,070	5,276
Peru	30,921	32,478	32,471	28,100	29,361	29,909
Uruguay	8,910	9,069	8,254	7,784	7,683	7,710
Venezuela	57,853	57,548	57,931	54,699	53,035	54,125
Total	759,270	760,443	751,837	730,609	754,463	781,424

*Preliminary estimates.
Source: Inter-American Development Bank and Central Intelligence Agency, based on official statistics of member countries.

interest groups in Latin America. Essentially, the gap between the wealthy elites and the rising middle class on the one hand, and the poor on the other, is enormous. Some people are "making it" in Latin America, but many others are clearly being left behind.

We need to be careful about these assessments, however, and draw some sharper distinctions. As shown in Figure 7.1, three groups are doing at least reasonably well in Latin America. The elite classes have seen their incomes rise both steadily and quite dramatically over the last four decades; the rate of increase slowed down in the 1980s but never flattened, and it accelerated again in the 1990s. The middle classes have also generally done well during this period. However, the rate of increase is not as sharp as that of the economic elites; also, income for many members of the middle class came close to leveling off in the 1980s, and they are feeling an economic bite even today. The Latin American working class, for the most part, also improved its lot

				Average Annual Growth Rates (%)		
1986	1987	1988	1989*	1961–70	1971–80	1981–89
92,357	94,555	91,142	85,730	4.4	2.5	−1.9
5,083	5,197	5,321	5,430	5.0	4.8	−0.8
321,791	328,286	326,073	336,072	5.4	8.7	2.1
25,529	26,949	28,925	31,809	4.3	2.6	2.9
39,552	41,645	43,250	44,663	5.2	5.5	3.5
4,284	4,481	4,625	4,873	6.0	5.4	2.2
4,831	5,184	5,244	5,450	5.1	7.0	2.6
12,273	11,789	13,065	13,132	5.2	9.1	2.0
5,264	5,390	5,473	5,517	5.8	2.6	−0.9
7,102	7,353	7,628	7,934	5.5	5.7	0.6
2,231	2,244	2,210	2,177	0.8	4.7	−0.8
4,031	4,245	4,457	4,549	5.3	5.8	2.3
159,080	161,806	164,267	169,472	7.1	6.7	1.2
2,999	2,970	2,659	2,600	6.9	−0.1	−1.7
5,286	5,395	4,518	4,478	8.1	5.1	0.0
5,264	5,496	5,856	6,207	4.6	8.7	3.1
33,492	36,606	33,694	29,257	5.5	3.5	−0.6
8,282	8,779	8,827	8,947	1.6	3.0	0.0
57,436	60,031	63,752	58,415	6.3	4.3	0.1
810,330	832,330	834,841	840,700	5.4	5.9	1.1

for several decades, saw many new workers (including women especially in assembly plants) join its ranks, but then in the 1980s experienced a loss of jobs and a decrease in real wages as austerity measures were imposed in the several countries. Note that while the income of the working class increased for a long time, its increases lagged behind those of both the elite and the middle class, and that the downturn in the 1980s was also harder on these workers than on either of the other two groups.

The one group whose lot has not improved is the unorganized poor, both rural and urban. Except for those lucky enough to emigrate abroad or find work in the cities, the standard of living has been falling. Moreover, they lag behind the other groups not only relatively but absolutely; that is, among these groups poverty has actually been increasing. We hasten to add that in few countries does this un- or underemployed element constitute the majority of the population. Rather, because of Latin America's generally quite dramatic

Table 7 ✦ 5 Gross Domestic Product per Capita (in 1988 $)

Country	1960	1970	1980	1989*	1992	Average Annual Real Growth Rates (%)		
						1961–70	1971–80	1981–89
Argentina	2,491	3,342	3,617	2,685	3,100	3.0	0.8	−3.3
Brazil	981	1,258	2,291	2,280	2,300	2.5	6.2	−0.1
Bolivia	659	849	1,052	763	630	2.6	2.2	−3.5
Chile	1,651	1,988	2,212	2,454	2,300	1.9	1.1	1.2
Colombia	747	922	1,273	1,432	1,300	2.1	3.3	1.3
Costa Rica	1,073	1,368	1,759	1,659	1,900	2.5	2.5	−0.6
Cuba					1,580			
Dominican Republic	413	496	761	777	950	1.9	4.4	0.2
Ecuador	626	758	1,350	1,272	1,070	1.9	5.9	−0.7
El Salvador	1,032	1,296	1,325	1,074	1,010	2.3	0.2	−2.3
Guatemala	639	825	1,085	888	1,260	2.6	2.8	−2.2
Haiti	369	326	431	341	440	−1.2	2.8	−2.6
Honduras	652	808	1,015	913	1,050	2.2	2.3	−1.2
Mexico	1,059	1,509	2,157	1,954	3,200	3.6	3.6	−1.1
Nicaragua	1,063	2,502	2,097	694	426	3.5	−3.1	−5.0
Panama	1,130	1,825	2,287	1,890	2,040	4.9	2.3	−2.1
Paraguay	741	874	1,497	1,493	1,460	1.7	5.5	−0.0
Peru	1,293	1,656	1,788	1,343	960	2.5	0.8	−3.1
Uruguay	2,224	2,357	3,058	2,908	2,936	0.6	2.6	−0.6
Venezuela	2,742	3,569	3,851	3,035	2,590	2.7	0.8	−2.6
Total	1,224	1,578	2,188	1,989	—	2.6	3.3	−1.1

*Preliminary estimates.
Source: Inter-American Development Bank and Central Intelligence Agency, based on official statistics of member countries.

development over the last several decades, we are talking in several countries mainly about *pockets* of poverty rather than a societywide *culture* of poverty. The poor social and economic condition of the lower classes, who may still number 40–60 percent or more of the population, is compounded by the fact that, politically, they are also the weakest group in Latin American society.

The Economic Structure

Latin America's economic structure has long been known as mercantilist. *Mercantilism* is a form of national economic organization that emerged after the decline of feudalism but before the full onset of modern capitalism—pre-

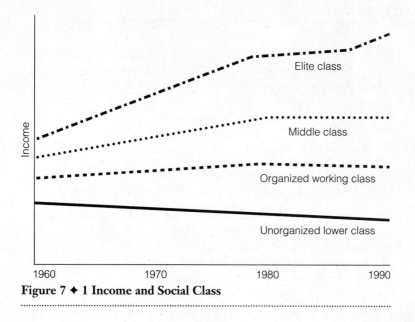

Figure 7 ✦ 1 Income and Social Class

cisely the situation in twentieth-century Latin America. In *mercantilism*, the *state* stimulates, guides, directs, controls, and polices economic growth, not individual entrepreneurs as in laissez-faire capitalism. It is the state that mobilizes capital, sets priorities, invests, and regulates wages, prices, and production rather than the marketplace.

Mercantilism is intermediary both in time and on the political-economic spectrum. Historically, mercantilism came after feudalism but before capitalism, so it is intermediary in that sense. But it is also intermediary in the sense that it falls between the other two better-known models of political economy, communism and capitalism, on a spectrum of systems going from left to right.

Let us explain further. If we set up a spectrum, as in Figure 7.2, ranging from pure communism on one side (complete state control of the economy) to pure capitalism on the other (completely based on free markets), we can then locate various countries at points on that spectrum. For example, the Soviet Union, prior to radical change beginning in 1989, was the most communist country in the world since approximately 96 percent of its gross national product (GNP) was generated through the state sector. In Poland, another formerly communist country, the figure was about 92 percent since Poland allowed somewhat greater private activity in the agricultural realm than did the Soviet Union. In Hungary, a communist country that had permitted a small capitalistic sector, the figure was about 85 percent; and so on down the line of communist countries. On the other end of the spectrum lies the United States, with only about 18 percent of its GNP generated through

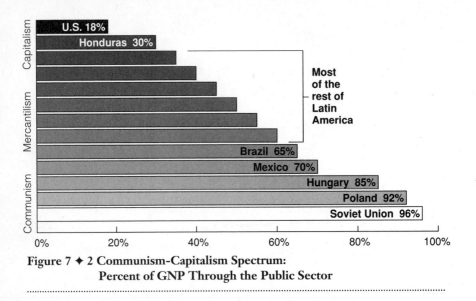

Figure 7 ✦ 2 Communism-Capitalism Spectrum:
Percent of GNP Through the Public Sector

the public sector; the United States is the most capitalistic, or nonstatist, country in the world. So let us say, using these criteria, that a country in which 75 percent or more of the GNP is generated through the public sector is communist or strongly socialist, whereas countries in which 25 percent or less of the GNP is in state hands can be considered capitalistic.

But that leaves a huge gap—fully 50 percent of the spectrum—between capitalism and communism. That is where Latin America with its mercantilist or perhaps state-capitalist economies fits in. The range is from Mexico on the higher end, with about 70–75 percent of its GNP generated through the public sector, to Honduras on the lower end, with only about 25–30 percent of its GNP generated through the public sector. Mexico, in other words, is close to being a socialist economy, while Honduras is far more a capitalist one. The other Latin American countries are strung out at various points along the spectrum between Mexico and Honduras.

If we ask, therefore, who owns Mexico or who owns Brazil, the answer is not General Motors, Ford, United Fruit, or some other big multinational corporation. Rather, the Mexican government owns Mexico and the Brazilian government owns Brazil. In the Brazilian case, the answer is a little more complicated because Brazil has a federal-type system like that of the United States. The Brazilian federal government generates 40 percent of the nation's GNP, individual states generate another 20 percent, and local government adds 5 percent more, for a total of 65 percent—close to the high-statist Mexican level. Keep in mind also that we are only measuring *officially countable* production here. A state like Bolivia has about 90 percent (fully socialist) of its officially countable income in the public sector; but if we add illegal (and officially unaccounted for) drug production into the total—drugs being mainly produced in the private sector—the percentage of total national production of goods and services generated through the public sector would actually be far lower. The "informal economy" (unlicensed, unaccounted for) makes up a significant share of the economy in other countries too, but that is still not enough to nullify the fact that these are basically statist or mercantilist economies.

In addition to the elevated percentage of the economy *owned* by the state, the mercantilist state is also a strict regulator of that part of the economy still in private hands. The Latin American state is a regulatory state, a directing state, a licensing state, far more than is the state in the United States. At one level, therefore, the Latin American state is powerful because it *owns* such a large share of the national economy; at another, it is powerful because it so tightly regulates the share of the economy that is in the private sector. Almost every business transaction in Latin America—even the most minor—requires a license, a permit, or a special dispensation. Almost everything falls under the regulatory umbrella (or maybe *tentacles* is the proper metaphor) of the state. The state often regulates prices, production, and wages, which in a truly capitalistic economy are left to the marketplace; it grants licenses (or monopolies) to start up a business; and it closely regulates all areas of national economic life. In Latin America, one simply can't just go out and open a business on one's own, unlike in the United States; rather, the process is enormously bureaucratic, regulated, burdensome, expensive, and time-consuming. That is a major reason there has been historically so little private business activity throughout Latin America.

Here, then, we have another insight into the nature of politics and the structure of power in Latin America. First, the state, as the largest generator—by far—of production and services in the country, is also the largest employer. If half or two thirds of the production is under state control, then half or two thirds of employment is usually generated by the state as well. *Everyone* works for the state, except for a few private entrepreneurs, some of the middle class, some workers, and the peasants. You do not rebel against a government that is paying your wages, so "everyone"—friends as well as enemies of the regime in power—gets put on the public payroll. The system is also heavily patronage-based: a job in the public sector is given in return for political loyalty and support. The state becomes a vast national patronage agency doling out jobs and favors to the "deserving"—that is, those who support and vote for the government providing the patronage.

Second, since the Latin American state has such vast licensing and regulatory powers, it has the ability to reward or punish whomever it wishes. The state in Latin America is not just a neutral referee; rather, it uses its powers to reward its friends and punish its enemies. Here is another key indicator of how power is organized. Those Latin Americans who have good connections or friends in high places or from whom the state wants something usually get an immediate and positive response to their petitions to the state, their requests for licenses to open a business, or their lobbying to be given a monopoly in certain sectors of the economy. Those people who are not well connected, do not favor the regime in power, or are too poor to pay the fees that unconscionable bureaucrats exact for the processing of what should be a simple paper transaction are likely to be kept waiting for months and even years, or ignored entirely. In sum, the system is responsive to those with money and the right political connections, but it is endlessly frustrating for those lacking funds or friends and relatives in the right place.

Third, the fact that the Latin American systems are so heavily statist explains why the competition for power there is often violent. The fact is, the stakes are far higher in a statist system where 50–70 percent of the GNP is generated by the state. In the United States and other capitalist countries, in which the state's share of the economy is small, the stakes are likewise quite small—only political power and prestige. But in Latin America, he who controls the state and its resources and the patronage flowing from them controls everything—or nearly so. With the stakes so high—livelihoods, jobs, wealth—the competition is intense, often leading to the use of violence, revolutions, or coups d'état. If the stakes were only political power and prestige as in the United States, that would be one thing; but with the economic stakes also so high in Latin America—basic livelihoods, jobs, wealth—it is small wonder that the politics are very intense and prone to conflict. And, of course, once in power, a regime or person tries to hang on to it as long as possible—giving rise in Latin America to what is called *continuismo* (continuism in office).

The statist or mercantilist economies of Latin America grew out of the Iberian colonial and historical past, and by now such systems have been around so long that they have acquired a certain resonance in the political culture of the area, similarly top-down and paternalistic. But statism emerges not just from history and culture in Latin America; it also grows out of real-life, present-day circumstances and pressures. Recession, debt, the desire for economic development, patronage requirements, central planning, and other social and political pressures all tend to increase the powers of the state. These pressures are being felt even as Latin America is under considerable international pressures to privatize and *reduce* the state sector. These contradictory pressures—on the one hand to expand the power of the state and on the other to contract its size—have added another element of tension to the Latin American political arena.

One final thought requires emphasis here: the close connection between statism or mercantilism in the economic sphere and statism or authoritarianism in the political sphere. Although these two may logically be separated—for example, one could have a mercantilist economy and a democratic political system—in Latin America in actual practice, statism economically has also generally meant authoritarianism politically. A top-down economic system implies a top-down political regime, with the two mutually reinforcing each other. The question now is whether the reverse correlation also holds. That is, as Latin America has moved progressively toward political democracy in the last two decades, will it also have to move toward a democratic, free, market-oriented economy? This as-yet unresolved question is so important that we return to it in Chapter 10, because if Latin America cannot sustain an economically open regime, it may not be able to sustain political democracy either.

Interest Groups

The preceding analysis has given us a background and context for understanding the structure of social, economic, and political power in Latin America. In examining the relative influence of different interest groups, we now turn to the power factor more explicitly.

Five general considerations must be borne in mind before beginning the discussion of specific groups and their influence. The first is that Latin America consists, for the most part, of small, intimate societies where everyone who counts knows everyone else who counts, as well as their families, life histories, and business. Even Brazil, with a population of about 150 million in a huge geographic area with diverse regional centers, is organized on this intimate, familial, personalistic basis. Politics and social life in Latin America often resemble that found in a small town: the people all know each other well and are intimately interrelated, and it is hard to keep secrets. Because of such close personal interconnections and the family-based politics, there is often little perceived need in Latin America for large, impersonal, bureaucratic interest groups as in the United States. Organized interest groups are usually seen as unnecessary in a context in which a friend or relative in high places and a quick meeting or telephone call serve the same purpose just as well.

Second, and related, it bears reiterating that the number of interest groups in Latin America is quite small. The United States has a myriad of community, parish, youth, professional, and church-related groups, to say nothing of city, county, state, and national interest groups representing every conceivable interest and point of view. Latin America lacks such diversity in its group or associational life. This is often referred to in Latin America as a lack of infrastructure, and outside of Latin America as a sign of underdevelopment. But in fact, with its close interpersonal connections, Latin America does not always think of itself as needing a U.S.-style interest group structure; it prefers a smaller number of easily defined, readily identifiable groups than what Latin Americans see as the "chaos" of U.S.-style interest group competition.

Third, and again related to the previous point, Latin American interest groups tend to be part of the state or closely connected to it, as compared with the greater independence of U.S. interest groups. That is what corporatism is all about. Corporatism means a *government*-regulated, -sanctioned, and even -licensed system of interest groups, as contrasted with the free associability of U.S. interest organizations. Just as it is hard to start a business in Latin America, one cannot easily organize an interest group and stage a rally as one can in the United States; rather, an elaborate process of state registration with its accompanying regulation is necessary. Of course, the power to recognize an interest group also implies the power *not* to recognize it, a tactic Latin American governments have frequently employed against trade unions and peasant associations—recall the discussion of the Latin American political process in Chapter 5. The overall result is far fewer numbers of and far less independence for Latin American interest groups than in the United States.

Fourth, *formal* Latin American interest groups may not be as influential as informal groups, about which we know little. Much of Latin American political life is organized on the basis of personal friendships, extended family ties, cliques or clan networks, informal groups within the military or extending across the military and civilian spheres, or economic "societies" or *grupos*. In Brazil, such groups are called *panelinhas*; in Hispanic America, a variety of other terms are used. Because these groups are based on informal ties, do not advertise their memberships, and are not formally registered anywhere, their workings and influence remain a source of some mystery. They usually have holdings in several sectors of the economy and have connections with all political parties so as to protect their interests no matter who comes to power. They are especially difficult for foreigners (scholars or embassy personnel) to penetrate and understand precisely because they are so private; one almost needs to have been born into and to have grown up in these groups to appreciate their importance. Behind a formally registered political party or interest group in Latin America, there often lies one of these informal groups.

Fifth, we need to say up front that the interest group structure in Latin America is terribly imbalanced. Some groups—the military, the economic elites—have great power; other groups, such as the peasants, have very little. Those with connections—again, the elites—have enormous power; those without such connections most often cool their heels for days, weeks, or years before their petitions are heard. This imbalance is reinforced by the fact that so much of Latin American politics takes place in informal settings, where the well-connected elements are even more influential. The imbalance among the interest groups is so pronounced that it is difficult to classify some Latin American countries as genuinely pluralistic, and hence democratic.

The Armed Forces

The armed forces are the ultimate arbiters of national politics in Latin America in that they can literally make or break a government.

A powerful role for the military has a long tradition in Latin America, going back not just to the early years of independence but to the colonial armies, and even to the military orders of medieval Spain and Portugal. The relations of the armed forces to the state were spelled out in what is called the *Fuero militar*, a document that enumerated the rights and responsibilities of both the military and the government. Even today in most Latin American countries, the armed forces occupy a special position constitutionally and legally as almost a fourth branch of government, with special powers in times of emergency to restore order, keep out foreign influences, and even stabilize the political system. So, when we read of a Latin American military taking over the reins of government, it is not always that the military is operating illegally or usurping the constitution; rather, the armed forces may be carrying out constitutional obligations. In short, the context of Latin American civil-military relations is quite different than in the United States.

Some militaries in Latin America *do* at times usurp power or intervene in the political process simply to promote their own interests or to protect or enhance their opportunities for graft and corruption. Recall that in Latin America, the government is where the money is—to paraphrase an old American saying about why one robs banks. At this point, however, the issue becomes murkier. Often, the military's constitutional role to preserve internal order and its self-interest roles may overlap. Or, the armed forces *may be* coaxed into playing an overt political role by civilians who want to use them for their own partisan purposes. Or else—even more likely—the armed forces will be split into various factions that *overlap* with various civilian factions, so that the issue is not military versus civilian but one military-civilian faction jockeying for power and influence against other military-civilian factions.

Overall, the armed forces in Latin America are playing a less overt political role and are more inclined to let civilians govern now than previously. The armed forces are better educated, more professionalized, and, like the rest of Latin American society, more exposed to how other, more developed countries do things. Recall also that the Latin American armies are no longer recruited from the elite families and do not see themselves necessarily as defenders of elite interests; rather, the officer corps has middle class roots and generally defends middle class—as well as its own professional—interests. Another factor explaining the declining frequency of coups is the fact that in the last thirty years the countries of the area have become more developed, more institutionalized, and stabler, thus giving the military less reason to intervene. Nevertheless, the armed forces still feel that special obligation—and usually have a constitutional or legal basis for it—to defend national integrity and to preserve domestic peace and order. These obligations may in some countries on some occasions oblige the military to step back into power.

Economic Elites

The economic elites of Latin America no longer comprise a single landowning class but encompass a plurality of bankers, businessmen, industrialists, financiers, importer-exporters, *and* landowners. They are no longer a single, monolithic "oligarchy," but a more diverse group with more varied interests.

The economic elites are powerful far out of proportion to their numbers—in most countries even more powerful than the armed forces. Although the military may be the ultimate arbiters of national politics, the economic elites are indispensable on an everyday basis. No government—leftist or rightist, military or civilian—can get along without them. They have the knowledge, the technical expertise, the connections, and the understanding of the world economy and finances that are absolutely necessary in today's interdependent world. In every government, therefore—even in full-fledged military regimes—civilian economic managers from the elite will be brought in to manage several cabinet ministries as well as the great variety of government institutes, public corporations, and agencies.

These economic elites often benefit themselves and their friends and families while also managing the public accounts—the line between the public interest and the private watering trough is frequently indistinct. The elites profit from their advanced and insider knowledge of pending government programs, from their ability to command vast patronage positions, from outright thievery of public funds, from their ability to buy into favorable investments, and so on. They may also shape public policy to advance their private interests. In sum, the economic elites use their privileged positions to take advantage of government programs, yet they are so indispensable to the administration of government that they cannot be excluded. On a day-to-day basis, the economic elites have enormous economic and political power.

The Church

Back in the nineteenth century, the Roman Catholic church was one of the three main pillars of the Latin American system—the others being the army and the oligarchy. The church was a major landowner and *the* voice of moral authority; its influence socially and politically was also formidable.

Since then, however, the church in most countries has fallen to sixth or seventh place in the ranks of major interest groups. The church has lost most of its property, it is woefully understaffed, its influence has waned, and it must increasingly rely on foreign clergy to carry out its functions. As Latin

America has modernized, it has also become more secular: while 90 percent of Latin Americans still call themselves "Catholic," only about 10–15 percent are active, practicing Catholics. The Catholic church also feels besieged by Protestant Evangelical churches, which are making increasing inroads among its flock.

Few people listen to the church anymore on political matters, and church and state have been formally separated. If the church presumes to tell voters for whom to cast their ballots (which it seldom does anymore), few people are inclined to listen. Even on such touchy moral (to the church) issues as divorce and family planning, the church has usually refrained from making a fuss—fearing that taking a stance or publicizing the issue will only harm the church. The result of this gradual loss of power is that the church rarely makes specific political recommendations anymore.

The church does maintain a pervasive influence on the culture and society, which is still Catholic in many of its precepts and values, and which still observes many Catholic holidays. The church may also sometimes seek to influence specific policies affecting its position in the society, and may have veto power over some issues. And in a crisis situation—such as in Nicaragua with the coming to power of a Marxist regime—the church may serve as a rallying point for those opposed to such a regime. But, in general, the church is a fading political influence in Latin America and is no longer one of the main pillars of the system.

The Middle Class

The middle class has emerged as the dominant element in the military officer corps, the clergy, small businesses, universities, political parties, trade unions, and the bureaucracy. Just listing those institutions indicates how influential the middle class has become. However, the middle class in Latin America doesn't speak as a single class and has no one single policy voice, which makes its day-to-day influence much less than its numbers in various sectors of the society might indicate. Moreover, the fact that many middle class persons ape upper class ways while others have dropped down on the social scale due to declining salaries gives the middle class very little homogeneity or solidarity.

The middle class is often organized through political parties and tends to vote in large numbers when elections are held. The middle class is also organized in various professional associations—engineers, pharmacists, dentists, architects, and the like—which make it *appear* that Latin America has an interest group structure like that of the United States. But the political activities of these groups are limited by law; in addition, since the legislatures in Latin America have generally been so weak, there is very little U.S.-style lobbying activity in the halls of congress. Instead, the interest groups in Latin America tend to focus on the individuals and institutions that do have influence: the executive branch and the bureaucracy. Once again, "pull" and "connections" are valuable assets. In some of the more developed countries of Latin America—Argentina, Brazil, Chile, Colombia, Mexico, Uruguay, Venezuela—interest groups are incorporated directly into the regulatory apparatus of the state, sometimes formally through a fixed number of positions in government agencies but most often informally through personal and family connections. This is another aspect of Latin American corporatism as distinct from U.S.-style liberalism.

A middle class group that commands special attention is the *técnicos*—those persons who work for the state in specialized or technical positions, such as economists, planners, and agronomists. Their skills have become especially valuable as Latin America has industrialized and modernized, and their positions *inside* the state bureaucracy give them special importance. Frequently, various *técnicos* are linked to rival military or civilian political factions that need their talents and connections, and they may—if the political chips fall the right way—rise to cabinet positions. The *técnicos* are thus important both in their own right and as links between the state system and groups outside the state.

The middle class has political influence through the vote, but since it lacks cohesiveness as a class as well as institutionalized channels through which to make its voice heard, its direct influence on everyday policy-making is often not felt. Fear of austerity and of loss of salary and privileges, as well as the desire for stability and now, increasingly, democracy, *do* tend to unify its members, whose ranks are still growing in every Latin American country.

Trade Unions

Latin American trade unions have been more oriented toward a political model of labor-employer bargaining than to the collective bargaining model of the United States. In part, this orientation stems from the radical and highly politicized (anarchist, Marxist, syndicalist) history of Latin American trade unions, but it is also a result of the immense social, economic, and racial gaps between employers and employees that make it virtually impossible for them to sit at a conference table together and bargain as equals.

The political model of labor bargaining means the use by labor of general strikes, marches on the national palace, violence, efforts to unseat an uncooperative minister, and other direct-action methods to try to get what it wants. The target of such political tactics is not employers directly; rather, the aim is to put pressure on the state to pressure employers, who will then grant wage increases, improved benefits, and so on. The main adversarial groups, unions and management, generally do not deal with each other directly but bureaucratically through the state's labor ministry or even the presidency. This aspect of corporatism fits in closely with our earlier discussion of how the Latin American political systems work.

Labor's influence in Latin America is limited by the low level of industrialization in many countries, the small percentage (10–15 percent) of the work force that is organized, and the deep divisions within the labor movement itself. There are, typically, unions sponsored by communists, socialists, social-democrats, Christian-democrats, and the U.S. embassy in each country, and these unions as often fight among themselves as with their "natural" antagonists: employers or management. In addition, employers and the government have numerous levers—police repression, nonrecognition of unions, refusal to bargain seriously, violence directed against the unions, and many others—that can be used to keep organized labor in its place. Recall the discussion of the Latin American political process in Chapter 5: an aspiring new group like organized labor must first demonstrate a power capability and a willingness to play by the rules of the system; those that do not are frequently forced to suffer.

More recently, with the end of the Cold War, the intense ideological battles over trade unionism in Latin America have begun to fade. In addition, collective bargaining is gradually supplanting political unionism as the preferred method of achieving labor's aims. But the traditions of the past die slowly, and all groups, including organized labor, still look to the state for redress of grievances.

University Students

University students have *in the past* in Latin America been an important voice politically—unlike in the United States, where students have little influence. The difference is due to the fact that in Latin America university education is still limited to a small elite (5–10 percent of the population), and that elite has long been presumed to speak for and be the leader of the less fortunate members of society. Workers and peasants, for example, may think of students as their intellectual mentors and as a political vanguard; one cannot imagine working class North Americans viewing college students that way.

The political tactics used by the students are parallel to those used by the trade unions with whom they often work in alliance: strikes, protests, demonstrations, marches on the national palace, some (usually limited) violence designed to establish martyrs and gain publicity for their cause. On some issues the university students are aided by high school students whose numbers help swell their ranks. Some public university campuses in Latin America have become well-armed camps; the police are forbidden to enter the university grounds because, like the church or the army in these corporatively-organized societies, the university enjoys a legal and contractually derived autonomy from the state.

Several factors help explain the declining political influence of the student groups. The spread of many forms of education (including vocational education) means that the university students are no longer such a privileged elite; also, numerous private universities now get the best students and are not so politicized. In addition, the better-organized trade unions are now able to bargain on their own. In broader terms, the general modernization and development of Latin America over the last thirty years has served to depoliticize somewhat not just society, but the universities. Finally, the fading away in the last decade of pro-Castro guerrilla groups, whose ranks were often filled with embittered students, has deradicalized student groups overall.

It used to be that a well-organized student movement, in alliance with unions, some middle class professional groups, and a faction of the army could topple a government, or at least a minister; but it is hard to imagine that happening very often now. Latin American student groups are still more influential than their U.S. counterparts, but, like the church, they have declined in influence as the society has changed.

Government Workers

We saw earlier that the Latin American state generates by far the largest proportion of GNP; a corollary of that is that the state is by far the largest employer, too. Fully 30, 40, 50, even 60 percent of the gainfully employed labor force may work for the state. In some Latin American countries, the state is virtually the *only* employer, particularly of educated persons.

These high numbers alone give state employees enormous influence; also important is the fact that the state bureaucracy is so central to national life. Recall that these are statist systems, so the state is involved in almost all economic, social, and political decisions, which in turn gives the people who work for the state enormous influence.

In some of the more advanced Latin American countries—Argentina, Chile, Costa Rica, Uruguay, Venezuela—state employees are organized into civil service unions and they have tenure, which means they are virtually impossible to remove. In the other countries, civil service laws exist, but the dominant mode of operation is through patronage: a job in return for a favor. And, once in office, these bureaucrats are often insufferable: not always showing up for work, demonstrating little sense of public service, extracting private payments in return for the processing of official papers, and so on. In the highly centralized, legalistic, and bureaucratic systems of Latin America, the bureaucracy can stall or stop virtually anything it wants—except for those fortunate few with the clout and connections to cut through the red tape.

In the 1970s, the Latin American bureaucracies often extracted vast entitlement programs (free health care, elaborate pension programs) from their governments. But they acquired these benefits without any commensurate rise in the quality of public service—indeed, the opposite occurred, and corruption increased as well. Now, even when everyone agrees that these bureaucracies are bloated, corrupt, and inefficient, and in need of reform and downsizing, their political influence and the government's utter dependence on them to get programs through make it almost impossible to streamline and reduce the bureaucracies. In fact, a Latin American president who wants his program to succeed will shower *more* benefits on the public sector, not less. The veto power of the bureaucracy explains why economic and political reform in Latin America is so difficult. The bureaucracy is therefore one of the increasingly powerful influences in Latin America, right up there with the armed forces and the economic elites, and ahead of the church, the trade unions, and university students. Recall also that the bureaucracy is one of the havens of the middle class, helping to explain why that element, with so many public service jobs available, has been growing in size and influence in recent decades.

Peasants

Peasants tend to be the forgotten people of Latin American politics. While numerically still the largest group (although with declining numbers), politically they are the weakest. To the extent that this large number of persons is still outside the political system, Latin America remains an incompletely pluralistic and therefore incompletely democratic society.

Because they are often illiterate, widely dispersed in an inaccessible countryside, and not often employed in large-scale production units (such as farms or factories), peasants are inherently difficult to organize. During the 1960s in a few areas of Latin America, peasant leagues were organized that, like the trade unions, were often affiliated with the main political parties. In addition, Peace Corps volunteers, university students, political parties and guerrilla organizers all sought to enlist the peasants in their causes and movements. This was also a time when agrarian reform was a hot topic in Latin America. The idea was that by dividing up the land and distributing it to peasants, the "oligarchy" would be stripped of the basis of its power and peasants would receive a greater stake in the system.

However, few of these organizational efforts among the peasants worked out very well. The peasant leagues still exist in some places, but they have not come close to organizing most or even very many peasants. The Peace Corps no longer places a high priority on such organizations, and the guerrilla groups in Latin America consisted mainly of disaffected middle class persons, not peasants. Agrarian reform may be socially and politically just, but dividing the land has proved to be economically unwise.

The peasantry, therefore, continued to languish. Meanwhile, more and more peasants began to "think with their feet" by moving out of the poor countryside and migrating to the cities or, ultimately, to greener pastures outside the country, chiefly the United States. In a sense, the "peasant problem" is being taken care of through mass migration; the peasantry as a class is beginning to disappear. The problem with this statement is that while the peasantry *is* declining in numbers, the peasant class—depending on the country—constitutes roughly 30–50 percent of the population and *still* has very little political representation.

Meanwhile, the mass migration of former peasants to the cities has added to the immense social problems there. Marx called this element a *lumpenproletariat*, a term that has stuck: urban dwellers, usually fresh from the countryside, who are largely illiterate and unskilled, often unemployed or underemployed, unorganized in trade unions, and potentially a very disruptive influence. They tend not to be organized politically, but they often do provide the "shock troops" in riots, demonstrations, and looting.

Women

Women are among the most recent groups to be organized in Latin America. As elsewhere, with women's higher life expectancy, women in Latin America constitute more than 50 percent of the population. But as an *organized interest*, women's groups are relatively new. And recall that it is *only* when a group is organized and receives recognition from the state in Latin America that it acquires legitimacy and the capacity to function as an accepted interest.

Latin American society has historically been patriarchal as well as patrimonialist. That means that women have long been in a more subordinate position as compared with their U.S. or Western European counterparts, although their position is far more elevated than that of women in India, China, or the Arab world. At the same time, Latin American women often have strong positions in the home and the family and with family finances. Recently, more and more middle class women have pursued professional careers, while lower class women are finding work in assembly plants and other industries. These employment and career changes are also changing the nature of home life.

Women's groups in Latin America are small and factionalized and have little real power as yet. Often, however, they have access to the power structure because the head of the women's group, like everyone else who counts in Latin America, is well connected in the elite power groups in the country. Nor is their agenda of issues fully developed as yet—for example, among professional women day care is not a major issue because most of them have maids. For politicians, therefore, the women's groups are something to consider in certain matters (property rights, justice in the court system), but they have little influence on most other issues.

Indigenous Groups

Other new sources of influence in Latin America are the indigenous Indianist and the Black power movements.

Historically, neither Black power nor Indianism have fared very well in Latin America. Racial and social prejudice was, and remains, strong: recall the early debates as to whether Indians or Africans had souls or not. But in Latin America the dominant orientation of Blacks and Indians has been assimilation rather than separation. That is, as a Black or Indian, one learns the national language, becomes Catholic, joins the money market economy, marries "up," seeks a place in Hispanic society, and gives up—as much as possible—one's older cultural habits, or at least learns to subordinate them. Thus, Black or Indian power movements, although not entirely absent in Latin American history, have seldom achieved much success.

Bolivia, Ecuador, Guatemala, Paraguay, Peru, and even Mexico (but to a declining extent) are known as the "Indian countries" of Latin America. Here, Indians may comprise anywhere from 40 to 70 percent of the population. This means that the percentage of people to be integrated into the national life may be *three times* as high as the unintegrated minorities in the United States. It is a daunting task. Neither military governments nor civilian ones, neither left-wing regimes nor rightist ones, have ever been able to solve this immense problem of integration of native peoples into Latin American society. Mexico had a revolution in 1910 that brought Indians into the political process for the first time, but eighty years later the percentage of unintegrated Indians had only been reduced from 70 to 40 percent. This is a long-term process as the Mexican case makes clear; there are no quick or easy solutions. Class prejudice, when combined with racial prejudice, is hard to overcome; and when it is not a small minority but a *majority of the population* that needs to be integrated (as in a few of the Latin American countries), the task is still more complex.

Black power movements in Latin America are largely confined to Brazil and the Caribbean countries. Elsewhere, the percentage of Blacks is too small for them to count for very much politically. Indianist movements have arisen in Bolivia, Ecuador, Guatemala, Mexico, and Peru aimed at empowering the Indian elements and instilling pride in Indian ways and culture, and perhaps reflecting a rising global emphasis on ethnicity. In fact, in 1992, an Indian leader, Rigoberta Menchu of Guatemala, won a Nobel Prize for her personal story, writing in support of such Indianist movements. But the dominant aspiration among most Latin American Blacks and Indians remains assimilation. Indigenous movements will probably continue to grow and to be heralded in the international media; but these groups are so diffuse, illiterate, unrecognized, divided, and poor that they are unlikely to become major political forces anytime soon. On some issues, in some countries, politicians need to pay attention to such groups; but for the most part indigenous elements are still unorganized, unrecognized, and therefore without influence in Latin America.

Social Movements and Community-Based Groups

During the 1970s, when Latin America was largely governed by military-authoritarian regimes, a variety of new community-based groups, usually composed of lower class persons, came into existence, some of which grew into full-fledged social movements. Many of these groups were initially organized, in both urban and rural areas, by the liberation theology wing of the Catholic church or by left-wing organizations that had been declared illegal, persecuted, and forced to operate underground by the authoritarians then in power. In the absence of a range of legal political parties and interest groups, also outlawed by these regimes, the community-based groups were often the only level at which people could organize.

With the restoration of democracy in many of these countries during the 1980s, the regular political parties and interest groups have reorganized and reemerged. In the renewed climate of freedom, there is no need for clandestine or semiclandestine organizations. The larger political parties and interest groups have often taken over the issues and agendas of the community-based groups. The result is that many of these community-based organizations and social movements have shrunk or disappeared—in much the same way that third-party movements in the United States are absorbed by the main parties and then disappear.

But many other grass-roots groups have continued on, and that is really the surprising story. Indeed, Latin America is presently dotted with more grass-roots community, neighborhood, and parish organizations than ever before. Its "organizational space" is beginning to be filled. The associational infrastructure that nineteenth-century political philosopher Alexis de Tocqueville recognized as necessary for democracy is being put in place. Latin Americans at the local level, as distinct from the "high politics" at the national level that has been our main focus here, are learning the lessons of organized, pressure-group politics. Often, these efforts are inchoate, limited, and not very well organized; and few of these groups have been legally recognized, with the result that their activities are still marginal. Nevertheless, grass-roots organizations represent a growing movement that promises to increase in influence and to change over time some of the main features, such as the lack of much interest group bargaining, of Latin American politics.

International Groups

As Latin America's historical isolation has broken down and as the region has become more closely interdependent with other nations, it has also been subjected to pressures emanating from outside its borders. In Chapter 11, we will be discussing Latin America's international relations; here, our focus is on those international groups that exercise influence *inside* Latin America.

The first of these is the U.S. embassy. The United States is not only the most important country in Latin America's international affairs; it is also one of the most important *domestic* actors—in some countries as important as the military or the economic elites. When a Latin American president makes a decision, the groups he checks with first are often the armed forces, the economic elites, and the U.S. embassy—and not necessarily in that order!

The embassy's influence is cultural, political, economic, social, and military; it covers labor affairs, peasant movements, political parties, leadership, economic development, agrarian reform—virtually all issues. During the long Cold War, the primary purpose of all these activities was to prevent any Latin American country from "going communist." To that overriding end the United States poured in vast amounts of dollars, aid, technical help, and political influence. In Brazil in the late 1960s, for example, the size of the U.S. mission reached over *two thousand* people—an immense and unprecedented number. All of these persons probably contributed, on balance, to Brazil's development, but the sheer weight of the U.S. presence was overwhelming.

In many countries (the Dominican Republic, El Salvador, Guatemala, Honduras, Panama, Brazil for a time) the U.S. ambassador functioned more as a proconsul, to help *run* these countries, and not just as the highest-ranking U.S. representative. His "country team" (for cultural, economic, political, labor, military, security, and other affairs) functioned almost as a "cabinet" for the host country. These officials wrote speeches for the president, told him whom to promote and remove, drafted legislation, formulated plans, and carried out programs. They often behaved as though they, and not the local government, were running the country.

The Vietnam War in the late 1960s and the growing U.S. budget crisis began to cut into this myriad of U.S. programs and the oversize of the U.S. missions. The end of the Cold War may accelerate this process. With the former Soviet Union no longer sponsoring guerrilla movements and fomenting revolution in Latin America, there is no need for such a large U.S. representation. In some countries where we are dealing with the legacies of crises of the recent past (El Salvador, Nicaragua, Panama; Peru because of the drug issue; Cuba in the future), the United States will continue to be a major presence. The newer issues of drugs, human rights, democracy, immigration, and the environment will also continue to command U.S. diplomatic attention. But overall, it seems likely that in this post–Cold War era the size of the U.S. mission, as well as its programs because of declining aid, will continue to shrink. In addition, the U.S. focus will shift away from Cold War/strategic issues and increasingly toward economic or political-economic ones.

A second major outside influence is multinational corporations, chiefly U.S.-based ones. Several decades ago, a number of these big companies

(United Fruit, Standard Oil, ITT, International Petroleum, Kennicott Copper) were so powerful, and the Latin American countries so weak, that the former could unseat governments almost at will. The bribing of local legislators, payoffs to the police, the paying of protection money, union busting, tax cheating—all were common practices (as well as the "stuff" of scandal-mongering news columns, television specials, books, and university lectures).

The current situation is more prosaic. Many of these and other big companies remain influential. But the main orientation now is lobbying, not trying to overthrow governments. The big companies work *with* the local governments for the most part, not against them. The nefarious activities of the past are not entirely absent, but the focus is on bargaining, not confrontation. The companies try to operate abroad much as they do in the United States, as interest groups trying to get fair or, if possible, advantageous treatment for themselves. They usually try to be good citizens, although there are instances in which the companies "dump" bad products in Latin America where the regulatory standards are not so strict. To accomplish their goals, the companies often join forces with local Latin American groups or companies. While these activities are generally strictly legal, the question remains whether a small, weak Latin American country—often desperate for investment—can keep these multinational giants under control or at arms length the way a better-institutionalized country like the United States can.

A third group of outside influences is made up of multinational lending agencies: the World Bank, the International Monetary Fund, and the Inter-American Development Bank. Latin America depends on these banks for loans; the banks in turn put conditions on these loans (austerity, belt-tightening, cutbacks) that became particularly onerous during the debt crisis of the 1980s. At times, the visiting missions of the lending agencies had more influence over Latin American economic and social policy than did Latin America's own governments. These banks still place conditions on their loans, but over the years they have learned how and when to cut back on the pressures. The international banks are a force to be reckoned with in Latin America, but they are not a vigorous everyday presence like the economic elites.

A fourth group of new international influences in Latin America comprises the various human rights, population control, ecological, religious, and prodemocracy forces that have sprung up there—often referred to as Non-Governmental Organizations, or NGOs. Many of these groups have local representatives, but they are also parts of larger international movements. These groups focus on the so-called new-agenda issues as distinct from the old-agenda, Cold War issues. By themselves, these groups have little influence in Latin America, but backed by an international organization—usually located in the United States or Europe—they can have a considerable impact. In the post–Cold War, more interdependent era in which we now find ourselves, many observers expect these groups to become more influential.

A fifth external force is the foreign embassies—German, Spanish, French, Japanese, Chinese, Israeli, and others—now active in Latin America. As was the case with the United States, these are *not just* diplomatic missions but often are active in internal affairs. These countries, like the United States, try to influence young Latin American trade union leaders, journalists, congressmen, mayors, and other future leaders through the granting of fellowships, travel grants, and other favors. One of the most interesting aspects of Latin America since the 1960s is that the United States, which largely had this entire area to itself, now must compete for influence with a variety of other countries. We return to this theme in Chapter 11.

Corporatism Versus Pluralism

Based on this survey of the Latin American power structure and interest group situation, it should be obvious that the Latin American interest group system is very different from that of the United States. There are fewer interest groups, they are licensed by the state, and they are often integrated into the state. The Latin American interest group structure is based more on a corporatist than a liberal tradition, or, at best, it represents a mixture of liberalism and corporatism. Moreover, much of Latin American political life is still based on informal contacts, through families, clan groups, networks, and personal connections, as distinct from the far more organized U.S. interest group system.

Nevertheless, in the last thirty to fifty years, there has been an *explosion* in the numbers and organizational base of the interest groups. It is not just the army, the church, and the oligarchy who are organized anymore, but also the middle class, workers, peasants, women, indigenous groups, university students, government workers, and internationally based groups. However, while there is thus a greater and newfound pluralism in Latin American society and politics, it is still a limited pluralism. The armed forces, the economic elites, the bureaucracy, and the foreign interests are well organized and strong; but the rest of the society is less well organized and often inarticulate. Argentina, Chile, Costa Rica, and Uruguay probably have a level and degree of pluralism that matches the United States; in other countries, there is less pluralism and hence greater political bias toward the privileged few rather than the many.

That raises the final question, therefore, of just how democratic Latin America really is. The four countries just mentioned are certainly democratic; Brazil, Colombia, the Dominican Republic, Panama, and Venezuela are approaching pluralist democracy; and other countries have *some institutions* of democracy but not the full social and political pluralism that democracy requires. This is an unfinished theme to which our discussion will return.

$$\frac{8}{\blacklozenge}$$

Political Parties and Elections

Political parties are usually thought of as indispensable agencies of competitive electoral politics and of democracy. Political parties help recruit people into politics, articulate and aggregate the views of diverse interests, devise programs and platforms, and select candidates to run in elections. Political parties are associated with being an advanced, developed country. Those, at least, are the views of political parties as derived from the Western European and United States' experiences. The question is whether parties perform the same functions and are viewed in the same way in Latin America.

The answer is, it depends. Actually, there are a great variety of political parties and party systems in Latin America, making it hard to generalize about the region as a whole. The significance of the parties also varies widely. Moreover, their functions are diverse, and not all of these conform to the U.S. or European patterns. In only five of the twenty Latin American countries can parties be seen as dominant actors on the political stage in the context of a democratic political system: Chile, Colombia, Costa Rica, Uruguay, and Venezuela. In several other countries, the parties are of growing importance but are probably not yet dominant: Argentina, Brazil, the Dominican Republic. A third category is countries where the parties are still secondary actors: Bolivia, Ecuador, El Salvador, Guatemala, Honduras, and Nicaragua. In Haiti, Panama, and Paraguay, the parties are still marginal actors, or all but nonexistent. In Cuba and Mexico, there are one-party systems, but the regimes are either monopolistic (Mexico) or communist (Cuba) in their control of public office. That means that only one fourth of the Latin American countries have functioning party systems in which the parties play a major role comparable to other Western democracies. What, then, is going on in the other countries in the region?[1]

Clearly, the European or U.S. model and system of political parties is faulty if it fails to explain 75 percent of the cases. Why is that? For one thing, the history of on-again, off-again authoritarianism in Latin America has not been propitious for the growth of political parties. Often, the army and not the parties has been the key actor in politics. For another, these are often small, close-knit, personalistic societies in which large, impersonal political parties are viewed as unnecessary. Third, and related, influential people in Latin America can easily bypass the political parties simply by contacting personally the appropriate government officials when they need to exert influence. Fourth, these are often patronage-dominated systems in which the parties, instead of writing platforms, presenting candidates, or running elections, serve as vast national patronage agencies. And fifth, there is a cultural factor: Latin Americans, like George Washington, have long viewed political parties as divisive, fractionalizing institutions that detract from national unity and integrity. All these factors help explain why political parties have not generally enjoyed the importance or gained the legitimacy in Latin America that they have in other countries.

But the situation is now changing. Latin America is far more developed than in the past, and an effective party system is related to increased levels of development. In addition, as Latin America has democratized, the parties have become more important as agencies of democratization. Oddly, Latin America may now be moving *toward* stronger party systems even as the United States and other advanced nations are moving *away* from them. We will have more to say on this intriguing paradox as the discussion proceeds. Furthermore, as Latin America has changed and democratized, so have the parties undergone change—toward better organization, larger memberships, and real ideologies and programs.

Features of Traditional Political Parties

We shall be dealing with these changes and the many varieties of parties later in the chapter, but for now let us look at some of the common features of traditional Latin American party politics.[2]

1. **Elitism**. Most political parties in Latin America are still elite or "cadre" parties rather than mass parties. They are run by—and often for—a small coterie of leaders. They serve as instruments to get these elites into power and not necessarily as agents of democratic participation.

2. **Patronage**. The parties in Latin America are often agents of patronage rather than agencies for enacting and carrying out public policy. They dole out funds, favors, inside information, and jobs to loyal supporters. At the same time, that is often why one joins a political party in Latin America: to get these same things for oneself.

3. **Absence of programs or ideology**. As patronage agencies, most parties in Latin America are not very ideological, nor do they have clear programs. Rather, their functions, to put it crassly, are jobs and money, not programs. Some of the newer Latin American parties are more ideological and program-oriented.

4. **Weak organization**. Few political parties in Latin America are well organized, in keeping with their character as elitist and patronage-dominated agencies. They often lack a popular base, they have weak national organizations, and their sectoral organizations (for women, students, peasants, and the like) are thin or nonexistent.

5. **Personalism**. Parties in Latin America are often one-man operations, based on the charisma and leadership of a single individual. As long as that individual does well, his followers and his party also do well. But when he disappears from the scene, his party, lacking an organizational and programmatic base, is likely also to disappear.

6. **Factionalism**. Because the parties in Latin America are so personalistic, they also tend to be torn by factionalism. The parties seem constantly to be splitting, dividing, and fragmenting—over personal issues as well as program goals. It is said in Latin America that when two people meet, you have a political party; when they part, you have two more. Such endemic splits explain why in some election campaigns, thirty or more "parties" may be competing.

7. **Relations to the state**. Parties in Latin America are often created by the government or person in power to serve as a political machine. They can act as official agencies of the state, dispensing patronage or mobilizing voters in support of the regime already in power. In this sense, Latin American parties are often closer to being official parties or even integrated into the state than is the case in the United States.

8. **Bad reputation**. For all the reasons listed previously, political parties are not held in high repute in Latin America. Many Latin Americans regard political parties as narrowly based factions that detract from

the grandeur of nationalism and the state. This is, again, a Rousseauian organic view. Hence, many political parties in Latin America are not called "political parties" at all, but "movements," "associations," or "rallies."

9. **Existence on the periphery**. Except in a few countries, parties are not the main actors in Latin America. Such interests as the military, the economic elites, or others often interject themselves *directly* into the political process, bypassing the parties. The informal networks, the family-based politics, and the interpersonal communication grids also enable well-connected groups and individuals to avoid political party ties or obligations. These alternative routes to power, of course, help further weaken the already weak parties.

Not all Latin American political parties conform to these characteristics. And many parties in the area are being strengthened, both because of Latin America's overall development and because of the recent wave of democratization that has thrust Latin America's political parties to the fore. But enough countries and parties (probably still the majority) *do* conform to most of these traits that the phenomenon of political parties is still not well institutionalized in Latin America.

History of Political Parties

Quite a number of Latin American political parties have been in existence for a long time, tracing their origins back to the nineteenth century. Initially, these political parties were largely concessions to a foreign fad: since the United States and Great Britain, the world's two leading democracies, had political parties, Latin America had to have parties, too.

These early "parties" were often a front for other interests. They were meant to be admired abroad—*para Ingles ver* ("for the English to see" and admire)—and they were taken to be symbols of modernity domestically; but they actually did little. Often, one group of elites would rally together to form a "Conservative Party," while another group would rally to form a "Liberal Party." But they were both elite parties, and there were often few programmatic differences between them. The situation was much like the old-fashioned fights for control of the country courthouse in the United States where one faction called itself "Democrats," and the other faction "Republicans," but there were few real ideological differences between them.

This situation, in both Latin America and the United States, changed over time as some real, but still limited, differences developed between the parties. The Conservative party in many Latin American countries usually represented the old landed elite, while the Liberal party often represented the business-commercial elite. Around the middle of the nineteenth century, the Conservatives also took on a more ideological orientation in favor of Catholicism and an established church, against the French Revolution of 1789 and its excesses, in favor of discipline and order, and against the mass revolutions in Europe in 1848. The Liberals, by contrast, often opposed an established church and favored the classic nineteenth-century freedoms of press, speech, and assembly, as well as free trade, which of course served their import-export interests. But both of these parties were still elite parties, and in some countries they alternated more or less peacefully in power for many years. In Colombia, Honduras, and Paraguay, these traditional Liberal and Conservative parties continued to exist into modern times.

At the end of the nineteenth century and the beginning of the twentieth, a number of new parties came into existence in several Latin American countries. The Radical Party of Argentina, patterned after the Radicals in France, was also liberal in the classic nineteenth-century sense (freedom of press, speech, assembly) but with one added ingredient: it was anticlerical, which was a quite radical position in traditionally Catholic Latin America. This party and a like-minded movement in Chile were instrumental in expanding the franchise and bringing the middle class into politics for the first time. In these and other of the more advanced nations (Argentina, Brazil, Chile, Uruguay), the first socialist or Marxist parties also date from the early twentieth century.

But it was not until the 1930s (again that defining period when many things changed in Latin America) that a variety of newer, more modern parties was formed. This was the time when the modern Latin American party systems as we know them today began to be organized for the first time. This period and the one just after World War II, reflecting the vast social and political changes taking place in Latin America and the world, gave rise to a number of new parties that were more oriented toward bringing about change and reform and providing a larger base for democratic participation and policy-making. Our discussion begins with the leftist parties and then moves toward the right of the political spectrum.

In most of the countries, Socialist and Communist parties were organized in the 1930s. Often, these parties had a mass base in the trade unions and agri-industry—reflecting the large-scale industrialization that occurred during this period. The leadership of these parties was not workers, however, but usually left-wing intellectuals, students, and even an occasional military officer. In Catholic and generally conservative Latin America, these parties seldom achieved much popular support; only in rare instances did they gain more than 5–10 percent of the vote.

Far more important were the parties of the democratic left whose orientation was, in European terms, social-democratic. These parties believed in progressive social reform, such as land redistribution, social justice, and greater mass participation in politics; but they believed in achieving those reforms through electoral, democratic means—that is, in evolution rather than revolution. Reflecting the vast social changes that had recently occurred in Latin America, these parties had strong support among the peasants, labor unions, and the reformist middle class. The "granddaddy" of the democratic-left parties was the Peruvian *Alianza Popular Revolucionaria Americana* (American Revolutionary Popular Alliance—APRA); other parties formed in this mold were the *Accíon Democrática* (Democratic Action—AD) party of Venezuela, *Liberación Nacional* (National Liberation—LN) party of Costa Rica, the *Partido Revolucionario Dominicano* (Dominican Revolutionary Party—PRD) of the Dominican Republic, and the *Partido Democrático Popular* (Popular Democratic Party—PPD) of Puerto Rico. In Honduras, the traditional Liberal Party also reformed itself in a democratic-left direction but retained its old name. Frequently, these democratic-left parties had to struggle against military dictatorships and repression, as well as against the power of entrenched conservative interests.

The leadership of this democratic-left movement reads like a roster of some of Latin America's greatest leaders of the last four decades: Victor Raúl Haya de la Torre of Peru, Rómulo Betancourt of Venezuela, José Figueres of Costa Rica, Luís Muñoz Marin of Puerto Rico, and Juan Bosch of the Dominican Republic. These parties and their leaders maintained close ties to the presidency of John F. Kennedy, and were chiefly responsible for trying to achieve the goals of Kennedy's Alliance for Progress. For a time, these parties were united in a "League of Popular Parties" through which they tried to present a common strategy and set of policies; many of them also joined the European-based Socialist International, an association of democratic-socialist parties. For a long time, and in some countries even today, these democratic-left parties were the largest, best-organized, and most popular parties in Latin America; but now and over time conditions have changed, several of them have split, and they no longer have the same degree of popularity or cohesion they enjoyed before.

Moving toward the center of the political spectrum, we find a number of Christian-democratic parties. The most prominent of these were organized in Chile, Venezuela, El Salvador, and Nicaragua. The Christian-democrats represented neither the most conservative Catholics in the traditional church nor the more recent leftist liberation theology types, but the centrist, middle class, moderately reformist elements. These parties also had strong support from the working class and the peasantry. Taking their inspiration from several reformist papal encyclicals of the twentieth century, the Christian-democrats stood for democratic reformism within a Christian/Catholic framework of brotherly love and mutual obligation. In this, they stood in marked contrast to the class-conflict model of Marxism, but not very far from the evolutionary reformism of the democratic-left.

The Christian-democrats enjoyed considerable success in the countries in which they were organized because, after all, they were both a reformist party in a hemisphere where reform was widely sought *and* a Catholic party in a region that was still overwhelmingly Roman Catholic. Their candidates were elected to office in several countries, including the presidencies in Chile, Venezuela, El Salvador, and the Dominican Republic. Gradually, however, these parties tended to gravitate toward a more center-right position as several countries evolved away from the extremes and toward a two-party system, with one party somewhat left of center and the other (often the Christian-democrats) somewhat right of center.

Moving farther to the right on the political spectrum, we find numerous anomalous situations. First, the political right in Latin America, including now both landed and business elites, has—until recently—seldom seen the need to organize in either large-scale interest groups or political parties. The right is usually so well connected that it does not need a political party to get what it wants; instead, personal or family connections serve just as well. And when these techniques failed, the right could usually call on the armed forces to nullify an electoral outcome not in the business elite's interests. Only recently, as Latin America has modernized and democratized, has the right seen the necessity of organizing into interest groups and a political party, such as the *Partido de Acción Nacional* (National Action Party—PAN) of Mexico, the *Unidad Nacional* (National Unity—UN) of Costa Rica, or the (since disbanded) *Partido Nacional* (National Party—PN) of Chile.

Fascism in Latin America has seldom enjoyed great support, although there was a time in the 1930s and during the early phase of World War II, when the Axis powers seemed to be winning, that fascism enjoyed some degree of popularity. But most governments in Latin America either snuffed out the fascists or co-opted those parts of their program (order, discipline, national development) that they found attractive.

Far more important than fascism was corporatism, on the center-right side of the political spectrum. Corporatism never had much popularity in the United States, but in Latin America in the 1930s and 1940s it was very popular. Corporatism was partially a product of the social teachings of the Roman Catholic church, but it also had secular origins. It favored a system of partnership among labor, capital, and the state based on class harmony, as contrasted with the class-conflict model of Marxism. It sought to give both labor and management, as well as other socioeconomic and functional groups, direct representation in the state—in either the legislature, a functionally representative council of state, or state regulatory and planning agencies—so as to guarantee that all voices would be heard. In this way, corporatism sought to respond to new groups and the pressures for modernization but without resorting to Marxism-Leninism or U.S.-style interest group pluralism. Corporatism presented itself as an alternative "third way," neither communist nor liberal-capitalist.

Corporatism was not a political party per se but an ideology and a way of organizing the relations between the state and its various societal groups.

However, it was incorporated into various political movements of the 1930s and later, ranging from Lázaro Cárdenas in Mexico on the left to Juan Perón of Argentina and Getulia Vargas of Brazil on the populist right. Eventually, it was absorbed in various forms into the Christian-democratic parties of the area and into other political movements of the left, right, and center. Corporatism as an ideology has by now been supplanted by the desire for democracy, but its ideals of stability, order, organic unity, class harmony, and functional representation are still very much alive in various political movements throughout the hemisphere.

During the 1960s, some new party developments occurred in Latin America. A number of these owed their origins to Fidel Castro and the Cuban revolution. For one thing, Castro's revolution helped give rise to a number of like-minded guerrilla movements and left-wing political parties throughout Latin America. For another, the Cuban revolution helped provoke a split in Latin America's communist movements between those who favored armed struggle and those who preferred peaceful coexistence. A third effect of the Cuban revolution was the split within democratic-left parties between those who admired Castro's nationalism and social programs and those who were critical of his totalitarian methods and alliance with the Soviet Union. A fourth result of the Cuban revolution was that it inspired rightist forces, heretofore largely lacking in political organization, to organize political parties in order to contest the *Fidelistas* and others in the political arena.

The Castroite challenge provoked in many countries later in the 1960s a counterrevolution of military and right-wing elements. However, the new military regimes in power in twelve of the twenty countries by the early 1970s proceeded not only to snuff out the pro-Castro movements but often to eliminate *all* political parties—again, evidence of the antiparty attitude that has long been powerful in Latin America. In some countries, most notably Brazil, the military then created its own political parties: usually a progovernment party to support the regime's own initiatives and a "loyal opposition" so that the regime could appear to be at least partly democratic. These creations of the military governments seldom lasted beyond the tenure of the military governments themselves, however; when the regimes disappeared, the "parties" they had created usually vanished as well.

As Latin America redemocratized during the 1980s, the parties that had been outlawed or forced underground during the preceding decade or more of military rule reemerged. So far as the party system is concerned, military authoritarianism did have one salutary effect in that it eliminated a host of small, personalistic parties that had previously served mainly to cause problems for the major parties. During this same period, other, newer parties or blocs were organized. Hence, during the 1980s, there began to emerge real, modernized parties and democratic systems in Latin America for the first time.

Types of Political Parties

Even with the reorganizations of recent years, there remains a considerable variation in the *types* of political parties in Latin America. Not all countries have all of the parties discussed here. Nevertheless, we should keep in mind the distinct kinds of organizations that call themselves "political parties."

Traditional Political Parties

The traditional Liberal and Conservative parties are still alive in several Latin American countries, most notably Paraguay, Honduras, and Colombia. Historically, these were elite-dominated parties, largely devoid of program, ideology, or organization. However, in several countries—especially Colombia but in others as well—the traditional parties are in the process of becoming modern ones—drawing supporters from across class lines, devising programs and platforms, and developing national organizations.

Personalistic Parties

By "personalistic" parties we mean organizations centered on the *person* of a single individual. These are often very small or "pocket" parties that, like the traditional parties, lack a programmatic, ideological, or national organizational base. These parties often consist of a single individual, his family members, and a few friends and hangers-on. These are seldom permanent parties, but in the months prior to an election, thirty to forty such parties may be organized in a single country.

These "mini" parties usually have little influence and no chance of winning an election. So why organize one? First, they often serve the egos of the persons heading them, who may think they are more important politically than they really are. Second, they often win these "leaders" invitations to government meetings or embassy cocktail parties that they would probably not receive otherwise. Third, and probably most important, these small parties are often political bargaining chips with which, in a close election, the leader of the party may be able to exchange his (however small) bloc of votes for a cabinet or other position. Such small, personalistic parties in Latin America thus serve much like third parties in the United States.

Patronage Parties

Some parties in Latin America have little intention of running candidates, devising party platforms, or contesting elections—the functions one might normally associate with political parties. Rather, they serve as gigantic patronage mechanisms. Their main purpose is not electioneering but distributing favors in return for loyalty, support, or votes. They may give toys to children at Christmastime, sewing machines to widows, wheelchairs to crippled soldiers, or food, clothing, and prescription drugs to the needy. They may help someone get a job in the government or bail someone out of trouble. On a larger scale, such patronage parties may also dole out government contracts, land, business opportunities, advance knowledge of pending government initiatives, monopolies, and so on to important groups or individuals whose loyalty the government wishes to keep. Or the regime in power may, in effect, turn over whole agencies of government to a group or faction (the agrarian reform institute to the army or the education ministry to the teachers' union) to "purchase" that group's continued support.

All political parties have such patronage functions, but in some Latin American cases patronage is virtually the only function. The best example is the Mexican *Partido Revolucionario Institucional* (Revolutionary Institutional Party—PRI), which has had a virtual monopoly on Mexican politics since the 1930s. In the absence until recently of serious competition, it serves as a huge patronage operation, doling out all kinds of favors in return for political support. If one doesn't support the machine, one's chances of getting a job or any other benefit or favor from the government are virtually nil. The party can create—and also break—vast fortunes, but it spends little time (until recently) on programs or elections. Such patronage-infused parties can be found throughout Latin America, but again, they are the reflections of tradition and are now also being called on to compete in the electoral arena.

Modern, Mass-Based Parties

More and more Latin American political parties are becoming modern, mass-based political entities—better-organized, more programmatic, and with a catchall, multiclass appeal. In short, political parties in Latin America are becoming more like their European or U.S. counterparts. Clearly, the social-democratic or democratic-left parties, the Christian-democratic parties, and now increasingly the right-of-center parties as well are all going in this direction. As modernization and democracy have spread, and as the electoral arena has been increasingly accepted as *the* only legitimate route to power, we are now seeing real, competitive party politics throughout the region for the first time.

Revolutionary and Fringe Parties

Many of the fringe parties, both leftist and rightist, that once played a more prominent role in Latin America are today in decline. Right-wing fascism and left-wing communism both had considerable followings in several countries in decades past, but during the 1980s and early 1990s both were in retreat and centrist democracy seemed to be triumphant. In country after country, democracy enjoyed the support of 85–90 percent or *higher* of the population, while the fringe parties were consigned to the margins, with seldom more than 5 percent support. These figures, and the overall trend toward democracy, tell us a great deal about what has been happening in Latin America in the last thirty years.

The revolutionary and fringe parties are hampered by the fact that their commitment to democratic politics is often suspect or, at best, partial. Nowadays, other than a few monarchists and a handful of fascists, there are few far-right parties in Latin America; the right-wing parties, such as ARENA in El Salvador, have now become center-right parties and opted for the electoral arena instead of an alliance with the military. The left-wing parties are also sometimes suspect in that they are often thought to favor guerrilla war over electoral politics and to use their "parties" as a political wing and cover for revolutionary action. With the end of the Cold War, however, the radical-left parties are moving away from guerrilla tactics and toward the electoral process. And in Brazil, Mexico, Venezuela, and Chile, we are beginning to see new-left coalitions that bring together the remnants of Marxists, socialists, and progressive social reformers. The Brazilian Labor Party, the Mexican Democratic Revolutionary Party, and *Causa R* in Venezuela are examples of the new-left parties opposed to centrist and center-right coalitions. We will have to wait and see how much electoral support they are able to garner.

Party Systems

"Party systems" refers to the type of system that the parties as a group form in an individual country. There can be one-party systems, two-party systems, multiparty systems, or even no-party systems, as well as hybrids of these several types.

One-Party Systems

One-party systems are usually associated with dictatorships or authoritarian regimes. Paraguay under General Alfredo Stroessner was for a long time a one-party dictatorship in which the Colorado Party monopolized political life. But now Stroessner is gone, Paraguay has embarked on a democratic opening, and other parties have begun to contest in elections. Many of the other old one-party dictatorships in Latin America—Somoza in Nicaragua, Trujillo in the Dominican Republic—have also been ousted from power.

In Mexico, the Revolutionary Institutional Party (PRI) dominated political power for over fifty years. But during the 1980s, faced with both domestic and international criticism, Mexico allowed the opposition to run largely unhampered and even permitted some oppositionist victories at the local and state level. At the national level, however, the PRI maintained its monopoly—except for those seats in Congress that it allowed the opposition to hold to give Mexico the *appearance* of democracy. So people began to call Mexico a one-and-a-half-party system: the PRI continued to dominate but the other parties were permitted to hold some positions. In recent years, however, the monopoly of the PRI has been increasingly challenged.

A special case is the one-party Marxist-Leninist and Marxist regimes: Cuba and (previously) Nicaragua under the Sandinistas. Cuba is a one-party totalitarian regime in which the Communist Party (CP) controls virtually all political life. It is modeled after the old Soviet/Stalinist regime. Freedom of expression is sharply limited, opposition activity is reported to the secret police, and no political parties besides the CP are allowed. Thus, the CP is a mechanism of control to keep the population in check rather than an instrument of democratic participation.

In Nicaragua, which was a less tightly knit and more pluralist regime, the Sandinista Party enjoyed a special position as the official party of the state. Opposition parties continued to function, however, even though they did not enjoy the favors of a special relationship to the government. Nevertheless, in the February 1990 election, a coalition of opposition parties managed to defeat the Sandinistas, thus returning Nicaragua to a kind of—though still unstable—democracy.

Two-Party Systems

Two-party systems seem to be the dominant trend in the world. In the United States and the nations of Western Europe and Latin America, the electorate seems to be dividing into two main blocks, which we will call the "party of change" and the "party of stability."

Several Latin American countries have long had two-party systems—even if interrupted from time to time by authoritarianism. Colombia is the largest country with a long-standing two-party system, although Uruguay, Paraguay, and Honduras have also been predominantly two-party systems for most of their histories. A complicating factor in both the Colombia and Uruguay cases is that the two main parties were deeply divided internally—so divided that the factions within the main parties often presented their own separate lists of candidates at election time. These were, in other words, quasi-multiparty systems masquerading as two-party systems. Recently, however, especially in presidential as distinct from legislative elections, the trend has again been toward two-party politics.

Another recent trend has been that formerly multiparty systems are moving toward becoming two-party systems. Argentina, Chile, and Venezuela have long been among the most prominent multiparty systems in Latin America; but in these and other formerly multiparty systems (Costa Rica, the Dominican Republic, Ecuador, El Salvador, perhaps Nicaragua), the tendency is now toward two-partyism. Many of the smaller parties in these countries are coming together to form coalitions or voter blocks. Once more, this trend is more prominent in presidential elections than in legislative elections. The process is incomplete, so we will have to hold off on a final assessment. But the trend seems to be toward two-party systems and perhaps toward the stability and peaceful alternation in power that such systems have long enjoyed in more advanced nations.

Multiparty Systems

Multiparty systems tend to emerge in countries where political opinion is deeply divided. The multiple parties usually reflect the wide diversity of views on political issues and the absence of national consensus on basic institutions or on the direction in which the country should go. Several of the less developed countries of Latin America, or countries just emerging from long years of dictatorship and still uncertain about their future political system or policies—such as Brazil—may have thirty or more parties competing in the political fray. After a couple of elections that sort out larger parties from "mini" ones, and in more established multiparty systems such as Chile, the number of parties usually "shakes down" to five or six.

Chile has long been the best example of a Europeanlike multiparty system in Latin America, although Venezuela and Costa Rica, and some others (the Dominican Republic, Argentina, Peru) on an on-again, off-again basis, are also interesting cases of multipartyism. Chile had six main parties: Socialist and Communist parties on the left, Radical and Christian-democrat parties in the center, and Liberal and National parties on the right. These parties competed vigorously as individual parties for parliamentary seats but were forced to form coalitions for the presidency. For example, the Socialist and the Communist parties often formed a popular front for electoral purposes, the Liberal and National parties joined in support of common candidates, and the centrist parties similarly tried at times to present a common slate. Or, when the left and the right ran against each other, they both tried to capture the centrist vote—as would be the case in the United States. Multipartyism reigned in the Chilean Congress, but the presidency provided greater unity and cohesion to the system.

Recently, however, these multiparty systems have gravitated toward two-partyism. The reasons for this include the unpopularity of the extremes (both communists and the far right), the rising importance of the middle class, which wants stability and centrism, dictatorial governments (such as Pinochet in Chile) that abolished the old political parties; and the gradual growth of national consensus on middle-of-the-road policies. Costa Rican politics, for example, has become basically a contest between the slightly left-of-center National Liberation Party and its center-right opponents. In Venezuela, the main contest over the past thirty years has been between the moderate-left Democratic Action Party and the moderate-right Christian-Democratic Party (COPEI); recently, however, both of these leading parties were discredited by charges of corruption and do-nothingness. In Argentina, it is the Peronists versus the Radicals; in the Dominican Republic, it's the moderate-left Revolutionary Party against a moderately conservative, reformist Social-Christian Party. Other countries, by fits and starts and with several minor parties still hanging around, also have moved toward a two-party system. Even Chile, the most established case historically of multipartyism, has moved toward a system of centrist politics and two large "families," one more liberal and one more conservative, that compete for political office.

No-Party Systems

Several countries in Latin America are either so underinstitutionalized (Haiti) that they lack effective parties, or so small and personalistic (Panama) that the parties play almost no role. In both countries, parties play a very limited role at best.

In some other weakly institutionalized countries (Bolivia, Paraguay, Guatemala), the parties play a very limited role as well. The parties and party politics occupy secondary positions; other institutions, such as the army and the economic elites, and direct-action techniques are simply more important than the parties. A mature, functioning political party system, therefore, is not something that springs up overnight; instead, it takes a long time to develop and to become institutionalized. In this way, political parties and a workable political party system are related to increased levels of national development, sociopolitical maturity, a growing middle class, and increased consensus on the ends and means of political activity.

The Future

Two-party systems seem to be the wave of the future in most Latin American countries. At both ends of the spectrum, there seems to be movement toward two-partyism. That is, such formerly single-party systems as Mexico, Nicaragua, and Paraguay have moved toward two-partyism; at the same time, many multiparty systems are also evolving toward a two-party or two-bloc system. Other countries, generally the less developed ones, have still not determined a clear political direction and have not yet institutionalized either their parties or their party system.

Other "Parties"

Latin America has not always been governed democratically, nor has legitimacy been conferred only through the electoral process. Instead, there have been several means (coups, revolutions, general strikes) to power, and therefore other actors besides political parties that functioned as agencies to acquire and stay in high office.

Hence, in Latin America, the practice developed of referring to some of these other actors, semiseriously, as "political parties." The armed forces, for example, would frequently be called the *Partido Militar*. It was not that the armed forces were a political party, only that they acted like one in sometimes presenting candidates for the presidency, making sure their voice was heard in national decision making, and frequently lobbying or maneuvering politically in ways similar to regular political parties. Other groups such as the church and the trade unions, although not political parties per se, sometimes acted like political parties and were thus referred to in the media and elsewhere as the *Partido Eclesiástico* (Church Party) or the *Partido Sindical* (Labor Party).

Such language is less common currently, and the reason lies in the changing nature of Latin American politics. In most countries, democratic elections are now viewed as the *only* legitimate route to power. Other groups that in the past functioned like political parties but used means other than democratic elections to acquire power now have a much harder time legitimizing their actions. Groups like the military or the Catholic church are still important actors, but now, at least in the bigger, more institutionalized countries, they function more like normal interest groups than direct participants in the contest for actual power. This is not to say that coups are a thing of the past in Latin America. But, because both the domestic and the international pressures are greater, it is harder to stage a coup or a power-grab and get away with it. Hence, the language of direct action, such as referring to the armed forces as a "party" as if campaigning for the presidency were a legitimate role for them, is also changing. Rarely nowadays, and usually with great difficulty or reluctance, do we see the direct involvement of such groups in political activities that in a democracy are reserved for political parties.

Voting and Elections

Democratic theory presumes a free and informed electorate that is able to make a rational choice among electoral alternatives. But in Latin America these conditions have not consistently applied. The electorate has not always been free or informed, and there has not always been a legitimate choice among alternatives. That is why voting and elections in Latin America sometimes do not conform to democratic precepts and why we need an expanded list of concepts to explain the different kinds of "voting."[3]

Affirmative Voting

Because of fear and/or inertia, many Latin Americans may vote affirmatively for an existent government or regime without considering alternative choices. The belief is that something bad will happen to them or their society if they vote the "wrong" way. This kind of voting is most typical of rural, uneducated, marginal people, who are the most susceptible to intimidation or whose existence is most precarious. But as Latin America becomes more urban and educated, and as international election observers oversee the process, such affirmative voting behavior may decline.

Patronage Voting

In patronage voting, issues and platforms are not at stake. Rather, it is a system of favors in return for favors. Such favors may not be explicitly stated; but if one attaches one's star to a budding *político* who does well, some reward—a favor or a job—is expected in return. Patronage voting is very strong in Latin America; moreover, there are no signs that it is abating. Indeed, the very success of securing democratic elections in Latin America may lead to more patronage voting rather than less.

Obligatory Voting

In many Latin American countries, voting is obligatory, not voluntary—one's ID card may be stamped, arm inked, or wrist lightly shaved. Ostensibly, this is to ensure that everyone fulfills their civic obligations and to prevent repeat voting, but in some countries it is also a means by which local military commanders or political bosses make sure voters choose their candidate. If one does not vote correctly, dire consequences may follow. So, while the aim of such procedures may be to make sure the electorate does its duty, they may also be used as instruments of intimidation.

Ritualistic Voting

Elections are usually held on Sundays in Latin America, with the day declared a national holiday. Thus, it is a day for car caravans, for gatherings of friends and family, and for trips back to one's home town. Voting in this context may be more a ritualistic act, a part of the festivities, than an exercise of public responsibility. Frequently, the meaning of the vote, of the careful exercise of choice, is lost among the day's many social obligations.

Plebiscitary Voting

Many Latin American dictatorships and authoritarian regimes have been careful to hold regular elections for the sake of maintaining the appearance of democracy. Generally, however, such elections do not offer the voters a choice; instead, they serve as opportunities for the electorate to vote "yes" on the government's programs or its continuance in office. These are plebiscites or plebiscitary elections aimed at demonstrating support for an already existing regime and in which a "no" vote is considered subversive, dangerous, and likely to get one in trouble. For example, Trujillo used plebiscites to show he had 95 percent, 98 percent, or even 100 percent (or more!) support for his policies; the Mexican PRI has also long run "elections" in which the issue was not choice but confirmation of the party in power.

Protest Voting

Protest voting has a long tradition in Latin America. If one doesn't like any of the parties or candidates, or one's party has been proscribed and eliminated from the ballot, or one wants to register disapproval of the political system as a whole, one can enter a protest vote. Protest votes may take the form of casting a blank ballot (in those countries that lack voting machines), spoiling the ballot, or perhaps smearing excrement on the polling station. Another way to protest is to abstain from voting altogether—the incidence of which also provides an indicator of a regime's popularity or lack thereof.

Rigged Voting

Rigged voting takes many forms in Latin America. The most blatant kind occurs after an election when the military or a defeated government, unsatisfied with the results, confiscates the ballot boxes and simply changes the totals. More sophisticated attempts at altering election results are usually focused on the period before the balloting. One can hire professional firms in Miami and elsewhere whose consultants are trained vote-riggers. They may play dirty tricks with the voter lists, bribe the local electoral commissions, pay voters to vote a certain way, or, often in cahoots with military commanders, use techniques of intimidation directed at voters. These methods, previously widespread throughout Latin America, are now on the wane.

Democratic Voting

After all these preliminaries, we finally get to real democratic voting: a clear choice among alternatives in a context of freedom and respect for civil liberties. Actually, these kinds of democratic elections have been far more prevalent in Latin America than one might think; furthermore, their importance has been growing in recent years to the point where fair and honest elections are now the norm and the other kinds the exceptions.

Two main forces have been at work here, explaining the trend toward democratic elections. The first is the general trend in Latin America itself, since the late 1970s, to more open democratic government. After long years of military rule, Latin Americans are demanding democracy and, with it, fair and honest elections. By and large, the military and other extra-democratic forces have acquiesced to these demands thus far. So long as the consensus on democracy remains strong and is supported by domestic pressures and a thriving economy in Latin America, honest, open elections are likely to remain the rule.

The other force leading toward democratic elections is international pressure. In the 1980s, the U.S. government and other international actors put strong pressure on Latin America to hold democratic elections. In El Salvador, the Dominican Republic, Nicaragua, Guatemala, Chile, Paraguay, Ecuador, Brazil, Panama, Honduras, Haiti, and other countries, the U.S. embassy was instrumental in urging an opening and helping to democratize the political system. Elections were the instrument to begin that process. After it became clear that the U.S. government was genuinely interested in promoting democracy abroad, a variety of human rights and prodemocracy groups, along with U.S. government agencies, began providing election observers—often dozens or even hundreds of them—to ensure fair balloting and honest vote counting. It gets harder and harder to rig or steal an election when literally hundreds of foreign observers are scrutinizing every move.

Parties and the Future

Political parties and the party systems of Latin America have undergone enormous development in the past four decades. From being essentially elite or cadre parties traditionally, we have seen these organizations grow into viable programmatic parties, well organized in many cases, and with a real mass base. Often suffocated under military repression, the parties—both old and new—have burst forth in the 1980s and 1990s as major actors in the political system. Development and democratization have both given renewed or newly found vigor to Latin America's often somnolent parties and the party systems.

While democrats have to be gratified by this political party development, a note of caution also needs to be sounded. The fact is, parties are rising in Latin America at the same time that they are in decline in the advanced industrial nations of Western Europe and North America. There, the parties are gradually being supplemented by other kinds of organization—corporatist structures linking the state to societal groups, think tanks, and political action committees (PACs)—that often bypass the parties and their intermediation functions to feed information and interests directly into the political system. It may be that Latin America will also gravitate eventually toward this newer, modernized form of corporatism—as distinct from the traditional medieval corporatism. But for now, let us celebrate the rise of Latin American political parties and party systems and the democracy that goes with them; we can worry about the new forms of corporatism if and when they become a reality.

Notes

1. The analysis here follows the categories used in Ronald H. McDonald and J. Mark Ruhl (eds.), *Party Politics and Elections in Latin America* (Boulder, CO: Westview Press, 1989); but the assessment and interpretation are my own. See also Scott Mainwaring and Timothy Scully (eds.), *Building Democratic Institutions: Party Systems in Latin America* (Stanford, CA: Stanford University Press, 1993).

2. This list is based on McDonald and Ruhl, but with the author's own analysis and assessment.

3. This list again derives from McDonald and Ruhl.

9

✦

Government, the State, and State-Society Relations

The Latin American state system has always been more centralized, more monolithic, more tightly knit, and more authoritarian than that in the United States. "Unity," said Simon Bolívar, the father of Latin American independence, "is to be prized above all else." Such strict centralization and control help explain why in Latin America the legislatures are frequently so weak, the judiciaries so timid, and local governments so ineffective; there is little separation of powers in Latin America. The model that best helps us understand Latin America is France, with its centralized institutions, where policy emanates from the central ministries in Paris and not so much from the local grass roots as in the United States. Indeed, to understand the role of the state in Latin America—at least historically—one needs to put aside comparisons with the United States and view the area in terms of its Southern European (France, Italy, Spain, Portugal) heritage. The question now is how much this has changed, both in the light of greater U.S. influence in Latin America and the region's movement toward greater pluralism and democracy.

In this chapter, we examine the history of Latin America's main political/governmental institutions and the origins of these both in continental Europe and in the indigenous civilizations of the area. We then move to a discussion of the functioning of these institutions—executive, legislative, judicial, local, and regional governments—as well as of the "bureaucratic phenomenon" in Latin America and the role of the military as almost a fourth branch of government. Next, we analyze state-society relations in Latin America, arguing that the corporatist or mixed corporatist/pluralist character of state-society relations is fundamentally different from the untrammeled interest group pluralism of the United States. Although a detailed treatment of social and economic policy is reserved for Chapter 10, here we briefly analyze the topic by focusing on the state's key role in guiding and directing national economic life.

History and Background

To understand the powerful role of the central state in Latin America, we have to go back to medieval Spain and Portugal. The authoritarian tendencies of the Iberian mother countries were reinforced in the Americas by vast spaces, impenetrable jungles and mountains, and the historical absence of national infrastructures. In the New World, the authoritarian traditions of the colonial powers meshed closely with the similarly authoritarian structures of the indigenous peoples. Let us examine these main influences on Latin America more closely.

In Iberia, recall, the emerging Spanish and Portuguese states had waged a centuries-long war to expel the Moors from the peninsula—a crusade that helped give birth to militarism and absolutism in the political sphere. The vast, empty, rugged terrain of Iberia also encouraged authoritarianism since, it was felt, only a strong ruler could tame such a fractured and violent land. Then, a succession of Spanish kings, culminating in Ferdinand and Isabella, sought to enhance their authority by snuffing out parliamentary and regional authority and all independent sources of power. The Hapsburg monarchy and the Hapsburgian model (see Chapters 2 and 6) of the sixteenth and seventeenth centuries cemented authoritarian institutions in place. It was these institutions that Spain and Portugal carried over to the New World.

In the Americas, the Spanish and Portuguese again found a vast, rugged territory populated by fierce and large-scale Indian civilizations. How to govern such a huge, wild, and unfriendly territory? To the Spanish and Portuguese *conquistadores*, the answer would naturally be the same authoritarian, top-down model and institutions that were used in the mother countries. The difference was that Latin America was even wilder, larger, and more primitive than were Spain and Portugal. Therefore, authority and authoritarianism in Latin America had to be even stronger than in Iberia itself.

The authoritarianism of the Spanish and Portuguese colonizers was matched by the authoritarianism of the indigenous groups. In some literature, the myth has grown up that before the Spanish and Portuguese arrived, the native Indians of the Americas were happy, peaceful, and blissful—"noble savages." In reality, the indigenous peoples of the Americas were often as nasty, violent, and brutal as the *conquistadores*. In addition, their political and governmental structures were just as authoritarian, if not more so. As we saw in Chapter 2, the method the Spanish used in governing these native peoples was to eliminate their leadership but to leave in place the control mechanisms and the hierarchical structure of Indian society—with the Spaniards as new "chiefs." In this way, the authoritarianism of the indigenous groups served to reinforce the authoritarianism of Spain and Portugal.

The top-down structure of colonial Spain and Portugal had a long history in the law, political philosophy, and culture of the two mother countries. Neither Spain nor Portugal had developed a system of checks and balances among the executive, legislative, and judicial branches, for example; rather, royal absolutism and strong executive power were dominant. Nor, in Spanish law, was there a perceived need to check executive power; instead, following the Aristotelian and Thomistic models, government was seen as inherently good and therefore in no need of restraint. In addition, in the long tradition of Iberian political philosophy, political authority was viewed as centralized, organic (all the parts tied together), unified, and hierarchical (king, viceroy, captain-general, local *hacendado*)—and as emanating from God. All these traditions pointed toward a strong state and a strong central executive authority.

These traditions of centralism and authoritarianism were largely continuous both before and after Latin America independence. Recall that the strongest influence on the newly independent Latin American states was not Jefferson or Madison or Locke, but Rousseau. In contrast to the North American advocacy of pluralism and separation of powers, Rousseau favored a centralized, organic, and unified state. His leader would know and personify the "general will"—without necessarily holding elections to check his policies or perceptions with the electorate. Hence, although the new Latin American states often borrowed entire sections from the U.S. constitution and even incorporated, in keeping with the style of the time, provisions for separate legislative and judicial branches, in fact their new constitutions made the executive branch supreme and endowed their presidents with such powers that they could rule as constitutional dictators.

These tendencies toward renewed centralism and authoritarianism were strengthened even more by the disruptive, centrifugal conditions prevailing in Latin America in the nineteenth century and in some countries continuing into the twentieth. In the immediate aftermath of independence, anarchy, chaos, and disintegration prevailed in much of Latin America. There was no infrastructure and little national organization on which to build functioning democracy. Everything seemed to be unraveling. Only a strong state, a strong leader, even a dictator appeared capable of holding the nation and society together against these disintegrative forces.

Then, as Latin America began to develop later in the nineteenth and early twentieth centuries, who helped engineer those developments? Again, it was the strong leaders such as Díaz in Mexico, Heureaux in the Dominican Republic, and Gómez in Venezuela. It was not the democrats who built the first roads, port facilities, docks, railroads, telephone and telegraph systems, banks, import-export facilities, and so on, or who ushered in the first sustained economic modernization. Rather, it was strong leaders and strong central states. Thus, in terms of both holding society together against disintegrative forces and achieving major national development, it was the strong, authoritative (if not authoritarian) states that achieved these goals—and were generally so perceived in the popular mind.

One final preliminary comment should be made about the strong role of the state in Latin American development. The central state in Latin America has often been stronger in aspiration than it has been in fact. Latin American constitutions, history, and political culture all enshrine a strong state; but in reality, the state's power and capacity to make its policies felt are limited. They are limited by impassable terrain, underdeveloped communications and transportation systems, the isolation and illiteracy of rural villages, and inept or ineffective bureaucratic agencies and grass-roots organizations that often have little or no influence outside of the major cities. These are all indicators of underdevelopment. If the country were more developed, then the state and its various agencies would likely be more effective. In other words, the Latin American state or government is often strong by design, by hope, and by aspiration; but its capacity to make its writ felt throughout the national territory is severely limited by the underdeveloped nature of the country.

Key Governmental Institutions

In Latin America, the government is a major actor. The government is not just a neutral referee of the interest group struggle as government is sometimes portrayed in the United States. Nor are government institutions merely the mirror images of class interests, as alleged in some of the literature. Instead, while *reflective* often of elite (middle and upper) class interests, the Latin American state and its various institutions also have considerable autonomy. These institutions therefore need to be evaluated independently in order to understand how things work or don't work in Latin America.

Law and the Legal Tradition

The Latin American legal systems grew originally out of Spanish and Portuguese medieval and feudal law. These laws were based on absolutist, top-down, scholastic principles that had a strong basis in the precepts of medieval Catholicism: the law derived from God and was therefore unchanging and unchallengeable. Legal training mainly involved rote memorization, chiefly of religious material, and application of deductive reasoning.

After independence, the Napoleonic code was adopted and superimposed upon the prevailing medieval legal structure. It was adopted both because it was fashionable at the time and seemed to represent the most advanced thinking, and because it represented continuity with the past. The Napoleonic code was a product of the more modern Enlightenment, but it was similarly top-down, deductive, and absolutist. The authoritarian and rigidly centralized systems of the new postindependence legal codes corresponded closely with the historical absolutism and top-down character of traditional society and the prevailing political system.

More recently, aspects of the U.S. legal system have been—often uncomfortably—conjoined with the Iberian medieval codes and the Napoleonic code, but without replacing these earlier codes. The U.S. legal tradition, stemming from the British system, is one of common law, precedent, the case method, and inductive reasoning. In such areas as political and human rights, constitutionalism, and commercial law, the U.S. legal influence in Latin America has been particularly strong.

The overlap of these very different legal traditions has given rise to a great deal of confusion and dysfunction. For example, the Spanish-French legal tradition gives precedence to group or corporate rights as distinct from the U.S. emphasis on individual rights. That is reflected in the fact that in Latin America, only after a group receives recognition from the state does it have the legal right to bargain in the political process (see Chapter 5). Another controversial area is human rights protection: U.S. law puts great emphasis on personal rights, whereas the Spanish-French codes tend to give greater importance to the rights and powers of the state.

The legal codes and legal system of Latin America help shape the prevailing political culture and the way public policy is carried out, as well as illuminating the frequent disputes between the United States and Latin America over human rights and other programs. No one doubts there are such relationships between legal systems and political behavior, but their precise nature is not always clear. In fact, the impact of the law and the legal system of Latin America on various aspects of society, economics, and politics is one of the least studied aspects of Latin American civilization.

Constitutions

Latin American constitutions are not just paper documents as is sometimes asserted, designed to be ignored, violated, or abrogated. Rather, these constitutions have major symbolic value, they spell out the institutions of government and how they should operate, and they often articulate goals (democracy, social justice, workers' rights, and so on) for the society to achieve. When these constitutions are ignored or abolished, it has major consequences for the government—and now more than ever. Nor should we judge constitutional stability in Latin America by the sheer numbers of constitutions, because while the United States has frequently amended or reinterpreted its constitution, the Latin American legal tradition is that an entirely "new" constitution is promulgated every time there is a new amendment or a new interpretation. The differences between the United States and Latin America in this area may not be as great as they appear.

Right after gaining independence from Spain and Portugal in the 1820s, most Latin American countries adopted constitutions based on the U.S. model. They provided for basically presidential systems and (in theory, at least) for the separation of powers, and they included long lists of human and political rights. But there was, as with the legal tradition and codes, a powerful French or Rousseauian tradition as well: strong central leadership, an emphasis on unity over checks and balances, and an organic or corporatist regime in which such agencies as the church and the army were integrated into the state.

While the early Latin American constitutions were quite liberal in orientation, the anarchic conditions prevailing in the region during the first few decades of independence caused much consternation. Democracy and liberalism were viewed as not working; it was argued that only a strong leader could hold these disorganized, fragmented societies together. As authoritarian dictators and the army moved into the power vacuum, they also wrote new constitutions that gave even greater power to the executive, severely limited the congress and courts, and made provisions for expanded emergency laws and the suspension of political and civil rights in times of crisis. Thereafter, much of Latin America's constitutional history could be written in terms of the alternations between these autocratic constitutions and the more democratic type.

In more recent decades, Latin America has experienced many constitutional innovations. First, there have been numerous attempts to try to limit excessive executive power by introducing measures that would force a president to share executive power (semiparliamentarism) with his cabinet or with the congress. Second, the Mexican Constitution of 1917 has become a model for many other recent constitutions incorporating provisions for agrarian reform, social justice, and workers' rights into the basic law of the land—thus also greatly increasing the length of the constitutions. Third, the congress and courts have gradually increased in power and independence over the decades. Finally, now that Latin America has begun to solve its problems of instability and historical lack of legitimacy for government institutions, there are increasing pressures to move toward a parliamentary system in which the legislature would be the supreme power, as distinct from the prevailing presidentialism.

The reestablishment of democracy in so many Latin American countries during the 1980s has given an enormous shot in the arm to *constitutionalism*, or a sense of government operating within the limits of law and constitution. The strong sense of legitimacy that exists for democratic institutions now makes it far harder for regimes to violate the constitution or for challengers to the government to seek to overthrow the constitution.

The Executive Branch

The presidency is the focal point of the Latin American political systems. It is the hub around which all the different spokes in the wheel of government revolve. The president has such vast power, both by tradition and by constitution, that he can rule as a virtual one-man government. He is the leader, the *jefe* (chief), the *caudillo* (man on horseback) of the regime. The noted Latin Americanist Frank Tannenbaum once observed that the president is the inheritor of the power once given to the Aztec emperor—or maybe the Spanish viceroy, or perhaps both of these combined.[1] Obviously, it is but a small step from all-powerful executive to full-fledged dictator, Caesar, or authoritarian.

Latin American presidents have broad constitutional powers as heads of state, with responsibility for both domestic and foreign affairs. They also hold wide emergency powers that in tumultuous Latin America have been frequently invoked: to declare a state of siege, to suspend human rights, to send the congress packing, and to rule by decree-law. In addition to their formal and administrative powers, most Latin American presidents command vast national patronage networks. In countries lacking a strong civil service and where personal loyalty is so important, the presidents may appoint everyone from cabinet members to janitors. They also dole out favors, contracts, and special privileges in return for support. As in the United States, the advent of television has focused even more attention on the *person* of the presidency.

Strong, personal leadership has long been a part of Latin American culture, and the presidency reflects that emphasis on personalism. But it is not just culture alone that explains the powerful executive. The economic crises of recent times, greater state responsibility in more areas of public policy, and political fragmentation and conflict all tend to focus more and more power, attention, and decision making on the president.

Over the years, various efforts have been made to check and limit excessive executive power. In some countries, for example, a cabinet minister must co-sign all legislation; in Uruguay, there is a history of plural executives, or government by committee. Some countries are flirting with semiparliamentary systems in which a president shares power with a prime minister, or perhaps even with the parliament. A parliamentary system would probably work best in such well-integrated and -institutionalized countries as Chile, Costa Rica, and Uruguay where there are also strong political party systems. In the other countries where parties are weak or there is fear of possible national unraveling and disintegration, a single strong president capable of holding the country together is still preferred.

The Legislative Branch

The congress in most Latin American countries has not been a major player. Traditionally, it has had very limited powers, has not served as much of a check on the executive, has had little in the way of staffing or technical capabilities as compared with the U.S. Congress, has frequently been prorogued (dismissed) by the president, and has often been something of a laughing-stock. Only in Chile, Costa Rica, and Uruguay has the congress been acknowledged as strong and independent.

But now this is beginning to change. In country after country, the congress is asserting its authority. It is staking out positions independent from the executive, even daring at times to frustrate presidential initiatives. In some countries, the congress is in the hands of a different party or parties than is the executive. The resurgence of democracy in the area has enabled the congress, even in such smaller countries as Ecuador, the Dominican Republic, and Honduras, to play this more independent, sometimes obstreperous role. The fact that many congresses in the area now have larger and better staffs, independent budget or investigative offices, and new committee and subcommittee systems, as in the United States, augments their more independent role. Nevertheless, it will be a long time, if ever, before the legislatures of Latin America have an importance equal to that of the executive.

The Judicial Branch

The courts are like the legislatures in Latin America: historically, they have played a secondary role and not been coequal with or independent of the executive. For example, in Latin American countries, supreme courts rarely declare laws unconstitutional, and in most countries the courts do not even have that power. As with the congress, the executive frequently rides roughshod over the courts, sends the judges home, or ignores the court's decisions. Never have the courts enjoyed a role as genuinely coequal and independent.

The court system, like the legal system in Latin America, is patterned after the French model—with a U.S. overlay. The courts are hierarchically organized: from courts of first instance, to appellate courts, to the supreme court. Special courts exist for commercial, religious, and military matters. Because of the underdeveloped nature of Latin American society, the lack of funds, the historically elitist nature of the society, and the privileged position of the armed forces, the cause of justice in Latin America is not always well served. Courts, jails, and the entire justice system have terrible deficiencies and injustices.

Many of these problems will be overcome as Latin America develops. The courts and the justice system will improve as they get more and better staff, facilities, and training. Judicial review of legislation and of presidential actions is becoming increasingly widespread and accepted in many countries. U.S. assistance in the legal and judicial realm is helping a number of countries to improve their court systems and judicial procedures.

But part of the problem is cultural as well, relating to the two different kinds of legal systems, code and common, that exist in Latin America and the United States, respectively. The code law system helps perpetuate and reinforce the authoritarian and top-down political systems that have long been present in Latin America. The system is rigid, bureaucratic, nonpragmatic, highly centralized, and unconducive to change. At the same time, the separate court system for the military helps prevent armed forces officers from being held accountable for human rights abuses and perpetuates the notion of the military as a separate and privileged group above the law. These historical and cultural factors will not necessarily disappear as modernization proceeds, although some of the worst abuses may well be ameliorated as a result of both Latin American and U.S. pressure.

Federalism and Local Government

At the time of its independence, the United States of America consisted of thirteen quite different colonies for which the principles of federalism reflected in the Constitution were a pragmatic response to existing reality. For Latin America, however, which had always been governed under the highly centralized control of Spain and Portugal, federalism was an artificial adaptation of a North American idea to a context where it had no history or tradition.

Only four Latin American countries actually adopted a federal-type system: Argentina, Brazil, Mexico, and Venezuela. All four of these are large, diverse, geographically spread-out countries where, it could be argued, federalism would make sense. But these are also highly centralized countries in which the states have never acquired the taxing or independent policy-making power of the United States. Nevertheless, federalism in these countries does have some importance: it is a reflection of regional differences, it serves as a very modest check on excessive central power, it provides jobs and patronage at a level below the central state, and it serves as a step (often a series of steps) in the career ladder of an ambitious politician. Additionally, the states in these four countries have *begun* to acquire some *limited* taxing and policy-making roles.

Local government in Latin America, like so many other things, was based on the centralized French model. It is the central government agencies in capital cities that make policy, not local officials. Unlike in the United States, Latin American cities and towns have almost no independent taxing or policy-making authority. Schools and education, health care, police, welfare—all are mainly controlled by the central government.

For a time, the United States championed "community development" as a way to encourage greater grass-roots participation and initiative in Latin America. But this idea, while laudable in theory, made no sense in the Latin American context, where centralism was the rule and where local mayors and town councils had no authority to instigate and carry out programs. Over the years, the U.S. approach has become more sophisticated; at the same time, within Latin America, towns and cities have begun to take on more responsibilities. But this is still very limited, centralism prevails, and it is unlikely this will change fast given the traditions of central state authority built up over five hundred years.

Bureaucracy and the Bureaucratic Phenomenon

Latin American governments consist of large public bureaucracies. Recall from Chapter 7 that the Latin American state sector may generate upwards of 60–70 percent of GNP; that also means that 60–70 percent of the labor force works for the state. In some countries, the government bureaucracy is virtually the only employer, particularly of educated persons.

These big, bloated bureaucracies are often dominated by corruption, inefficiency, and patronage. This is frequently difficult for Americans to understand because the North American expectation is of honesty and efficiency from government bureaucrats—or else we try to get them removed. Not so in Latin America, where bureaucracy often serves patronage functions first, and efficient administration of the public weal only secondarily. Generally, it takes a very long time to process even simple bureaucratic procedures in Latin America, frequently a "fee" has to be paid for the service performed, the procedures are not very efficient, and people sometimes seem to go to their jobs mainly to collect their paychecks but not to work. In addition, some especially privileged persons and elites seem to have the capacity to cut through all this red tape and get their requests acted upon quickly, while humbler petitioners may have to wait days, weeks, or forever.

In recent years, under the pressures of modernization, these traditional habits have begun to change in favor of greater efficiency and rationality. But the old ways often die slowly, so that most Latin American bureaucracies show a considerable overlap between the traditional patronage-oriented behavior and the newer efficiency. For example, most Latin American countries now have civil service laws to give the bureaucratic career greater professionalism and permanence, but few bureaucrats are actually protected by such laws, and the president or cabinet minister still appoints most functionaries on a patronage basis (a job for you in return for support for me). Most counties also have civil service trade unions, but again, only a small percentage of government workers may be covered. New standards of honesty, efficiency, and even downsizing have been introduced; but usually for every bureaucrat fired, two more are hired.

Bureaucratic growth has been especially strong in the autonomous agencies and state-run corporations that are prevalent in Latin America. These are not the usual cabinet ministries (although they, too, have grown) but the new plethora of agrarian reform institutes, water resource agencies, government development banks, housing institutes, and so on that have emerged in the last three decades as the state has been increasingly called upon to provide services in these areas. In addition, remember that much of the industrialization in Latin America since the 1930s has been through state-run steel mills, petrochemical complexes, railroads, and so on. All of these agencies over the years have become gigantic patronage agencies, rife with corruption and inefficiency, and yet protected from reform by their statutes of autonomy. Due to demands for greater honesty and efficiency, efforts are now being made to improve the performance of these agencies and reduce their size, but the old patronage ways are deeply entrenched, and reform will take a long time.

We entitled this subsection "Bureaucracy and the Bureaucratic Phenomenon." The latter term refers to the fact that most Latin American states are bureaucratic states as distinct from liberal states in the North American sense. That is, the various groups in the system (let us say, labor and capital, university students, or others) tend to deal with one another indirectly, through the bureaucracy, rather than directly. Labor and capital seldom bargain directly with each other; rather, they *both* work through the state apparatus, trying to get the president or maybe the labor minister to put pressure on the other party to reach an agreement. Again, the state, or more likely the president personally, is the focal point of the entire national system, with all groups working through it, using the state for their own advantage, or trying to capture it (or parts of it) for themselves. This "bureaucratic politics" phenomenon in Latin America is quite different from the U.S. system of direct, laissez-faire bargaining among diverse interest groups.

Fourth and Fifth Branches of Government

Since the eighteenth-century French political theorist Montesquieu, we have been accustomed to speaking of the three-part division of government: executive, legislative, and judicial. But growing out of Iberia's and Latin America's distinct history is another tradition that precedes Montesquieu, one in which the Catholic church and the armed forces are regarded as almost fourth and fifth branches of government.

We have already discussed in Chapter 7 the role of the military and the church as interest groups and need not repeat that material here. However, we do need to reiterate the special role of these two and perhaps other groups in Latin American constitutional history. It all goes back to the notion of the *fuero* (*foro* in Portuguese) in medieval Iberian law. *Fuero* means "right," in the sense of a fundamental, *God-given* right. A *fuero* would refer to the fundamental *rights* of a group, such as the armed forces, the church, or the university. *Fueros* were usually stated in the form of a social contract or organic law that spelled out the rights and the obligations of the groups affected and the emerging state. Recall that many of these *fueros* preceded the formation of a Spanish or Portuguese central government.

That tradition was continued in part in postindependence Latin America. The church and the army were such important institutions that almost all Latin American constitutions contain separate sections dealing with them. Catholicism was the established religion, and the church had many obligations in the areas of morals, education, and welfare. Similarly, the armed forces were given constitutional obligations in the maintenance of public order, social peace, and domestic tranquility. These powers often were so vast that, in effect, they made the armed forces and the church into fourth and fifth branches of the government. Language usage ran parallel to this reality; journalists and others would sometimes use the term *poder militar* (military power) or *poder ecliástico* (religious power) to refer to these institutions.

Such usage is now in decline. The Catholic church has been disestablished as the official state church, Catholicism is no longer the only or official religion, the armed forces are *beginning* to be subordinated to civilian authority, and the military's constitutional role as "balancers" is being curtailed. Thus, it may no longer be accurate to speak of these groups as fourth and fifth branches of government. In fact, some scholars now refer to the emergent government-owned corporations as the new "fourth branch" of government, replacing the church and the armed forces. It is important to recognize the fluctuations in power and constitutional role of these groups, but it is also important in understanding Latin America to know that historically—and to an extent today—the armed forces and the church occupy special and privileged positions in Latin American jurisprudence.

State and Society

The "state" here refers to the entire gamut of institutions discussed in the previous section (laws, constitution, government branches); the state is the legitimate, authoritative, public policy-making and -implementing apparatus in the country. "Society" refers to the social actors (classes, interest groups) that participate in the national social and political life. State-society relations, therefore, refers to the interrelations between the government and its component societal parts.

The United States has long been dominated by a liberal or pluralist system of state-society relations in which the social and interest groups exist independently from the state. By contrast, in command or totalitarian systems, social and interest groups are completely subordinated to or perhaps even snuffed out by the powerful state juggernaut. Once again, as with its economic system, Latin America occupies a third or intermediate position, between the nearly absolute group freedom of liberalism and the absolute control of totalitarianism. We call that third way *corporatism*; it has long been the prevailing system of Latin America—although it is now giving way, partially, to liberalism.

By corporatism in state-society relations, we refer to a system of still limited pluralism in terms of numbers of interest groups (usually nine or ten in Latin America, in contrast to the unfettered pluralism of the United States), which are generally licensed and regulated by the state (in contrast to the total control of totalitarianism). The *corporate groups* that are generally a part of this system are those already discussed here: the armed forces, the Catholic church, the economic elites or business groups, organized labor, university students, the bureaucracy, peasants, women. Each of these groups usually has a contractually defined relationship with the state; before being recognized and licensed by the state, and thus being afforded legal political standing, each group must generally have its internal character, membership roles, and purposes scrutinized and approved by the state. In this way, the state allows a limited degree of pluralism (unlike totalitarianism) that the state hopes does not get out of hand and lead to anarchy and breakdown; at the same time (unlike liberalism), the state's licensing procedures and power of recognition or nonrecognition give it enormous power over these groups in terms of both numbers and functions.

Corporatism grew historically out of the medieval struggle between an emerging state system seeking to control an anarchic national territory and the prior existence of these groups seeking to retain their autonomy. Corporatism was carried over to the New World in Spanish and Portuguese colonial administration, where a caste or racial element (Whites, Indians, Blacks, *mestizos*, mulattos, and so on) was added to the rather weak, often disorganized system of sectoral or functional corporations. In the early part of the twentieth century, corporatism in Latin America was closely associated with Catholic political philosophy and the attempt to develop an alternative (the "third way") to both liberalism and Marxism. Each group (labor, capital, farmers, military, and so on) was to be integrated into the state under the licensing procedures described earlier, so that some degree of social pluralism would be allowed, but not U.S.-style liberalism. More recently, various regimes in Latin America abandoned this Catholic and ideological view of corporatism in favor of a system that enabled them to exercise authoritarian control over interest group activity while also permitting some officially sanctioned adaptation to modernization and pluralism.

The arena of labor relations is often considered *the* most critical in the corporatist schema, and a key reason for wanting to have a corporatist system. The reason this arena is so crucial is that industrial and labor relations often form the anvil on which the structure of modern society is hammered out. On the one hand, it is absolutely essential for any regime trying to develop to stimulate economic growth, and that can only be done through the on-again, off-again encouragement/control of the business groups. On the other hand, the very economic growth that the state wishes to encourage also gives rise to trade unions whose strikes disrupt the system and whose ideology, if radical, might lead to instability or even revolution. Hence, the state under corporatism tries mightily to harness and control both big business and organized labor (with the main emphasis on the latter) while also encouraging both to work together harmoniously, under state auspices, for national development. The state may seek to encourage while also closely regulating big business; at the same time, it seeks to control the unions and enforce labor peace. This can require considerable authoritarianism on the state's part.

Since the 1970s, as most countries of the area have moved toward democracy, they have also begun to move away from corporatism. In *all* countries, the process is incomplete. The first step is a move away from a closed, authoritarian, dictatorial kind of corporatism toward one that is more open and democratic. For example, Brazil has largely repealed its earlier corporatist labor legislation, but in actual practice the state still regulates large areas of labor relations. Argentina has similarly moved toward democracy, but corporate interests were still strongly represented in the unions, the government, and the business sector. President Carlos Menem began the process of reforming and reducing this corporatist structure. Venezuela has been a democracy since 1958, and yet its political parties and interest groups are still heavily dominated by top-down sectoral organization and patronage. Peru moved back to democracy, but that seemed for a time to strengthen corporatism in the economic sphere rather than weaken it. And Mexico, even as it moves toward closer ties with the United States and responds to pressure for democratization, still has a dominant single-party system (the PRI) organized on a sectoral (workers, peasants, popular elements) or corporative basis. But these are "open" and quasi-democratic forms of corporatism, not the closed, dictatorial systems of the past.

Only three countries seem to have moved away from corporatism altogether and toward full, free, unfettered democracy and pluralism: Chile, Costa Rica, and Uruguay—and perhaps now Argentina as well. In these countries, there are few if any restrictions in place on freedom of association or the ability to form interest groups and to bargain in the political process. However, corporatism of one sort or another is so deeply ingrained in the society and politics of Latin America that the movement away from it is likely to be very slow at best. What is most likely to emerge in most countries is various mixed forms. We could, and probably will, see free elections, representative government, democracy, and constitutionalism in the political sphere. That certainly is the trend in most countries. At the same time, in the system of interest representation, labor relations, and policy consultation and implementation, the state may well continue to exercise some degree of control over group licensing, regulation, and compulsory (under state auspices) collective and political bargaining. In sum, democracy and corporatism are likely to continue to coexist in most Latin American countries—not always comfortably.

Recently, in Europe, Japan, and other advanced industrial nations, new forms of corporatism (as distinct from the quasi-medieval hangovers that still exist in parts of Latin America) have emerged. The rationale behind this neo-corporatist development is that modern economics are too complex and too interdependent to be subject to the disruptions of strikes and worker-man-agement conflict. It is better, these countries suggest, to head off such disruptions by incorporating workers, farmers, employers, and so on into the normal consultative, regulatory, and decision-making bodies (ministries, agencies, and the like) of the modern state or to create economic and social councils that incorporate labor, business, government, and other groups. However, the consequence of bringing labor, capital, and the state under one big collaborative umbrella is a new, modern form of corporatism. That is, in fact, the direction in which much of Latin America will probably go: away from the old-fashioned, almost feudal form of corporatism of the past, but not necessarily in most countries toward U.S.-style unfettered pluralism and laissez-faire interest group liberalism. What's more likely is a movement toward a new form of European-style consultative corporatism, in which democracy in the political sphere is comingled with corporatism in the socioeconomic arena.

The State in the Economy

The Latin American state is a large state, a mercantilist state, a regulatory state. With the state sector generating such a high percentage of national GNP (30–75 percent), and with an equally high percentage of the population working for the state, the state has an enormous influence. The state is a center of jobs, patronage, contracts, spoils, licensing, and power. The competition to control it, to gain special access to it, or to find a place or position in it is often intense and sometimes brutal. Working in the state bureaucracy—and securing in it places for one's family, friends, and political cronies—can be a lifelong preoccupation.

Because the state economic sector is so extensive, it has sometimes been called a fourth branch of government—rivaling the church or the army for that honor. The state's involvement in the economy is far more extensive than in the United States. Often, the state sector in Latin America will monopolize or have a near-monopoly in such areas as television, insurance, banks, liquor, steel, petrochemicals, public transportation, mining, and utilities.

In other economic areas, the state may be in partnership with private investors in various kinds of arrangements, but all of them implying extensive state involvement. The Latin American state is like a spider with its web or perhaps an octopus with its tentacles, reaching into virtually all areas of the national economic and political life.

The extensive reach of the state and the large numbers of peoples on its employment rolls mean that the public bureaucracy has become one of the most important influences in the country—right up there with the army and the economic elite as a political force. Because it is so large and important, and because there are so few alternative sources of employment, efforts to reform or downsize the Latin American state have not been very successful.

The state is not just a large economic presence in most Latin American countries; it is also a vast and virtually unlimited source of political patronage—in systems that largely function on the basis of patronage. For a Latin American politician, including now-elected ones, the state becomes a place to reward one's friends with jobs and favors—and even one's enemies, since an enemy on the public payroll is not likely to rebel against a government that is paying his or her salary. That also explains why it is so hard to reduce the state's size, because as a politician one's public support depends on one's ability to reward one's supporters—or else, the "else" meaning withdrawal of their support and loss of influence or even position.

Hence, in the current climate where there is a lot of pressure, both domestic and international, to reduce inefficiency, corruption, and the size of the bureaucracy, politicians are having a hard time. In Mexico, for instance, under pressure from the International Monetary Fund (IMF) to streamline the bureaucracy, the state fired 35,000 workers in one week with great public fanfare; but in the following weeks it quietly put 50,000 more on the public payroll. In the key countries of Argentina and Brazil, the government announced major privatization and downsizing plans with vast publicity, but then quietly forgot about many of these changes as it faced the harsh reality of patronage demands. Only Chile among the Latin American countries carried through a serious privatization and public sector reduction program, but it did so under one of the most brutal and repressive dictatorships ever to come to power in Latin America; recent democratic governments have slowed the process considerably.

On the international front, the pressure to downsize and privatize is also easing. The IMF and the World Bank have become far more relaxed about enforcing their recommended austerity measures and have learned how and when to pull back if a government administering this harsh medicine is politically threatened. Similarly, while Presidents Ronald Reagan and George Bush (especially the former) were in power in Washington, the downsizing and free-market pressures emanating from the United States were intense; but under a Democratic president, Latin Americans think there will be less antistatist pressure, so that they can slow or halt the privatizations and thereby also protect their patronage base.

In sum, a large state sector is likely to be a more or less permanent feature of Latin American politics. Such a large state system has political and particularly patronage functions that are quite different from the private sector–dominated system of the U.S.; the Latin American statist systems have a rationality and dynamics all their own. Because the stakes are so high, it seems doubtful that these statist systems will be changed quickly or easily.

The Future: Final Comment

Latin America is moving toward greater efficiency, rationality, and honesty in the management of the public sector. It is similarly moving toward filling the organizational space, the historical absence of associations and associability, that has long plagued the area, kept it from developing, and frequently forced its politics to alternate between chaos and dictatorship. Government institutions are also becoming more responsive and effective.

But that process, as this chapter makes clear, will be long and difficult, and may never result in Latin America looking exactly like the United States. The first reason for this is cultural and historical: a large, centralized, top-down, mercantilist state, in aspiration if not always in actual practice, is part of the Latin American tradition and culture stretching back at least eight hundred years to the mother countries of Spain and Portugal. Second, many currents in the modern world—the desire for economic development, the need for central planning and economic regulation, the demand for greater social services, the presence of large bureaucracies—force the state to assume a larger role, not less. And third, given the strongly patronage-based nature of much of Latin American social and political life, a large state is quite rational.

Here is where economic rationality and political rationality come in conflict. While economically it makes good sense in Latin America to downsize, rationalize, and privatize these large and often bloated public sectors, politically it may make no sense at all since an elected government's continued popularity and even its capacity to stay in power depend in great part on its ability to reward its friends and supporters. This contradiction between economic and political rationality lies at the heart of the Latin America policy and development dilemmas, as we see even more clearly in the following chapter devoted to public policy.

Note

1. Frank Tannenbaum, *Ten Keys to Latin America* (New York: Vintage, 1962).

10
✦
Public Policy

In recent years, Latin American governments have been called upon to provide a variety of public services that they had no history of providing before: agrarian reform, community development, rural electrification, sanitation, housing, water supplies, family planning, health care, education, economic development, legal reform, human rights, and a host of others. These new demands grew out of the rising political consciousness of Latin America, the changing political culture that has undermined the old fatalism and raised popular expectations, and the notion that it is government's role to provide more goods and services.

Quite a number of these pressures for reform also emanated from the international environment, chiefly from the United States. Fearful of a "second Cuba" in Latin America (that is, a Marxist-Leninist regime, allied to the Soviet Union, and allowing its territory to be used as a base for Russian missiles), the United States began pressuring Latin America for reforms as a way of heading off the possibilities for Castro-like revolution. At one level, therefore, the Latin American and the U.S. recognition of the need for reform came together—as, for example, in John F. Kennedy's Alliance for Progress. But, unfortunately, many of these reform programs were hastily conceived, based on a U.S. model that had little to do with Latin American realities, and very unevenly implemented. Some of these reforms proved more destructive than constructive, contributing to instability and, though that was not intended, to the wave of military coups that swept over Latin America in the 1960s and 1970s.

These implied criticisms, however, should not detract from a recognition of the overall policy accomplishments since the 1960s. The Latin American populace is now better educated, more literate, and healthier, and has a longer life expectancy; Latin American society is more urban, more democratic, more industrialized, more middle class, and more economically developed than at *any time in its history*. This development is uneven, to be sure, and many problems remain; but we should not minimize the changes. Along with Asia, Latin America in the last four decades has been one of the most economically dynamic areas *in the world*. How that could occur when the actual policies pursued were so often misconceived is one of the mysteries this chapter seeks to unravel.

We cannot possibly deal in a single chapter with all of the public policy programs that Latin America has pursued in recent times. But since many of them were conceived in the United States or in the dynamics of U.S.–Latin American relations, they often went through similar life cycles: they were born with great fanfare, Latin American governments were persuaded to adopt them, the programs then began with considerable enthusiasm, the results often proved disappointing, and eventually the programs faded into oblivion—although seldom disappearing altogether. Because so many of the programs followed this same pattern, we need not deal with all of the programs but only a representative sample of the most important ones: agrarian reform, family planning, economic development and the debt issue, social welfare, and the environment. All of these cases show the dynamics between Latin America and the outside forces pushing it toward change.

Traditional Latin American Public Policy

Traditionally, Latin American governments have not been called on to provide very much in the way of public services. These tended to be patronage regimes—jobs and favors in return for support—and not program-oriented. In the largely rural, agricultural, and subsistence economies of nineteenth-century Latin America, the populace expressed—indeed, because of underdevelopment, had no mechanism to express—few demands for land reform or very many other public services. In addition, in the traditionally Catholic societies of the time, the church, not the state, was expected to provide alms to the poor and to care for orphans, beggars, and the sick. Hence, the Latin American state in the nineteenth century was a very limited state. It usually had a foreign ministry, a ministry of the army, a ministry for government and administration, and perhaps a ministry of public works—that was about all. Clearly, as the shortness of the list of ministries and their limited functions suggests, government could not—and was not expected to—carry out very many public programs.

This situation changed very slowly as Latin America entered the twentieth century. The economic growth that began toward the end of the nineteenth century required some government involvement in the building of roads, telephone and telegraph systems, and port facilities, and in the chartering of such institutions as banks. However, the main stimulus for these projects was not local Latin American governments but foreign capital, private ventures, or (in some countries) U.S. Marine occupation forces. In the 1930s and 1940s, as Latin America began to industrialize, often with government support, the size of the state began to increase, as did the number of ministries. But through the 1950s, the Latin American state remained limited in size, with limited responsibilities, and with still limited demands and expectations placed upon it.

All of this was altered fundamentally in the 1960s and thereafter. One cause was rising Latin American demands for government programs and services: the "revolution of rising expectations." Radio, television, more and better roads, Peace Corps volunteers fanning out into the previously isolated countryside—all these influences, and others as well, helped raise popular consciousness and made Latin Americans want more things. The other cause was U.S. pressures to offer more programs as a way of defusing popular discontent and thus heading off the potential for violent, Cuba-like revolution. Indeed, it was often the United States, even more than the Latin Americans, that pushed for new planning ministries, agrarian reform institutes, housing agencies, development banks, government-run corporations, and so on. It may be that the Latin Americans also wanted some or all of these agencies, but we do need to be careful in sorting out where the pressures came from. In some instances, the pressures were home-grown; in others, the new government agencies were imposed from the outside—as a condition for qualifying for U.S. Alliance for Progress economic assistance. Because it seemed logical and rational, the United States pushed for agrarian reform, for example; but it never bothered to ask Latin Americans if they wanted such a program or in what form. The United States simply *assumed* that they did, that what it advocated was also good for Latin America. But if such programs were imposed from the outside, and not necessarily in accord with Latin American wishes, then it would not be surprising if they failed to work very well.

The answers, unfortunately, are not as clear as we would like them to be for the sake of arriving at a definitive, unambiguous conclusion. On the one hand, Latin American demands for more and better public services were rising. On the other, public opinion surveys also showed that what Latin Americans wanted *most* from the state was to be left alone, not to be beaten up, to be allowed to carry out their activities without government interference.

That attitude might suggest internal pressures for a continued small or minimalist state. It also suggests that at least some of the many government agencies established in Latin America from the 1960s came about because of U.S. pressures and insistence, and not necessarily as a result of Latin American demands.

Agrarian Reform

Nowhere is this phenomenon better illustrated than in the policy field of agrarian reform. Agrarian reform was largely pushed on Latin America by the Kennedy administration, which made the enactment of an agrarian reform law a precondition of U.S. aid. No one knows if the Latin American people favored agrarian reform because no one bothered to inquire; probably some peasants favored it, but certainly Latin American governments (often dominated by people who own land) were against it. Essentially, the United States pushed agrarian reform on a reluctant or at least wary Latin America to serve its own security interests. The United States believed, rightly or wrongly, that agrarian reform would help head off the spread of communism.

This discussion should not be construed as opposition to agrarian reform or any other programs in general—provided the Latin Americans want them and see them as useful. We are against the effort to impose such programs on an unwilling Latin America, particularly programs conceived, hatched, and largely implemented by U.S. officials without adapting them to the realities or culture of Latin America. Unfortunately, there were a large number of such programs imposed on the area from the outside in the 1960s, a practice that often continues in different forms even today.

The case for agrarian reform looks superficially appealing. After all, the popular image of Latin America—often shared by U.S. policymakers—is that it consists of two classes: rich landowners and poor peasants. Social justice demands that the wealth, including the land, be shared more equitably. In addition, the argument went, land redistribution would create in Latin America a society of middle class family farmers just like in rural Wisconsin or New England: well-informed, landholding, participatory, democratic citizens with a stake in the system (land) and thus able to resist communism. This last consideration was most important from a U.S. foreign policy point of view, which is why the United States so strongly pushed for agrarian reform in Latin America.

Unfortunately, the U.S.-sponsored agrarian reform efforts were misguided for a number of reasons. First, some crops, such as sugarcane, require large landholdings, seasonal labor, and expensive machinery; such crops cannot be grown profitably by small, independent family farmers. Second, studies have repeatedly shown that when land is divided into smaller farms, productivity and therefore national income go down. Thus, while agrarian reform may still be justified on moral or foreign policy grounds, it simply doesn't make sense economically. Third, Latin American governments were wholeheartedly opposed to agrarian reform. They would pass the legislation in order to qualify for Alliance for Progress aid, but then not implement it. There is only so much the United States can do to pressure a government into doing something it clearly does not want to do. Fourth, the agrarian reform model the U.S. government applied in Latin America came originally from Japan and Taiwan; it had little to do with the Latin American situation and was never adapted to take account of a very different culture and society.

Fifth, and perhaps surprising, many Latin American peasants did not take kindly to the program. Many chose to sell the land they received rather than to farm it—especially since they lacked tractors, fertilizers, or knowledge about markets. Many preferred the existing system, in which they often worked for the landlord for two or three days per week and then had the rest of the time to themselves. Being an independent owner implied hard, grinding work and a degree of uncertainty many farmers preferred not to shoulder. In addition, the movement toward agrarian reform corresponded to the beginning of a tremendous rush toward urbanization in Latin America: instead of staying on the land, millions of peasants migrated to the cities, leaving many areas of the countryside completely abandoned. The "agrarian problem," in a sense, was solving itself—while adding to the problems of the cities.

As all these uncomfortable realities began to have an impact on the plans of the agrarian reform advocates, agrarian reform itself went through a process of redefinition. The original conception had been broad and revolutionary: it implied a fundamental social, moral, economic, and political transformation of the Latin American countryside. But when that didn't work for all of the reasons noted previously, the U.S. government formulated a far more modest plan that encompassed little land redistribution but emphasized better fertilizers, better breeding of farm animals, better land use, and new crops. That was a far cry from the original conception and generated little enthusiasm. Finally, when military regimes swept into power in the late 1960s and 1970s, the land that was once destined for redistribution was often doled out to armed forces officers for their private use—a massively corrupt perversion of the original agrarian reform conception. By this time, agrarian reform was pretty well dead in Latin America as a public policy issue.

One still hears calls for agrarian reform in Latin America, and doubtless a case can be made for such a program. But the conditions are now so different that agrarian reform no longer generates the enthusiasm it once did. The problems of maldistribution of land, for example, and an impoverished, often landless peasantry still exist. But Latin America is 70 percent urban now, as compared with 70 percent rural in the 1960s when agrarian reform programs first began, so agrarian reform will clearly have far less impact now. The conditions have changed (people are abandoning the countryside) and the problems are different (urban rather than rural), so the solutions have to be different as well. A well-conceived agrarian reform program would probably still be useful in some Latin American countries, but one should have modest expectations about what can be accomplished and not view agrarian reform as a way of effecting societywide transformation.

Many of the original and grandiose programs conceived under Kennedy's Alliance for Progress went through the same life cycle as agrarian reform. They were conceived with great enthusiasm—chiefly by U.S. planners and visionaries. Then they faced the realities of Latin America, where they were undermined, subverted, or used for purposes (such as the land grab by military officers) other than the intended ones. Meanwhile, the United States also lost enthusiasm. Few of these programs ever ended completely, however; rather, they continue to hang on and to attract some enthusiasts even today. But few believe anymore that agrarian reform will solve Latin America's major problems, which are now far more complex. So agrarian reform—and many other like programs—has gone through this life cycle: birth, initial enthusiasm, then reality, failure, cynicism, and ultimately not so much death as oblivion, a slow fading away.

Population Policy

If agrarian reform was the great panacea of the 1960s in Latin America, family planning was the favorite program of the 1970s. Once again, the logic seemed unassailable: in virtually all countries of Latin America, population growth, usually in the neighborhood of 3.5–4.0 percent per year, was outstripping economic growth (GNP grew about 2.5 percent per year). That meant that people's living standards were, on average, steadily getting worse from year to year because the modest economic growth achieved was being submerged by even higher population growth rates. Even in a growing economy, the per capita income was being reduced. The policy response was to try not only to stimulate economic growth but also to reduce population growth, which, according to the numbers, would produce an equally beneficial result.

Most Latin American governments were not entirely persuaded by these arguments. For one thing, the Catholic church opposed most forms of birth control, and few governments in the region wanted to antagonize the church. Since most birth control techniques are essentially abortive—that is, they take effect after conception—the church opposed them. Moreover, Latin American *machismo* is such that few men wanted to use any form of birth control, and many Latin American women also pride themselves on the size of their families. In addition, in rural Latin America, it makes sense to have large families, because more children means more hands to work in the fields and to care for the parents (who usually have no social security) in their old age. Finally, many Latin American governments wanted a larger population to fill their vast territories, as well as equating population size with national power.

The opposition to population control was such that the United States and the several international population agencies felt it necessary to launch the program through stealth rather than openly and directly. For one thing, it was called "family planning" but not "birth control." For another, the program was run through ostensibly private family planning associations, which were largely set up and funded by the United States, so as to avoid the appearance of it being an "official" program. Moreover, great efforts were made to disguise that the birth control techniques used were essentially abortive. Finally, the programs were presented (to avoid church and host government opposition) under the guise of maternal-child health care rather than in terms of population control.

These secretive and often deceptive techniques did not always endear the international family planning agencies to the Latin American governments with whom they were supposed to cooperate. Many resentments arose—and remain. Nevertheless, even with all these obstacles, family planning began to take hold and achieve some success. More and more family planning clinics were opened, more contraceptives were distributed, family planning became more accepted, and in many cases governments actually took over and made official (albeit usually on a small scale) previously private programs. Most importantly, the rate of population increase began to decline, from 3.0, 3.5, or 4.0 percent to 2.5 percent in most counties. In other words, the rate of population increase began to fall back to the level of economic increase or below, making most countries and their peoples better off on a per capita basis.

A major controversy continues to surround this issue, however, over the *causes* of the decrease in the population growth rate. Was it really the family planning programs that all Latin American countries now have? Some skepticism is warranted because even the best national programs in Latin America succeeded in reaching only a very small percentage (maybe 15–20 percent) of women of child-bearing age, and many of these discontinued use of contraceptives after a while. Or was the cause mainly "natural" factors: better education, better health care, rising literacy, and greater urbanization (it makes far less sense to have many children in crowded, big-city slums than in the countryside)? Probably, both causes are important. In any case, there is no doubt that the rates of Latin American population increase are falling—often dramatically—although the region (except for Argentina and Uruguay) still has a long way to go to reach the more or less stable birthrates of the United States, Western Europe, or Japan.

The family planning program was in many ways similar to the agrarian reform program and went through much the same life cycle. First, it was principally a U.S. plan imposed from the outside; Latin America was far less interested in it and had little to do with its original formulation. Second, the program was based on a model derived from other cultures and areas (Japan, Taiwan, Western Europe) and had little to do with Latin American realities. Third, when it was introduced in Latin America, it immediately ran into trouble with Latin American governments and influential groups such as the church. Fourth, the program was enacted *only* because, like agrarian reform, the United States made the granting of any additional aid conditional on the country having a family planning program. Fifth, Latin American governments enacted the program reluctantly and failed to implement it effectively. Therefore, the program sputtered along, never abandoned but never carried out properly, either. Finally, despite all these negatives, the program did actually produce some positive, although limited, results.

That is, essentially, the story of *dozens* of other public policy programs hatched in the United States but carried out at best fitfully in Latin America. What the United States did was to take a program—community development, legal reform, central planning, and many others—that seemed to work somewhere else and applied it to Latin America without taking account of the special culture and sociology of that area. A presumably "global" model was applied to an area where it did not fit, or did not fit very well. It is not surprising that such ethnocentrism (the failure to understand and come to grips with other cultures on their own terms) produced so many false starts, unintended consequences, and meager results. What is surprising is that these programs, despite their many flaws, produced *some* positive results at all.

Economic Development

When we talk about economic development, unlike agrarian reform or family planning, we are talking about something that all the participants—the United States and the individual Latin American governments—wanted. Here, the differences were not over the goals themselves but rather the best ways to achieve those goals. On that matter, the United States and Latin America for a long time went their separate ways, fueling a debate that is still going on today.

Latin American Versus U.S. Approach

Latin America has long been committed to a statist or mercantilist model of political economy. That means that, as in France and other European countries, it is the central state that guides, leads, and directs economic development, and not so much private entrepreneurs and a laissez-faire marketplace. When Latin America began industrializing in the 1930s, it was the state that led the way and not so much the private sector. One can say that from the colonial period on, Latin America has consistently been dominated by a political economy of mercantilism and state capitalism.

The U.S. approach, of course, has always been to emphasize private markets and private engines of growth. This conception will always clash with the preferred Latin American method of statism. Early in the Kennedy presidency, however, when all the big U.S. assistance programs were first gearing up, these differences were blurred considerably because the Democratic administration and the economists manning the Alliance for Progress also believed in Keynesian economics, central planning, and a strong state role in the economy. There were still frequent tensions between the U.S. advisors and the Latin American governments over priorities and emphases, but not so much as in the agrarian reform and family planning areas. On this basis, U.S. and Latin American goals could be advanced in tandem. Only later, under Lyndon Johnson and then a succession of Republican administrations, would the commitment to having the central state play a key role begin to slacken and eventually lead to conflict.

There was, however, another larger issue over which Latin America and the United States strongly disagreed. The chief purpose behind the U.S. economic assistance programs during this period was strategic: to build up sufficient prosperity to prevent any country of the area from succumbing to a Castro-style revolution. The assumption of the U.S. economists who formulated the program was that, by pouring in sufficient money and getting the pump of economic growth primed and running, a larger middle class would be created and democracy inevitably would follow from this greater affluence. The assumption was that democracy was the necessary and inevitable product of economic development.

Latin Americans saw things quite differently. First, they were more interested—naturally enough—in getting money from the United States and not so much in the Cold War strategies the United States was pursuing. Second, democratic Latin Americans found the assumptions underlying the U.S. programs to be naive and flawed. They did not believe—correctly so, as it turned out—that democracy flowed inevitably from economic growth; instead, their argument was that first an honest and democratic government needed to be established that was oriented toward genuine development and that did not simply line its own pockets with U.S. aid. When, in the later 1960s, a wave of authoritarian regimes swept to power throughout Latin America and, despite the considerable economic growth of the decade, snuffed out a whole string of democratic governments, the argument for the inevitability of democracy flowing from economic development seemed awfully hollow.

As it turned out, both views were partially correct. The Latin Americans were correct in the short run: with a rash of dictatorial governments in power in the 1960s and 1970s, there was obviously nothing inevitable about democracy flowing automatically from economic growth in their region. But, in the long run, the U.S. economists who designed many of these programs were also partly correct. For, by the 1980s and 1990s, as Latin America bore the fruit of the earlier economic development (a larger middle class, more affluence and prosperity) *and* returned to democracy, the earlier correlations between development and democracy began to seem more valid.

Competing Economic Theories

Three main economic theories competed for prominence in Latin America during this period: Marxian, neoclassical, and import substitution industrialization. The Marxian theory of complete state ownership, or socialism, was popular among some intellectuals but seldom among the public; it was applied only in Cuba, for a short time and incompletely in Chile and Nicaragua, and in partial and greatly attenuated form in a handful of other countries. But now, with the collapse of socialism in Eastern Europe and the former Soviet Union and its failures in Cuba and Nicaragua, almost no one wants to follow that route anymore. Nowhere does Marxism-Leninism have the support of more than 3–4 percent of the population.

For a long time, the neoclassical theory, which emphasized capitalism and a laissez-faire, free-market system, was not very popular in Latin America either. Neoclassical economics was associated with economist Milton Freedman and the so-called Chicago School. But most Latin American economists, planners, and government officials favored a state-directed economic system in which *they*, and not the "unseen hand" postulated by Adam Smith, would be in charge. The first breakthrough for the neoclassical school occurred in Chile under Augusto Pinochet when a number of Chicago-trained economists put the free-market ideas into effect with spectacular success. But their success was ascribed also to the dictatorship of Pinochet, who kept labor in check and ruled with an iron hand, so that many doubted if that model could be applied elsewhere and in democratic contexts.

However, during the 1980s, the neoclassical school gained adherents. Part of this was due to the example and pressure of the Reagan administration in the United States, which also stressed privatization and free-market competition. Part of it was due to the failure of the two other alternatives in Latin America, the Marxist and the mercantilist. Part of it also was due to the spectacular success of the East Asian countries (Japan, South Korea, Taiwan, Hong Kong, Singapore), which similarly used capitalism to achieve phenomenal economic growth and which Latin America sought to imitate. Regardless of the precise reasons, by the late 1980s many Latin America countries were moving away from statism and toward privatization, free markets, and export-led growth. Moreover, using these strategies, they began to recover from their prolonged debt crisis and to move toward renewed, dynamic growth. Whether the neoclassical model would remain dominant, however, remained an open question.

The third strategy, which in fact was the main one during almost all of the period under review, was import substitution industrialization (ISI), which represented an updated, modernized version of mercantilism. Until the 1930s, Latin America had been overwhelmingly an agricultural and raw material–producing area that had to import almost all manufactured goods. Over time, however, the price the Latin American countries had to pay for manufactured goods began to outpace what they earned from their primary agricultural and raw material exports. Therefore, Latin America began to *industrialize* so that it could *substitute* its own manufactured goods for those previously *imported*—hence the unwieldy term *import substitution industrialization.*

It was the *state* that led and directed the process of industrialization, not the private sector. This was the period, under ISI, when the state's share of GNP began to reach the 50, 60, and even 70 percent range, as described in Chapter 7. And, it must be noted, that from the 1940s through the 1960s, the ISI strategy was quite successful. It was not as successful as the then–West German economic miracle or those of the East Asian "tigers," but it was not that far behind. Under ISI, several Latin American countries, especially Brazil, Venezuela, and Mexico, achieved growth rates of 5–7 percent per year and even higher in some years. Several other countries moved out of the stage of underdevelopment and toward the status of being NICs—Newly Industrialized Countries.

Eventually, the ISI strategy outlived its usefulness. The quadrupling of oil prices in the 1970s (Latin America imports most of its oil), the debt crisis of the 1980s, and the incompetence of many of Latin America's military regimes during this period all helped kill it. But the main factor was that, while ISI was appropriate at an early stage of economic development—when a state-directed economic system was useful and necessary—at a later, more developed stage a more complex, less bureaucratized, less statist, more free-market, and more export-led strategy was necessary. That is what the Chicago School provided.

For a time in the late 1980s and early 1990s, the free-market, export-led strategy seemed to be becoming dominant and produced major successes in Argentina, Chile, Mexico, and other countries. However, many Latin Americans still preferred a state-run, neomercantilist strategy; and when the string of Republican, free-market-oriented administrations in the United States came to an end in 1992, these Latin Americans felt that the pressure to privatize was off and that they could return to the centrally planned systems of the past. Hence, there seemed to be some slippage away from the free-market strategy that had seemed so promising for Latin America. Doubtless the free-market versus neomercantilist debate will continue into the future.

Within these various economic development strategies, the focus of attention of the major international aid donors also shifted over time. In the 1960s, the emphasis was on large infrastructure projects—roads, dams, port facilities, highways, heavy industry—that would provide a foundation on which future economic growth could be based. In the 1970s, however, the emphasis shifted to basic human needs: efforts to feed and care for people at more elementary levels. By the 1980s and 1990s, foreign aid to the Latin America region began to dry up, and what assistance there was went mainly to help Latin America out of its debt doldrums or else to such crisis countries as El Salvador and Nicaragua. By the time of President Bush's Enterprise for the Americas Initiative (EAI), there was very little assistance money left, and the emphasis was chiefly on trade, not aid. Under President Clinton, the focus shifted again to population and environmental issues, but with very little money to carry out these programs.

Policies Versus Results

Over the long run, these shifts in emphasis on the part of the big donors and their up-again, down-again program focus, which often looked confusing and disorganized at the time, probably did not matter all that much. The important thing is that, whatever the program, it got some sorely needed money flowing into the Latin American economies. Probably the assistance programs would have been just as effective had the United States dropped the money randomly from helicopters. That the agrarian reform and other programs that the United States pushed did not always produce their intended consequences turned out, in the end, not to have made that much difference. It mattered, but not too much, for the main accomplishment was that the flow of dollars for all these programs helped stimulate economic growth. It was the overall growth that was important, and not so much the specific programs, because with the stimulus, the pump priming, provided by this growth, Latin America could pull out of underdevelopment and move toward self-sustained modernization. In that sense, the U.S. aid program could be considered something of a success—even if its specific programs were not always so.

The Debt Crisis

The great debt crisis of the 1980s is now winding down, but for a time it threatened to bring down a variety of banks, a number of Latin American governments, and potentially the entire international financial system. The debt crisis provides an example, unlike a number of those policy issues previously discussed, of close cooperation between the United States and Latin America—but not without tensions here, too—to solve the problem.

The debt crisis began in 1982 with Mexico's admission that it could not pay its foreign debts, a tacit admission of national bankruptcy. Most of the other Latin American countries were facing a similar situation. The total

Latin American debt owed to foreign lenders was $400 billion and increasing by about $40 *billion* annually. The debt was unpaid and unpayable.

The origins of the debt crisis lay in the 1970s. Because of the quadrupling of oil prices during that decade, the oil-producing countries of the Middle East had an abundance of dollars ("petrodollars"), which they were depositing in U.S. banks. The banks, therefore, had surplus capital that they were eager to loan out—in many cases pushing it in the direction of Latin American governments whose credit worthiness had not been carefully checked. The Latin American governments, in turn, were eager to borrow to pay for expensive construction and social programs, for military hardware, and in some cases for outright graft. The U.S. government encouraged these private loans as a substitute for public foreign aid, which was then declining. All parties to this arrangement believed it could go on indefinitely because there would presumably be an endless supply of petrodollars and Latin America could therefore always contract new loans to pay off the old ones.

But the U.S. recession of 1979–82, which quickly became a global recession, in conjunction with the glut and hence declining price of oil, ruined this rosy scenario. There were fewer petrodollars for new loans, the United States imported less, Latin America could not export its products as these markets dried up, and therefore it did not have the earnings to pay back its earlier debts. In 1982–83, because of the sheer size of these unpayable loans, the world financial system teetered on the verge of collapse.

The issue was immensely complicated by the fact that no one could admit publicly that there was a problem of such severe dimensions. The banks could not admit to their stockholders that they had all these uncollectible loans on their books because the banks themselves might go under. The Latin American governments could not admit that they were broke because they would then not be eligible for any future loans and their assets abroad (national airlines and so on) might be seized. The U.S. government could not admit the severity of the problem because it would be obliged to bail out both the banks and Latin America at the U.S. taxpayers' expense—clearly politically unacceptable.

This was a real conundrum. What to do? The stakes were very large: the banks, Latin America, the international financial system, and the U.S. treasury. All could go under.

Basically, there were three alternatives. One was to treat the issue as a purely private matter between the banks and the Latin American governments. But the stakes were too high for that purely laissez-faire approach—although, to calm public nerves, the United States did try to keep the issue low-key. A second option was for the U.S. government to pay off, forgive, and itself absorb the Latin American debt—but that was deemed politically unacceptable since voters would object strenuously. A third approach was ad hoc: help some of the debtors in real emergency, but meanwhile hope that the world economy recovered sufficiently so that the banks and the Latin American countries could begin to recover on their own.

The United States opted for the third approach, while Latin America naturally favored the second: debt forgiveness. The United States provided emergency loans to Mexico to help it get through the immediate crisis of 1982. But the next year, Brazil, which had an even larger foreign debt than Mexico's, similarly threatened to go under, and so the United States again provided emergency relief. By then, however, Peru, Bolivia, and several other countries were in *de facto* bankruptcy; the United States could not bail out all of them. The ad hoc option seemed to be failing. Something more was needed.

The "Baker Plan," named after then-U.S. Treasury secretary, James Baker, emerged from this realization that "ad hoc-ism" was not enough but that a complete bailout of Latin America at U.S. taxpayers' expense was politically unacceptable. Baker proposed a "menu" approach that included a number of in-between solutions: programs to lure U.S. private investment to Latin America with U.S. government guarantees so that the region could begin to *grow* out of its debt problems; proposals to U.S. banks to roll over and renegotiate their Latin American loans indefinitely rather than write them off as uncollectible; pressures on Latin American governments to reform and streamline their internal economies; pressures on U.S. and international lending agencies to allow aid money to be used for debt payments; tax benefits for the banks if they would forgive some of the loans; the ending of subsidies and the imposition of austerity measures in Latin America; and so on.

Using these means, the debt problem in Latin America was not solved in any final way, but it did gradually begin to look less dangerous. At the least, the threat that the banks, Latin America, the U.S. Treasury, and the international financial system would all go belly-up was alleviated. But Baker's proposals proved after a while to be insufficient, and hence some additional steps were taken, called the "Brady Plan" after Baker's successor Nicholas Brady. The Brady corollaries encouraged the banks to replace some of their old and uncollectible Latin American debt with new loans that would be guaranteed by the U.S. government, helped facilitate the process by which the banks could sell their debt holdings on the open market (for below face value, but that was better than zero return), provided massive infusions of U.S. funds to the World Bank, the IMF, and the Inter-American Development Bank so that they could bail out Latin America without it appearing to U.S. taxpayers that they were doing so, and even forgave some debts outright.

By these means and others, the debt began to seem less troublesome. Over a five-year span, most of the banks had managed to extract themselves from the worst aspects of the crisis by carefully managing and unloading their Latin American loans while rolling up large profits in other sectors. Most Latin American governments still had debt hangovers, but not so severe as before: they had similarly managed to extract themselves from the worst aspects of the crisis, had not had to declare bankruptcy, and by the end of the 1980s were beginning to show positive economic growth again. The United States also extracted itself from this crisis: it brokered the deals between the banks and Latin America, provided much-needed assistance when necessary, and helped bail out the other parties without the taxpayers discovering the sleight of hand. By these smoke-and-mirrors measures, the debt crisis was contained.

Some Latin American countries are still plagued by debt problems and must continue to follow austerity programs (wage freezes, reduction of the bureaucracy, elimination of perks, price rises for basic goods, fewer imports) imposed by the IMF and other lending agencies. In these countries, the debt continues to be a hardship. But most countries of the area have broken out of the grip of the "lost decade" of the 1980s and have again moved in the 1990s toward renewed and sustained economic growth. In fact, quite a number of the Latin American economies are really taking off. Through an elaborate shell game, the banks, Latin America, and the United States have now largely put the debt issue behind them.

Equity and Social Programs

During the economically difficult 1980s, most Latin American countries did not pay serious attention to equity or social issues. *Equity* refers to how the wealth is divided, or who gets what share. In difficult economic times, that concern is usually subordinated to the issue of generating economic growth and raising the GNP. Unless there is growth and development, in the minds of most political leaders it makes little sense to talk of equity; then, all one is doing is redistributing the poverty. But now that Latin America in the 1990s is again on the road to economic growth, equity and social justice issues are being talked about again.

Social conditions in many countries are still at abysmal levels. Poverty and illiteracy are still too widespread. The housing, water supplies, electrification, and sanitary conditions in many urban slums are unacceptable. Disease and malnutrition stalk the young and old especially. In too many countries there are children with bloated bellies, persons with missing or malformed limbs from lack of medical care, persons debilitated or dying from such treatable diseases as malaria, tuberculosis, dysentery, and cholera. In Brazil, the problem of unwanted and abandoned children living precariously in the streets where they are preyed upon or often murdered has reached epidemic proportions.

But Brazil is hardly alone in this regard. In many countries, the poverty and disease are mind-numbing. This may be the strongest impression that visitors from the First World of modern industrial states have when they encounter the Third World, including parts of Latin America. The poverty, disease, and fetid conditions in some countries remind one of the images we see of Ethiopia, Somalia, Bangladesh, or the Sudan. Food riots, protests, looting, and rising crime and violence are adding to the political tensions in Argentina, Venezuela, Peru, the Dominican Republic, and other countries. It is these conditions, often made worse by the debt crisis and economic downturn of the 1980s, that have prompted renewed attention in Latin America to equity issues.

And yet, some perspective is necessary. Almost nowhere in Latin America, except Haiti and perhaps one or two other, especially troubled areas, do we see the same nationwide levels of poverty, malnutrition, or disease that we see in Somalia or Bangladesh. Recall that Latin America consists chiefly of transitional economies on the way to modernization. There are many problems, to be sure. But for the most part in Latin America, what we are seeing at present are *pockets of poverty*, not societywide poverty. Poverty may afflict 20, 40, or in the worst cases, 60 percent of the population; but it is no longer 80–90 percent as in the poorest countries of Africa or Asia.

The poor in Latin America are mainly people who got left behind as modernization has proceeded. The percentage of these is certainly too high by Western standards. But that is not to imply that these are hopeless countries that have made no economic progress at all. Rather, these are countries that have achieved some truly miraculous economic growth in the last forty years. The situation is reminiscent of that portrayed by Charles Dickens during Great Britain's great surge to industrialization in the nineteenth century. Some people were left behind and victimized by the often-cruel process, but more people benefited than suffered in the long term—and eventually even the sufferers were brought along through social welfare policies.

That is precisely the situation that Latin America is in today. In countries undergoing rapid industrialization and economic development, some people get left behind, often cruelly. But that is quite different from the condition in other, far-worse-off Third World countries where there is no economic development at all. And to say there are pockets of poverty, even big pockets in some cases, is far different from saying the country is characterized by societywide poverty. Poverty is unacceptable in any form and in any country, but we still need to distinguish between levels and types of poverty. Surely a poverty rate of 30 or 50 percent is less catastrophic than a poverty rate of 80–90 percent.

That is the issue that most Latin American governments are being called upon to address. Now that economic growth has resumed after the dismal 1980s and new investment funds are again flowing in, how should the continuing problem of poverty be addressed? What is the proper balance of funds to be reinvested in the programs that are necessary to continue modernization versus the funds to be funneled into social programs to help the poor? These are often difficult choices; they involve trade-offs between two desirable goals. Clearly, however, in the future Latin American leaders will be wrestling with this issue as they have not always done in the past. In Venezuela, Argentina, Brazil, Mexico, Peru, and other countries, the social agenda has become an explosive one, threatening to topple or undermine elected governments unless something is done about it. Because of this threat, and the perceived need to switch from emphasis on economic development exclusively to one in which development and social justice are pursued together, we can expect to see considerably more attention in Latin America to issues of poverty, illiteracy, and other social problems.

The Environment

Environmental concerns are a relatively new issue in Latin America. The *environment* is one of the so-called new-agenda items in U.S. foreign policy after the Cold War—along with human rights, democracy, immigration, drugs, and hunger.

The push for policies on the environment has come chiefly from the United States and from such international groups as Greenpeace. In this sense, the environmental issue is very much like agrarian reform or family planning—that is, initiated from the outside. The environmental issue in Latin America has not, generally, been locally generated; rather, the pressure has come mainly from the international actors. It is not that Latin America is against measures to preserve the environment, but the issue has not been a high priority there. The real impetus to programs on behalf of the environment has come from countries and organizations that are already developed, industrialized, and affluent.

But that is precisely the problem from Latin America's point of view. Latin America argues that it is fine for rich, already-industrialized nations like the United States to elevate environmental concerns to major proportions. But for poorer nations such as those in Latin America, too-strict environmental controls and regulation will hinder their development. Such controls will keep Latin America from developing the heavy industry and factories that are essential to jobs and economic growth. The Latin Americans argue that environmental concerns are the product of affluent, already-developed countries that can well afford them, but for Latin Americans, development and growth must take priority over the environment. For example, Brazil, Mexico, and other Latin American countries used to blatantly advertise in the U.S. media: "Send us your polluting industries; if environmental regulations become too strict in the United States, come to our country." In other words, Latin America sees development and the environment as competing issues and argues that developing nations must focus first on growth and only later on the environment.

In addition, there are nationalistic concerns. The Latin Americans say to the United States: "Who are you, foreigners, who have been polluting and despoiling the earth for centuries, to tell *us* what we should do with our forests, minerals, and waterways? This is a national matter, not one with which international groups should be concerned." To the Latin Americans, the issue of sovereignty is central. They often think the United States and the environmental groups are infringing on *their* right to develop *their* countries as they please. Latin America tends to see the issue in nationalistic terms, not from the viewpoint of a global environmental agenda. "The earth may be all one ecosystem," they concede, "but preserving it as is means you in the already-developed world will always remain rich while we are condemned to perpetual poverty." That is intolerable. It also explains why public defenders of the environment in Latin America, such as Brazil's Chico Mendes, are sometimes thoroughly disliked in their own countries (Mendes was actually killed, but by large landowners) even while they are hailed as heroes by foreign environmentalists.

Can there be a meeting of the minds on this issue? Yes, but not without great difficulty—and probably in ways that are similar to Latin America's earlier "compliance" with agrarian reform and family planning initiatives, which were similarly pushed on the area from the outside. The United States will pressure Latin America on environmental concerns. The U.S. government and foreign private groups will push Brazil to stop burning the Amazon rain forest, Mexico to clean up its environment, and so on. These countries will complain about how hard it is for them to do that, so the United States and the environmental groups will "sweeten the pie" by forgiving their debts or promising them aid. Eventually, Latin America will adopt legislation to protect the environment because having such laws in place will be a condition for receiving foreign aid. But then most Latin American countries will either ignore the laws on the books, fail to implement them completely, or drag their feet. The process and response will be similar to those of the Spanish viceroys in colonial Latin America when they received inconvenient or inappropriate royal directives from the mother country: "I obey but I do not implement." Meanwhile, a handful of countries like Costa Rica will carry out a real, effective environmental program.

What kind of public policy process and outcome is this? Actually, it's not as bad as it sounds. It represents a compromise between U.S. and Latin American differences over this issue, without either one having to back down or lose face. It enables all sides to come away happy: the United States gets environmental protection laws officially approved in Latin America, while Latin America qualifies for much-needed aid. And, in the process, some progress in the care of the environment will be made because everyone will be more conscious of the issues, some enforcement mechanisms will be in place, and Latin America will have to do *something* to comply. Brazil will not stop burning the rain forest and Mexico will not stop polluting right away. But *something* will be done—limited at first and more later. Perhaps that is as much as we can realistically expect for now. In any case, that is how the public policy process works in Latin America, particularly in those areas such as agrarian reform, family planning, and the environment, where international as well as domestic forces are involved.

A Changed Latin America?

The public policy process in Latin America, as portrayed in this chapter, is often murky. It frequently produces unexpected results and unanticipated consequences. The process often proceeds by fits and starts. Smoke, mirrors, and subterfuge abound. Hypocrisy and dissembling are common. Examining the operations of these political systems, one could easily and understandably come away with a quite cynical view.

Such cynicism would not be justified, however. First, cynicism must be distinguished from realism and, as described above, this is how the Latin American policy process actually does work. Second, if one examines Latin America closely, the results achieved over the last thirty years—even within this "murky" political process—have been remarkable, and the changes have been nothing short of phenomenal. Let us briefly review the record of accomplishments.

In 1960, Latin America was 70 percent illiterate; today it is 70 percent literate. In 1960, only 2 percent of the college-aged students attended universities; today it is 12 percent. In 1960, Latin America was 70 percent rural; now it is 70 percent urban. In 1960, life expectancy throughout Latin America was in the low 60s; since then it has risen into the 70s—close to that of the United States. In 1960, Latin America's per capital income per year was about $340; today it is about $1400—a four-fold increase! In this thirty-year period, Latin America has rapidly industrialized, become a services and manufacturing area, and diversified away from its earlier heavy reliance on agriculture and other primary products. Almost all households now have radio sets, and most have television sets as well. The population is now healthier than ever before, as well as better fed, better housed, better educated, and more prosperous. The middle class has grown enormously; the range of government institutions has also swelled to keep pace with the new demands. Political parties and interest associations have emerged to fill the historical institutional void. The conditions of democracy and human rights are better than ever before. The record of accomplishment is really quite remarkable.

All this is not to minimize the problems that continue to exist: the disease, the poverty, the squalor, the slums, the malnutrition, and so on. But remember, these are no longer society- or culturewide problems; rather, they are increasingly confined to pockets of the population. The conditions are still horrible in some regions and countries, although by now most countries and more and more people are making impressive progress. Our assessments, therefore, should focus not just on the part of the glass that remains half (or 30 percent) empty but on the part that is half (or up to 70 percent) full.

Several important conclusions may be drawn from the preceding analysis. The first is that Latin America has truly made impressive progress on many policy fronts since the 1950s. The second is that this process has rarely conformed to neat or rational formulas of how public policy ought to unfold; rather, it has been disjointed, sporadic, and messy. Third, the policy has not been the result of very much central state planning; instead, it has taken place countless times at the individual level when people determined that they could take charge of their lives and improve themselves. As the old Brazilian adage puts it, "The country develops at night while the government sleeps." And finally, let us emphasize that while some of the programs pursued were sometimes wrongheaded (we have explored several of these in this chapter), the fact that they brought investment dollars and technical expertise into the region meant that countries developed even if the individual programs sometimes went astray.

11

✦

Latin America in the World Arena

Throughout its history, Latin America has been isolated from the outside world, and the various countries of the area isolated from one another. Latin America has long been considered to lie outside the mainstream of modern, Western civilization. We indicated earlier that during the colonial era the region was bypassed by all the great currents that we associate with the making of the modern world: the Enlightenment, the Industrial Revolution, the scientific revolution, the Protestant Reformation and the movement toward religious tolerance and pluralism, the trend away from feudalism and toward capitalism, and the trend toward liberal, representative, limited government. Even after independence and on into the nineteenth century, the German philosopher Hegel argued that Latin America had experienced no development and therefore had "no history," while Marx similarly portrayed the area negatively as dominated by fatalism and awaiting the great motor of capitalism to start up. Until about 1850, Latin America's trade, diplomatic relations, and contact in general with the outside world and its influences were extremely limited.

Nor did the Latin American countries have much contact with one another. Separated by vast distances, impenetrable jungles, and towering mountain ranges, the countries of the area lived in not-so-splendid isolation. Before the construction of modern roads and communication networks and the advent of jet travel, there was almost no commerce, tourism, or interchange among the Latin American countries. Even after modern communication systems began to develop, the focus was still on contacts with or through the United States or Europe, not directly with each other. For example, a simple telephone call across the estuary of the Rio de la Plata could not be made directly from Argentina to Uruguay; instead, the call had to be routed from Buenos Aires to New York and then all the way down to Montevideo again. That is symptomatic of the lack of direct contact between the Latin American countries.

Now all this is changing very rapidly. Latin America has opened up to the outside world. International cultural influences—rock music, blue jeans, Coca-Cola, consumerism, democracy, human rights—are all having a profound impact on the area. Latin America's ties with the outside world—trade, tourism, diplomatic relations—are also expanding greatly. It is not just the United States but also Western Europe, Japan, China, and the Middle Eastern countries that have forged new trading, diplomatic, and political relations with the area, helping to break down its traditional isolation. At the same time, the contacts among the Latin American countries themselves, in the form of diplomatic arrangements, economic integration efforts, and tourism, are also greatly expanding. Latin America is rapidly becoming a part of the *modern, interdependent* world.

European Interlopers in the Nineteenth Century

During the long, three-hundred-year history of Spanish and Portuguese colonialism in Latin America, the two mother countries tried to maintain a monopoly on all trade with the area and to keep other foreign powers out. They wanted to keep Latin America all to themselves—unlike the situation in Asia and Africa where the early Spanish and Portuguese colonial presence was largely supplanted by British, Dutch, French, and German influences.

In their monopolistic ambitions, Spain and Portugal were remarkably successful. The Dutch invaded northeast Brazil and held it for thirty years; they also took some small Caribbean islands and what is now Suriname on the South American mainland. The French seized Haiti, French Guiana, and several small islands in the Caribbean; and the British captured Jamaica, some small islands, and what were then seen as two worthless enclaves on the mainland: Belize and British Guiana. British, Dutch, and French pirates were also active in the Caribbean, bombarding Havana, Santo Domingo, and Panama and seeking to capture the Spanish treasure ships carrying gold and silver back to Spain. But, by and large, the Spaniards and Portuguese were able to maintain their monopoly on trade to and from Latin America and to bar foreign interlopers from virtually all of South and Central America. (Popular books such as *Robinson Crusoe* and *Treasure Island*, as well as many TV shows dealing with pirates and buccaneers, took place in this time and setting.)

During Latin America's wars for independence in the early nineteenth century, the British were active in aiding the independence forces in the hope of gaining access to the ports and trade long denied it by the Spanish and Portuguese colonial monopolies. Great Britain was the foremost naval and imperial power of the time, and hence it is no accident that most of the early banks, railroads, port facilities, and import-export houses in many of the new Latin American republics were built with British capital and for the profit of British investors. Great Britain also sought territorial aggrandizement in British Guiana and Belize and along the Caribbean Coast of Central America from Guatemala to Panama.

While Great Britain was the first major colonial power in Latin America after independence, other nineteenth-century European imperialists also sought conquest and new colonies in the area. During the 1860s, for example, France occupied Mexico for a time but was eventually driven out by Mexican forces. Spain, the former colonial power, not only held on to Cuba and Puerto Rico until 1898 but also sought, unsuccessfully, to reincorporate some of its former colonies into its domain. The Dutch were more interested in trade than in acquiring new colonies, but they did hang on to their earlier possessions. Germany, while not seeking new colonies as it had in Africa, established sizable German immigrant communities in Argentina, Brazil, Bolivia, Chile, Colombia, Cuba, and Mexico, and later sought to use these German-speaking colonies to advance its interests during World Wars I and II.

The United States, still a small and weak power in the early- to mid-nineteenth century, was not a major actor in Latin America during this period. The United States had expressed sympathy for the Latin American independence movements but did little officially to assist them. In 1823, President James Monroe issued the famous doctrine that bears his name, urging the European powers to keep their hands off the new Latin American republics; but at this stage, the United States was unable to back up its moral injunctions with military force. The United States acquired Florida from Spain by treaty and took Texas and the Southwest from Mexico by force, but these acquisitions were more a part of the continental expansion of the United States, of "manifest destiny," than they were of anything resembling a U.S. foreign policy in Latin America. There were also occasional incursions into the Caribbean and Central America by private U.S. filibusters, land speculators, and would-be acquirers of new slave states for the pre–Civil War Confederacy; but these were often equivalent to comic operas—although colorful and sometimes tragic. Until after the Civil War, the United States simply was too weak militarily as a nation and Latin America too unstable and disorganized for there to be much in the way of relations between the two.

Nor did the new Latin American nations during the early nineteenth century have much contact with one another. They were still isolated, couldn't afford the costs of maintaining very many embassies abroad, and had little trade or commerce with their neighbors. The small Central American countries, for example, had relations with one another and Mexico, and that was about it. Argentina, Brazil, Chile, Colombia, Peru, and Venezuela usually had some form of relations with one another, but not usually with the smaller countries (unless they were next-door neighbors) in the region. Most of the Latin American countries tried to have a representative in the major capitals: Washington, London, Paris, Berlin, and Madrid; relations with other areas or countries were either nonexistent or carried out irregularly and on a part-time basis by itinerant businessmen. In sum, the nineteenth century was not a time when Latin America had a large number of external relations or played a significant international role.

The U.S. Role

The United States does not have entirely clean hands in its dealings with Latin America. During the last hundred years, the United States repeatedly intervened in the area, exploited it, sought arrogantly to re-create Latin America in its image, and often ran roughshod over Latin American institutions and sensitivities. On the other hand, the United States has seldom been as exploitive as other colonial powers and has often made positive and helpful contributions to Latin America. The picture is not wholly pretty, but it is not entirely bleak either.

Serious U.S. interest in Latin America began after the Civil War, corresponding to domestic population increases, the gradual settling of the western territories, industrialization, and emergence as a world military power. During the 1870s, there was increased U.S. investment in Central America and the Caribbean, and by the 1880s the United States was beginning to supplant Great Britain as the dominant investor and trading partner in the circum-Caribbean—even though Britain's economically dominant position in South America continued until World War II. At several points in the 1880s and early 1890s, the United States flexed its economic and military muscle in Latin America, but the turning point was the Spanish-American War of 1898. In defeating Spain, the United States secured control of Puerto Rico, established a protectorate over Cuba, and emerged as the prevailing economic and military power in the region. Latin America's fears and sometimes loathing of the United States, and its efforts to try to establish a diplomatic counterweight to U.S. power, increased correspondingly.

In the early decades of the twentieth century, the United States expanded its economic influence, especially in Central America and the Caribbean (the policy was baptized "dollar diplomacy"), while simultaneously increasing its political, diplomatic, and military presence. In 1902, the United States assisted Panama in securing its independence from Colombia so that it could have a compliant country through which to build and administer the Panama Canal. Between 1905 and 1925, the United States militarily occupied the following countries (some more than once): Cuba, Haiti, the Dominican Republic, Panama, and Nicaragua. In Mexico, the United States intervened militarily on several occasions but recognized that Mexico was too large to occupy. During a number of these military occupations, United States' forces built roads and made other improvements, introduced baseball and chewing gum, and sought—arrogantly—to rebuild these countries in the U.S. mold. By the time of World War I, with the United States occupying half the countries of the region, the Caribbean had become an American lake—"our backyard."

The motives for these repeated armed interventions were several. First, the United States was beginning to acquire a considerable economic stake (sugar, banks, minerals, utilities, fruit plantations) in the area and wanted to protect its interests. Second, the United States had always considered itself a special nation with a higher, noble, and idealistic purpose: when President Woodrow Wilson proclaimed that he wished to "make the world [including the Latin American part of it] safe for democracy," we should not doubt that he was sincere.

But the major reason was strategic. On east and west, the United States is protected from any potential enemies by vast oceans, and to the north lies friendly Canada. But to the south (the "soft underbelly," as it was referred to in the strategic literature of the time) lay small, weak, underdeveloped nations that appeared to be chronically unstable. It was not that any of these small countries posed a direct threat to the United States. Rather, the fear was that the weakness and instability of these countries would enable a larger power (France, Spain, Great Britain in the nineteenth century; Germany during World Wars I and II; the Soviet Union during the Cold War) to move in, take advantage of the situation, and establish bases from which to threaten the United States. That is what the Soviet Union did in Cuba in 1962 when it based missiles aimed at the United States, and what the U.S. government feared *might* happen in Nicaragua and El Salvador in the 1980s.

Most of the U.S. military interventions of the early part of the twentieth century ended in the 1920s under Presidents Calvin Coolidge and Herbert Hoover. The earlier German threat appeared to be over, and the U.S. public had tired of the role of Caribbean policeman. This epoch in U.S. diplomatic history came to an end definitively under President Franklin Roosevelt's "good neighbor" policy. Roosevelt promised not to intervene in Latin America; unfortunately, in some ways, nonintervention was as destructive as intervention because it meant the United States would not intervene on human rights grounds against such brutal dictators as Rafael Trujillo in the Dominican Republic, Anastasio Somoza in Nicaragua, and Fulgencio Batista in

Cuba. In addition, the United States *did* intervene during World War II to neutralize the sizable German colonies in Latin America and prevent them from becoming a "fifth column" to advance German interests against the United States, but this took the form of forceful or (occasionally) coercive diplomacy rather than military intervention.

For a short time after World War II, before the Cold War began in earnest, the United States sought to advance a liberal trade agenda in Latin America of open markets and also took steps to push some dictators aside and establish democracy. But these efforts proved short-lived once the Cold War began. In 1954, the United States intervened in Guatemala to oust a leftist regime that had communist support and communists in the government—thereby precipitating wild and violent swings of the Guatemalan governmental pendulum that continued for over thirty years. In 1959–61, after Fidel Castro in Cuba had declared himself a Marxist-Leninist, broken with the United States, and allied himself with the Soviet Union, the United States tried various ways to oust that regime and maintained an economic stranglehold of the island that also continued for over thirty years.

During the 1960s, the U.S. role was both positive and negative. The negative part was to prevent any "second Cubas" (Marxist-Leninist regimes allied with the Soviet Union, allowing the Soviets to use their territory for military bases) at almost any costs. To that end the United States intervened in the Dominican Republic in 1965, in Chile in 1970–73, in Central America beginning in 1979, and in Grenada in 1983. The positive part was the Alliance for Progress, the Peace Corps, and a host of U.S. assistance programs launched in the 1960s. The United States realized it could not intervene militarily every time communism raised its head; far better to provide assistance to Latin America that would make the countries of the area more economically developed, middle class, socially just, and democratic. That way, they would be able to resist communism by themselves; furthermore, by becoming more developed, the conditions would be removed that cause communism to take root and grow in the first place.

The results of these programs—as we saw in the previous chapter—were terribly mixed, particularly in the short run. Just the fact of pouring in all this assistance money undoubtedly helped Latin America's economic development. But many of the programs were based on the wrong or inappropriate models; took insufficient account of Latin American culture, politics, and sociology; went off in wrong directions; and produced a host of unhappy and unanticipated consequences. For example, by helping to mobilize lower class groups in Latin America, the United States severely frightened the upper classes and the military, which staged a series of coups beginning in the 1960s. Hence, instead of producing moderate, democratic, middle-of-the-road regimes, the U.S. policies inadvertently helped produce right-wing authoritarianism, which polarized the Latin American countries and precipitated a new wave of guerrilla movements and revolutions (El Salvador, Nicaragua)—precisely what the U.S. programs had been designed to prevent.

During the forty years of the Cold War in Latin America, U.S. policy was mainly reactive and defensive. It was aimed at containing communism: keeping it from emerging stronger or coming to power in countries where communism was weak, and keeping it from spreading from countries like Cuba where it was already established. U.S. policy may also be characterized as *derivative*: the main focus was the Cold War with the Soviet Union. The United States was chiefly interested in Latin America only when and to the extent that the Cold War came to Latin America's shores. Several other corollaries flowed from this overwhelming Cold War focus: the United States largely ignored Latin America unless there was a Cold War issue involved; it paid insufficient attention to democracy and human rights issues; it never fashioned a mature, long-term policy for the region; and it focused almost exclusively on the small Central American/Caribbean countries to the detriment of relations with the larger, richer, more important countries of South America.

Latin America's reaction to the overriding U.S. emphasis on Cold War issues was a mixed one. On the one hand, many Latin Americans shared the United States' dislike and suspicion of communism; on the other, many thought the United States had exaggerated the dangers and/or had gone about pursuing its anticommunist strategies by inappropriate means. But the United States was big and powerful, and the Latin American countries generally smaller and much weaker, so they often had no choice but to go along with U.S. policies. In some, this produced anger, bitterness, and anti-Americanism. But the cleverer Latin Americans often paid lip service to or went along with U.S. policies at some levels while pursuing their own agendas at others. In such agencies as the Organization of American States and other bodies where Latin American interests were represented, there was often a tug-of-war between the need to follow the U.S. lead and the desire to strike off in independent directions.

During the 1980s and on into the 1990s, U.S. policy began gradually to produce better fruit. The United States returned to an emphasis on democracy and human rights, not just on idealist grounds but as the best way to protect its interest in stability and development. In addition, all the economic aid poured in over the preceding two decades began, finally, to show positive results in the form of a larger middle class, greater affluence, and more people with a stake in the system. Latin America moved, and in several key cases the United States pushed, away from authoritarianism and toward democracy. The United States and Latin America gradually overcame the debilitating debt crisis of the 1980s and moved on to an agenda emphasizing trade, development, and greater mutual consultation. Central America (El Salvador and Nicaragua) was a divisive, polarizing issue for a time; but as these regional issues moved toward resolution in the late 1980s, the debate over them became less frenetic as well.

The End of the Cold War and the U.S. Policy Dilemma

Since the late 1940s, it is fair to say, U.S. foreign policy—including in Latin America—was driven almost exclusively by Cold War considerations. That meant excluding the Soviets and their proxies from establishing any toeholds in the Western Hemisphere or, as in the case of Cuba, containing them and keeping them from expanding once they were established. In short, the United States was interested in Latin America—stripping away all the romantic reasons and justifications frequently offered—simply because the Soviets were interested in Latin America.

But now, with the end of the Cold War and the Soviet Union, Russia has almost no interest in Latin America. From the Russian point of view, Latin America is far away, Russia has no strategic interests there, and it has very little trade or tourism with the area. Russia is even giving up its support of, pulling out its troops from, and terminating its economic assistance to Cuba, its longtime ally and satellite in the Americas. The key question arising out of the end of the Cold War, therefore, is, if the Russians aren't interested in Latin America and their presence was the chief reason for U.S. interest there, then without the Russians why should the United States show any continuing interest in the area?

The logic behind this argument is compelling, at least superficially. During the Cold War, there were legitimate reasons for the United States to be concerned about a Marxist-Leninist regime in Cuba, for example, allied to the Soviet Union, brimming with missiles aimed at the United States, and being used as a military and political base to destabilize regimes throughout Latin America friendly to the United States. It was not Cuba's Marxism that was a problem, but rather the fact of all that Soviet presence and threat directed at the United States. Now, however, there is no significant Russian threat or presence. So, in today's circumstances, absent the Russians, if some obscure country in Latin America wants to "go Marxist," why would the United States care, let alone send in the Marines? With no threat from anywhere in the area, what difference should Latin America make to the United States? If Latin American politicians now run to U.S. embassies abroad or to Washington—as they've often done in the past—and say, "You must help us or the communists will take over," the U.S. response now might be: "Well, that's too bad. We're sorry if you become communist. But since we're no longer threatened by the Cold War or anything that happens in your country, you're on your own. There is no *vital* or *compelling* reason for us to help you, bail you out, or come to your defense." Is this the logic that should now apply?

This is tough logic to overcome, but it does not present the whole picture. There are many reasons why the United States should retain an interest in Latin America, even after the Cold War:

1. **Drugs**. Illegal drugs have become a major foreign policy issue; most of the drugs used in the United States come from Latin America.

2. **Military/strategic considerations**. While the Cold War is over, the United States still has ongoing strategic interests in Latin America: the post-Castro transition in Cuba, stability in Mexico, Panama and the Canal, continuing commitments in El Salvador and Nicaragua, drugs and insurgency (the notorious and bloody *Sendero Luminoso*) of Peru, potential political instability in Brazil and Venezuela, arms control, and nuclear nonproliferation (mainly affecting Argentina and Brazil). Not all of the United States' strategic concerns ended with the Cold War.

3. **Democracy and human rights**. Democracy and human rights are legitimate U.S. foreign policy concerns. But not only are democracy and human rights *morally good*, but a policy in favor of them also promotes U.S. *interests*. For example, democratic regimes do not start wars, they do not send guerrillas into other countries, they do not try to destabilize their neighbors, and they are better for trade and overall relations. In addition, support of democracy and human rights gives U.S. foreign policy a unifying purpose.

4. **The new agenda**. With the Cold War now over, a host of new foreign policy issues have come to the fore: immigration, drugs, pollution and the environment, democracy, human rights, humanitarian aid (Haiti), ecology (the Amazon rain forest), and so on. For one reason or another, almost all of these new issues of interdependency resonate most strongly in Latin America.

5. **Interdependence**. The United States is now interdependent (we need them almost as much as they need us) with Latin America in a great variety of ways—all of the issues listed above plus water rights, labor supplies, trade, investments, diplomacy, and more. It used to be we studied U.S. policy *toward* Latin America; now we need to look more at the complex interrelations *between* us.

6. **Oil**. Oil is the lifeblood of modern, industrial society and absolutely essential to the continued health of the U.S. economy. Increasingly, the United States imports petroleum and natural gas from Mexico and Venezuela. No more needs to be said on this subject, whose importance is self-evident.

7. **Mexico**. Mexico is a case all by itself; along with Japan, Russia, and Germany, Mexico may be one of the most important countries in the world as far as the United States is concerned. Mexico is interdependent with the United States for all of the reasons given earlier; it is also the focus of all the new-agenda issues: drugs, immigration, pollution, and so on. Mexico is, additionally, the United States' third-largest trading partner, and its economy will become increasingly tied into ours as the North American free trade area comes into existence. In addition, Mexico is *the last country in the world* the United States would want to see destabilized since even the slightest tremor of either economic or political instability will send tens of millions of Mexicans fleeing toward the porous U.S. border, with enormous consequences for U.S. domestic social, economic, and political life.

8. **Economics and trade**. With Latin America's economic takeoff of the last forty years, its rising industry and growing prosperity, the region looks like a prime area for U.S. trade and commerce. Indeed, with Russia in chaos, the European Economic Community more and more closed off by protectionist barriers and trade restrictions, and Japan forming its own closed market in Asia, Latin America looks better and better from a trade viewpoint. One would have to be blind not to see a future, almost inevitable common market arrangement here: the United States has the technology, know-how, capital, and markets; Latin America has abundant labor supplies, raw materials, booming manufacturing, and rising markets. We return to this important theme in the final chapter.

9. **Mutuality of interests**. It used to be that Latin America was far removed from the United States, not only in terms of miles but also psychologically. Cultural differences between the two parts of the Americas still exist, but the common interests are now at least as important: democracy, human rights, trade, economic development, free and open markets. These common-agenda goals have reduced the differences between the United States and Latin America and also made it much easier than in the past for the two Americas to work together.

All these factors should help bring the United States and Latin America together despite the end of the Cold War; they reflect a newfound commonality of interests, and provide abundant reasons for continued close involvement there. Indeed, in this new era of mutual interdependence on such a wide range of issues, Latin America may be more important to us now than it was during the Cold War.

Other Actors in Latin America

It used to be that the United States pretty much had Latin America to itself. In the familiar metaphors of an earlier time, the Caribbean was "our lake" and the entire Western Hemisphere was "our sphere of influence." As we have seen, this notion of U.S. hegemony in Latin America had its origins in the nineteenth century, but it reached its high point during the Cold War. Until the 1960s, as one former secretary of state put it, the United States was "practically sovereign" in the Western Hemisphere.

Beginning roughly in the 1960s, other actors began to play a role—though often still comparatively small—in Latin America. These included the Soviet Union, Germany, France, Great Britain, Spain, Japan, Israel, the Republic of China (Taiwan), as well as other countries. The presence of all these other actors on the Latin American stage made the international politics of the area much more complicated.

The reasons for this new interest in Latin America by other outside nations were diverse. The Soviet Union was interested in expanding its strategic and commercial ties, and in causing problems for U.S. policy. Most of the European countries as well as Japan—now much more prosperous than previously and thus able to afford a larger international role—were mainly interested in commerce and trade relations with Latin America, but they also had political and diplomatic interests in the area. Spain had special ties of history and culture to Latin America that it wished to expand. Israel and Taiwan, both isolated nations internationally, wanted to augment their diplomatic support from the Latin American nations. At the same time, Latin America itself, long isolated from the world historically, wished to expand its trade and diplomacy with other nations and thus reduce its heavy reliance on the United States.

Let us look individually at each of these countries and their interests in Latin America.

Russia

The Soviet Union saw Latin America as an area in which its diplomatic, trade, and strategic interests might be advanced, and as a way to embarrass the United States in its own backyard. The Soviet Union had long sponsored communist parties and communist trade unions in Latin America; after Cuba's revolution in 1959, the Soviets also had a reliable ally and military base in the region. With the Cubans often leading the way, the Soviets during the 1960s and 1970s helped sponsor guerrilla movements, terrorism, and subversion throughout Latin America—all aimed at causing problems for the United States and tying up U.S. resources. By the late 1970s, with ongoing revolutions in Nicaragua, El Salvador, and Grenada, and countries like

Guyana and Jamaica going radically to the left, Soviet policy seemed to be succeeding.

But Soviet power and global reach were stretched very thin, and the Soviet Union was probably not as great a threat as many thought at the time. As the Soviet Union began to crack and eventually crumble in the 1980s and the Cold War came to an end, the Soviet threat also ended and the Russian presence in Latin America largely evaporated. Russia still has some trade interests in the area, mainly in Argentina and Brazil, and a kind of residual interest in Cuba. But for Russia, Latin America is distant, only limited interests are involved, and therefore we can expect continued declining ties to the area. An additional consequence of the Soviet Union's disintegration has been the decline of the formerly Soviet-sponsored communist parties in the area, of Latin American sympathy for Marxist solutions, and of most of the guerrilla movements that once were so prominent.

Germany

The Federal Republic of Germany (West Germany) began to show a rising interest in Latin America during the 1960s. Germany's interests were mainly in trade and commerce, but also included political and diplomatic interests. Both on a governmental level and through the foundations associated with Germany's two main political parties (Social Democrats and Christian Democrats), Germany sought to influence Latin American trade unionists, peasant leaders, political party heads, university students, and government officials. Though German foreign ministry officials often worked closely with U.S. government officials, in many areas the United States and Germany plainly were competitors—which generated some friction. In the 1980s, Germany also staked out different positions on Central America and other issues.

But now, with the reunification of Germany and Germany's proximity to and interests in Eastern Europe, Germany has its hands full in its own neighborhood. Germany is still a significant actor in Latin America, but a declining one. Its trade, diplomacy, and military/strategic ties are overwhelmingly in Europe, while its Latin American interests seem no longer as important.

France

France has the advantage of exerting a great deal of cultural influence in Latin America. French ideas since Rousseau and the Enlightenment have had a strong impact on Latin America; for educated Latin Americans, French was (now it is usually English) their second language; and the French newspaper *Le Monde* is often displayed prominently (but seldom read) on Latin American coffee tables. There are French schools throughout Latin America and many French cultural events; at the same time, when Latin Americans travel, Paris is one of the places they *must* see.

French commercial and diplomatic ties with Latin America, like Germany's, began to increase in the 1960s and 1970s. In addition, France began to distance itself from U.S. policy in the region. But now France, again like Germany, is preoccupied with Europe—with the Common Market and with European integration. Its interests in Latin America have therefore been in decline in recent years.

Great Britain

The story is largely the same as regards Great Britain. During the 1960s, the country developed a large number of new Latin American studies centers, and it expanded its commercial ties with Latin America. But during Latin America's economic downturn in the 1980s, Latin America came to look less attractive from an investment standpoint; furthermore, Great Britain was also wrapped up in the great issues of the future of Europe and not so much that of Latin America. A special factor in Great Britain's case was its 1982 war with Argentina over the Falklands/Malvinas Islands, which soured British–Latin American relations. So, like Germany and France, Great Britain seems to be less interested in Latin America.

Spain

Because of common ties of language, law, culture, and history, Spain's relations with Latin America are special. Unlike the other European countries, Spain has an ongoing and expanding interest in Latin America—quite independent of fluctuating trade relations.

Spain had long sought to reestablish a presence in Latin America—even after its expulsion from the area in the nineteenth-century wars of independence and its defeat by the United States in the war of 1898. But Spain was a poor country, and for a long time its Latin American relations were limited to nostalgic references to past ages and glories. More recently, however, Spain has sought to present itself to Latin America as a model of democracy and human rights. Spain is also more prosperous now, and its investments in Latin America are expanding. The Spanish king, prime ministers, and cultural groups have made repeated visits to Latin America seeking to enhance Spain's presence.

But Spain still has few resources to spend in Latin America, and its institutional infrastructure (Latin America research centers and the like) for dealing with Latin America is still quite limited. Furthermore, Spain is itself now a member of the European Economic Community, and it has European loyalties and obligations. Spain wants to be "in" Europe but also to have a "special relationship" with Latin America, and it is sometimes a struggle to do both.

Japan

Japan's interests in Latin America are almost exclusively commercial. That means that its ties with the area are chiefly with the larger, stabler countries that have large resources and large internal markets: Mexico, Chile, Argentina, Brazil, and Venezuela. By building factories in Mexico, Japan feels that it will be better able to export goods to the United States once the North American Free Trade Agreement takes effect. There are also sizable Japanese immigrant communities in such countries as Brazil and Peru. On the diplomatic and strategic front, Japan recognizes that Latin America is largely a U.S. preserve, and therefore it has not been very active in these areas.

Israel

Israel's relations with Latin America, in contrast to the other countries, are not commercial but almost exclusively political and diplomatic. Because of its treatment of the Palestinians, Israel was for a long time considered a pariah state by the Third World and isolated by it. To counter this tendency Israel opened embassies throughout Latin America, sent technical experts to help these countries, and sought to expand the number of Israeli scholars and diplomats with expertise on Latin America. Israel is less isolated now, but it still seeks to keep a small although active mission in all of the Latin American countries.

Republic of China (Taiwan)

The Republic of China (Taiwan) is in some ways like Israel: a small, isolated country that is something of an outcast in world politics. That is because the "other" China, the People's Republic of China, is so much larger and has insisted that countries wishing good relations with it cannot have relations with Taiwan. Thus, Taiwan has been cast out of the family of nations at some levels and must struggle for international support and recognition. Rather like Israel, therefore, Taiwan has opened embassies and missions throughout Latin America, promoted very active programs in the region, and arranged for numerous Latin American heads of state to visit Taiwan.

But Taiwan's interest in Latin America has also been commercial. Taiwanese trade missions are frequently present in Latin America, Taiwan sells its finished products to Latin America, and it buys primary products from the area. Taiwan, though a small country, has followed an aggressive commercial and diplomatic policy in Latin America.

Other Countries

Most of the other European countries—Holland, Italy, Belgium, the nations of Scandinavia—have small and limited interests in Latin America. They have modest diplomatic missions, small aid programs, and limited commerce with the area. Some of these countries, despite their limited acquaintance with Latin America, have nonetheless been strongly critical of U.S. policy in the area. Among other things, that posture enables them to be anti-American and thus keep the domestic left in their own countries happy, but to enjoy the luxury to do so in an area of the world where they have very little interest.

Saudi Arabia is now opening up relations with more Latin American countries, especially other oil producers. Iraq, Iran, Syria, and Libya are developing political and commercial ties in the area. Australia, also occupying the Southern Hemisphere, is beginning to develop an interest in Latin America. Canada has joined the Organization of American States (OAS) and has both trade and humanitarian interests in the area. China (the People's Republic) is also establishing a presence in the area.

Perhaps the most striking feature of this survey is that most of the major countries—Russia, Germany, France, Great Britain—have declining interests in Latin America. The reasons are varied, but the practical result is that Latin America has now been thrown more than ever back into the arms of the United States. For good or ill (mostly the former), the United States is once again the overwhelmingly dominant and most important power in Latin America. All of Latin America's efforts in the past two decades to diversify its trade and diplomatic relations and thus reduce the hegemony of the United States have produced a situation in which the United States is again dominant and will be for a long time to come. None of the other countries mentioned, now or in the foreseeable future, can replace the United States as the dominant power in the region. Most Latin American countries and leaders have reacted pragmatically and realistically to this trend. It is a theme to which we return in the Conclusion.

Relations Among Latin American Countries

Historically, the Latin American nations had only limited relations with each other as well as with the outside world. Their ties, when they had any, were with Madrid, Paris, or Washington, but seldom with one another. We often speak of "Latin America" as if it were one entity with a single interest; but, in fact, the region is exceedingly diverse, and the countries of the area have no one single interest that they try to protect, nor do they present a common front diplomatically. Only in recent decades have we begun to see concerted Latin American efforts to develop common policies and the institutional structures to carry them out effectively.

Here we focus on three agendas: economic, diplomatic, and strategic. As regards economic integration, the fact is that most of the Latin American countries are competitors with one another rather than being economically complementary. They all (or almost all) produce bananas or coffee or sugar or other primary products. In addition, the countries of Latin America are often intensely jealous of or have hard feelings toward each other (Chile and Argentina, for example, or Argentina and Brazil, Colombia and Venezuela, Costa Rica and Nicaragua, El Salvador and Honduras, Haiti and the Dominican Republic). These differences are political and nationalistic, but they are often also social, cultural, and racial, which makes them nastier. So, even though these are often small and poor economies with small markets and slim resources that need to be integrated into larger units, in practice such integration has proved to be very difficult.

The movement toward economic integration in Latin America began in the 1960s. A Caribbean Common Market, Central American Common Market, and the Andean Pact all came into existence; in addition, an Institute for Latin American Integration (INTAL) was created as a subsidiary of the Inter-American Development Bank to help further integration. These efforts produced *some* positive benefits for intraregional trade, but overall the results were disappointing for the reasons given above, and Latin America never achieved the level of integration of Western Europe. In the 1970s and 1980s, integration efforts continued to sputter.

But with Latin America's economic recovery, and even boom, in the 1990s, economic integration efforts were revived as well. With the settlement of the troublesome Nicaragua and El Salvador conflicts, the Central American Common Market was revived, the Andean Pact began to take on new life, and Argentina and Brazil as well as the smaller states on their borders came together to form MERCOSUR (the Southern Market). There are still many difficulties—political as well as economic—in advancing Latin American integration efforts; but such efforts *do* help (although still marginally) in Latin America's economic development and they *do* provide, albeit in small ways, a means to bring the Latin American countries together.

On the diplomatic side, Latin American has long been interested in countering the fact of overwhelming U.S. power in the Western Hemisphere. Since the end of the nineteenth century and especially since the Spanish-American War of 1898, the Latin American states have recognized the far greater power of the United States as compared with their own and have tried to hem that power in. At numerous conferences dating back to the 1880s, Latin America has tried to limit U.S. might, to force the United States to consult with Latin America, and to prevent intervention. However, these efforts did not deter the United States from acting unilaterally or intervening repeatedly in Central America and the Caribbean during the early decades of the twentieth century.

Following World War II, the United States and Latin America created the Organization of American States (OAS) and signed the Rio Treaty and the Act of Chapultepec. The OAS was fashioned as a regional body, comparable to the United Nations at the global level, designed to deal with Latin American issues at the hemispheric level before they became larger, world problems. Most of the Latin American states envisioned the OAS as a check on the United States, whereas the United States, as the Cold War began to heat up, saw the OAS as a U.S.-led alliance to prevent communism in Latin America.

The Rio Treaty and the Act of Chapultepec helped provide mutual defense arrangements under which an attack on one member (the United States and the Latin American countries) was to be considered an attack on all, requiring a common response. But neither the OAS nor these mutual defense treaties served to prevent the United States from intervening militarily in Latin America when it felt its interests were affected. Such unilateral interventions by the United States occurred in Guatemala in 1954, Cuba in 1960–61, the Dominican Republic in 1965–66, Chile in 1970–73, and Panama in 1990. Moreover, when, in 1982, Argentina got into a war with Great Britain over the Falklands/Malvinas Islands and expected the United States to assist it as part of the Rio Treaty's mutual defense obligations, the United States instead supported its historic ally Great Britain, thus rendering the Rio Treaty all but null and void.

Because of these and other reasons (lack of interest on the part of member states, ineffective leadership within the organization, a cumbersome bureaucracy, budget shortages), the OAS was widely viewed in the 1980s as a worthless organization. In addition, the collective security arrangements of the Rio Treaty were in tatters. The OAS, for example, was all but completely useless in helping to solve the major crises in Central America (El Salvador and Nicaragua) during the 1980s. As a result, some of the Latin American countries began to operate outside of the OAS framework through more informal groups of nations to try to accomplish what the OAS could not. The Contadora group (so named because of the Panamanian resort island on which their leaders met), for example, consisting of Panama, Colombia, Venezuela, and Mexico, sought to mediate the Central American conflicts and helped provide political support to Costa Rican President Oscar Arias, whose peace plan assisted the United States and the several contending factions in El Salvador and Nicaragua in finding a way out of their conflicts. The Latin American countries are demonstrating a new vigor in pursuing a stronger, more diverse, more independent foreign policy.

But by the late 1980s, the OAS had also begun to revive. The United States paid some of its arrears, appointed an ambassador who actually spoke Spanish and knew Latin America, and began to take the organization seriously. Latin America also contributed to the OAS' revival.

The mutual defense/collective security arrangements of the Rio Pact remained uncertain, although efforts were also underway to revive it. Here, the key agency is the Inter-American Defense Board (IADB), which is the military arm of the OAS. In the wake of the Cold War, however, when there doesn't seem to be any external enemy, the functions the IADB would serve are no longer self-evident; in addition, Latin America remains suspicious of any agency that might be employed in a military exercise directed at them. The United States would like to see the IADB take up new activities: counternarcotics, disaster relief, and nation-building activities (building of roads and the like). But Latin America remains wary, and so far the idea of creating a permanent inter-American defense force to police border disputes or to mediate in strife-torn countries like Haiti, or of creating an associate membership in NATO (*North Atlantic Treaty Organization*) for the Latin American states, has foundered. Hence, while on the diplomatic front there are signs of revival of the inter-American system, in the military field there has been far less change.

At the heart of this discussion over Latin American foreign policy has loomed the issue of bilateral versus multilateral approaches. Because they are mostly small and weak, the Latin American states have long favored a multilateral approach to foreign policy, thinking that there is strength in numbers and that it is the only way to counter overwhelming U.S. power—hence their support for such multilateral agencies as the OAS and the Contadora group. The United States, in contrast, following a strategy of divide and conquer, has long preferred bilateral or one-on-one diplomacy whereby it can deal with each state individually. Bilateralism serves to enhance U.S. power while multilateralism offers the possibility of checking that power.

Recently, these positions, which prevailed during most of the history of U.S.–Latin American relations, have begun to change. The United States is now much more favorable toward multilateral bodies, recognizing that in the post–Cold War era it is useful to work through such agencies as the UN and the OAS. At the same time, the larger Latin American states such as Mexico, Brazil, Argentina, Chile, Colombia, and Venezuela are now sufficiently strong and self-confident that they usually prefer to deal with the United States directly and on a bilateral basis on most issues rather than on the basis of unwieldy multilateralism. For all states of the area, bilateralism and multilateralism now exist side by side, with each country using both of these depending on the issue and circumstances.

Latin America in the World Arena

For a long time, Latin America was known for the ability and cleverness of its international lawyers, quite a number of whom sat on international courts of justice or fashioned innovative principles of international law. Without demeaning these significant accomplishments, we should also say that they confirm another, realistic principle of international relations: strong states do things, while weak states produce international lawyers.

Actually, Latin America is now much more involved in the world arena than its past history, or the aphorism stated above, would indicate. The Latin American states are members of both the UN and the OAS, with Brazil starting to talk—because of its size and importance—about a permanent seat on the UN Security Council among the world's superpowers. Almost all the Latin American countries are members of such international bodies as the Universal Postal Union (UPU), the World Health Organization (WHO), the International Labor Organization (ILO), and many others.

It used to be that the Latin American countries maintained embassies in the United States and some (Spain, France, Germany, Great Britain) of the larger European countries, but that was about all. Their relations with one another and with the smaller European countries were mainly handled by consuls—often nationals living in a foreign country—or by itinerant businessmen. But now, the Latin American countries' webs of international relations are far more extensive than they were previously—with each other and with the outside world. As a Pacific nation, Chile has established growing relations with Australia and the larger South Pacific; Brazil has had a vigorous foreign policy in Africa. Argentina sent peace-keeping troops to the former Yugoslavia and is examining an associated role in NATO. Mexico has advisors in El Salvador and Nicaragua as part of a UN team. Venezuela aspires to be a regional power in the Caribbean while Brazil plans to replace Portugal as the international leader of the Portuguese-speaking world. Cuban troops and trainers were in more than twenty countries in the 1970s and 1980s serving both Cuban and Soviet foreign policy goals; Brazil sent a significant contingent of troops for the Inter-American peace force in the Dominican Republic in 1965; and Argentinian forces provided training in Central America in the 1980s. Both Argentina and Brazil seemed to be developing nuclear capacities in the 1970s and 1980s but later backed away from the development of nuclear weapons.

Throughout Latin America, the world of diplomacy, of contacts with the outside world, and of participation in international conferences and events has expanded enormously in the last thirty years. Not only is Latin America an active player in the international arena, but several countries of the area have taken on the role of regional or middle-level powers.

Toward Maturity in International Affairs

Latin America has long been isolated from the main currents of world history and of international affairs. But now that isolation is ending: not only is the outside world—the "global culture" of rock music, blue jeans, Coca-Cola, consumerism, and democracy—having its impact on the area, but Latin America itself is reaching out to make *its* impact on global politics. Clearly, we are in a new era in international affairs.

Latin America is no longer so defensive about its historical isolation and underdevelopment, nor does it feel that it must overcompensate for its weaknesses by being aggressive internationally—as Cuba was in the past. Instead, the task for Latin America and for those countries who have extensive relations with it—such as the United States—is to develop normal, regular, mature relations on a wide variety of issues of mutual interest. Both the United States and Latin America need to develop the same kind of mature, regular, multifaceted, almost "boring" relations that the United States has long had with Western Europe.

In the past, U.S. policy in Latin America has alternated between dramatic interventions on the one hand and benign neglect (which usually turned out to be not so benign) on the other. We need to put that history behind and to go forward on the basis of the pragmatic and mutually beneficial resolution of issues of common interest. On that basis, the United States and Latin America can develop good relations for the future that allow the mutual suspicions, ill will, and bad relations of the past to be put to rest.

12

✦

Conclusion

In 1992, we commemorated the 500th anniversary of Columbus's discovery of and encounter with America. The anniversary served as a reminder of both the long history of Latin America and the vast differences between the United States and its neighbors to the south.

Latin America, in contrast to the United States, was founded in the fifteenth and sixteenth centuries on an essentially feudal and medieval basis. Politically, that meant a hierarchical, authoritarian, top-down, centralized, and absolutist system of government; economically, it meant mercantilism, statism, exploitation, and inefficiency; and socially, it implied a rigid, unyielding, two-class system, reinforced by racial criteria, that kept the Latin American people locked in place. Religiously, it meant a similarly authoritarian, absolutist, top-down system that reinforced the social and political structure; while educationally and intellectually, it meant a focus on the traditions of absolute truth, rote memorization, and deductive reasoning. In contrast, the United States, settled and colonized a century and a half later, was founded on a modern (rationalist, pluralist, democratic, capitalist, and more secular) basis that goes a long way toward explaining why the United States forged ahead while Latin America lagged behind.

Much of Latin America's history over the last five hundred years can be read in terms of the effort to come to grips with—and eventually to overcome— the feudal/medieval legacy of its colonial past. Now, finally, although unevenly, by fits and starts and with the ever-present possibility of reversals, Latin America seems to be entering a new and more modern age. Change is everywhere in the air in Latin America, and the region is almost unrecognizable compared to what it was before.

The "New" Latin America

With independence in the early nineteenth century came republicanism and constitutionalism, but for a long time democracy was not a glove that fit very well in Latin America. Economic stimulus came in the late nineteenth century, and industrialization in the 1930s, but these occurred under state auspices and thus perpetuated the old mercantilism. Social change also accelerated beginning in the 1930s, but even with all the changes, the fundamentally two-class and semifeudal nature of the society was largely perpetuated. The more things changed in Latin America, the more they seemed to stay the same.

The most impressive and far-reaching changes in Latin America have come since the 1960s. Latin American life expectancy on average is now over 70 years, almost matching the life expectancy rates of the more developed countries. From being 70 percent illiterate in 1960, Latin America has now exactly reversed that percentage: 70 percent literate. A similar change has taken place with regard to urbanization (another index of modernity): thirty years ago Latin America was 70 percent rural; now it is 70 percent urban. These indicators mean that Latin America is no longer the "sleepy" area of "banana republics" that it was in decades past; rather, it has become dynamic, vibrant, alive. By every index of modernization, Latin America has become far more developed and modern.

Such vast social changes—commencing earlier but now more widespread—began in the late 1970s to restimulate political change and modernization as well. Recall that in 1977, twelve of the twenty countries were under military-authoritarian rule, and in five others the armed forces served as the power behind the throne. But by the 1990s, in one of the most remarkable transformations of the late twentieth century, eighteen of the twenty countries had become democratic. Only Haiti and Cuba remained as holdouts in this stirring shift to democracy, and even they offer some hope that democracy might be in the future. Of course, in several countries, democracy is still incomplete or partial, there are human rights abuses, and in a few countries democracy could conceivably be reversed. Moreover, we must recognize that democracy means not just the holding of elections but civil liberties, genuine freedom, real pluralism, and social justice. Nevertheless, even with these qualifications, the transition to democracy in Latin America of the last twenty years is an inspiring, stirring undertaking.

The economic reforms that followed the political changes have encountered more difficulty. Almost all of Latin America has now begun to abandon its earlier mercantilist or statist philosophy in favor of a reform program that emphasizes privatization, downsizing of government bureaucracies, greater honesty, free trade, and open markets. But it has been harder to implement these programs than to enact them in law. A lot—money, contracts, patronage, government jobs—is at stake. Most governments have ventured slowly into this new economic policy terrain; only a few—Mexico, Chile, Argentina—have made major reforms. Virtually all the countries of the area recognize that with foreign aid decreasing, they must now assume responsibility for their own economic futures; and this neoliberal economic reform package seems to be the only way to do it. The debate, unlike in past years, is no longer over whether to carry out open-market reforms, but only over how quickly and how deeply the changes should be made.

The final area of change—and to my mind the most important—is in the area of values. After all, it is relatively easy to change institutions and policies; but if the underlying values and practices do not change correspondingly, nothing much will have been altered. In Latin America, some of the most significant advances toward modernization are occurring in the area of values and attitudes, or what we earlier called "political culture."

Latin Americans are trying to hang on to those values that they (and others) believe are worthwhile in their culture: the emphasis on the family, on strong interpersonal relations, on being gracious and *simpático*. At the same time, however, they recognize that other, not-so-attractive values will have to go if they are to be considered modern nations and no longer outcasts among the family of nations. This includes the cronyism that leads to corruption, the authoritarianism that leads to widespread human rights violations, and the favoritism that excludes the bulk of the population from any consideration. In addition, Latin America recognizes that the United States is no longer able, financially and otherwise, to bail them out anymore; that no one else (Europe, Japan, China) will provide much in the way of assistance; and that they can no longer, as in the Cold War, play off the United States against the Soviet Union and thus get favors from both. To put it bluntly, Latin America has learned that it needs to shape up, to improve its educational system, to reduce corruption, to produce and compete rather than live under an umbrella of paternalism and protectionism, and to take charge of its own destiny and future since *no one* else will do it for them.

Modernization, Stability, and Change

Such sentiments, which are still unevenly spread throughout Latin America, can be seen as *both* a hopeful sign of modernization *and* a potential source of instability, even in democratic countries. Argentina, Brazil, and especially

Venezuela may be "models" in this regard. For example, Venezuela is a leader in Latin America: it had for a long time the highest per capita income in the hemisphere, it is highly literate and advanced by all indicators of social modernization, and it has been governed democratically and stably for almost forty years. Yet it is precisely because it is so advanced that Venezuela is currently in trouble. Its people are educated and sophisticated, and they share the sense of dignity that is part of Latin America's new value system. The Venezuelans are fed up with favoritism, with corruption, with special privileges, and with impunity. In the past, corruption was not only tolerated but expected. But now, among a literate population no longer willing to accept the historical levels of corruption in the country, there are widespread protests over government corruption, waste, and self-enrichment. Indeed, these protests have become so vocal that they may well destabilize the Venezuelan government. And remember, this is an elected democratic government, not a repressive or illegitimate one. Venezuela may therefore be a leader in Latin America not only toward development and democracy but also toward ridding itself of governments or leaders that violate these new norms of probity and good government.

While nearly all of Latin America has made enormous progress toward democracy in the last decade and toward development over several decades, some countries have made far more progress than others. We usually talk of and treat Latin America as a whole, and that is fine up to a point, but we also need to distinguish between countries. Thus far, it is the larger countries—Mexico, Colombia, Chile, Argentina, Brazil, Venezuela—those that are richer in resources, have larger internal markets, and are generally better institutionalized, that have been the success stories. To these we must add Costa Rica, Uruguay, and the formerly British Caribbean nations—all smaller and with limited resources but with a solid political infrastructure. All of these countries have made it into the ranks of Newly Industrialized Countries, or NICs. They are no longer poor countries but genuinely *developing* ones that have broken out of the interlocking vicious cycles of underdevelopment and are now achieving sustained growth. They are sufficiently affluent that they have "graduated" from poverty and are no longer eligible for U.S. foreign aid.

These successful counties must be distinguished from the less successful ones: Bolivia, Ecuador, Peru, and Paraguay in South America; Panama, El Salvador, Nicaragua, Honduras, and Guatemala in Central America; and the Dominican Republic in the Caribbean. These countries lack the natural resources of the larger countries, have small internal markets and therefore quite finite developmental possibilities, and have weak political institutions. These are countries in which a reversion to authoritarianism might still be possible.

But these are not countries for which one would predict a complete descent into chaos and disintegration—although Peru with its murderous guerrilla movement, Nicaragua with its severe economic problems, and El Salvador and Guatemala with their fratricidal social conflicts could conceivably experience such a fall. More likely is a scenario in which these countries, dragged along on the coattails of the more successful modernizers, also experience growth but at a slower pace than the NICs. In other words, all or virtually all of the Latin American nations will rise like ships on the ocean as the tide of economic growth comes in, but some will rise higher and faster than others, and the slow risers are more likely to be buffeted about by the storms that accompany the tides.

Almost nowhere in Latin America do we expect to see complete "basket cases" of social, political, and economic breakdown, comparable to Angola, Bangladesh, Somalia, or the former Yugoslavia. Among the Latin American nations, only Haiti falls in this "hopeless" category. Nicaragua, Peru, and perhaps El Salvador might conceivably be candidates for national breakdown; however, it's more likely that these deeply divided countries will continue to limp along without suffering a full breakdown. Cuba, as one of the last remaining communist countries in the world, is also in deep economic and political trouble; we can expect little change there until the regime of Fidel Castro is gone.

Among Third World areas, therefore, Latin America stands out along with Asia as one of the world's major success stories. Asia has its "tigers" (South Korea, Taiwan, Hong Kong, Singapore), but Latin America has Mexico, Chile, Argentina, Venezuela, Brazil, Costa Rica, Uruguay, and Colombia (without the drugs)—all of which have also done very well economically and politically. Asia also has its "second tier" (China, Thailand, Malaysia, India, Indonesia), which lag behind the leaders but are now starting to do well economically, just as in Latin America there is new dynamism in Central America, the Caribbean, and the smaller counties of South America. Finally, Asia has its problem cases: Cambodia, Burma, the Philippines—just as Latin America also has countries that have not yet quite made the breakthrough to modernity. But in both areas, the *overall* dynamism, progress, and change from past practices are very impressive. Latin America is now poised, we can realistically say, on the verge of a potentially unprecedented, long-lasting period of stability and growth.

U.S. Policy

The final question is, what should U.S. policy be in response to these changes in Latin America and to the "new Latin America" that has come into existence? Historically, the United States has not always done well by Latin America: we have ignored it, disparaged it, repeatedly intervened there, and given it as a low priority.

But now Latin America has changed markedly. It is no longer poor and backward. It is a major trade partner of the United States. The governments are more stable and democratic, which makes it easier for the United States to get along with them. The human rights situation is much better. The area has begun a major economic and political reform program, which will also make it easier for the United States to invest in, trade with, and deal with the area. In addition, the United States is now much more interdependent with Latin America on a host of issues including the environment, immigration, tourism, oil and natural gas, markets for U.S. products, investment, labor supplies, natural resources, and so on. Finally, what makes Latin America look better and better as a trading and commercial market is that other areas are getting harder and harder to penetrate: Japan is a tough market to crack, Europe is closing its doors, and China and Russia may be too chaotic and underdeveloped to be major markets.

That leaves Latin America. To make the most of this exciting opportunity, the United States must do several things. First, it needs to put its relations with the area on the same normal, regular, mature (as distinct from "benign neglect" or military interventions) basis that it has long maintained with Western Europe. Second, it needs to continue to monitor, encourage, and sometimes prod Latin America not only to maintain but to deepen its democratization and economic reform effort. Third, it needs to complete the shift now well under way by which open and free trade with Latin America replaces foreign aid as the main basis of the relationship. And fourth, now that the Cold War is over, it needs to elevate Latin America, which is a natural partner, in its list of priorities and begin thinking of the area no longer as a potential threat but as a partner in opportunity. On these bases, both U.S. interests and the developmental aspirations of Latin America can go forward at the same time.

Suggested Readings

Adie, Robert F., and Guy E. Poitras. *Latin America: The Politics of Immobility.* Englewood Cliffs, NJ: Prentice-Hall, 1974.

Anderson, Charles W. *Politics and Economic Change in Latin America.* Princeton, NJ: D. Van Nostrand, 1967.

Bushnell, David, and Neill Macauley. *The Emergence of Latin America in the Nineteenth Century.* New York: Oxford University Press, 1988.

Cardoso, Fernando Henrique, and Enzo Faletto. *Dependency and Development in Latin America.* Berkeley: University of California Press, 1978.

Cespedes, Guillermo. *Latin America: The Early Years.* New York: Knopf, 1974.

Chasteen, John Charles, and Joseph S. Tulchin (eds.). *Problems in Modern Latin American History.* Wilmington, DE: Scholarly Resources, 1994.

Collier, David (ed.). *The New Authoritarianism in Latin America.* Princeton, NJ: Princeton University Press, 1979.

Collier, Ruth Berins, and David Collier. *Shaping the Political Arena: Critical Junctures, the Labor Movement, and Regime Dynamics in Latin America.* Princeton, NJ: Princeton University Press, 1991.

Cortes Conde, Roberto. *The First Stages of Modernization in Spanish America.* New York: Harper & Row, 1974.

Dealy, Glen Caudill. *The Latin Americans: Spirit and Ethos.* Boulder, CO: Westview Press, 1992.

De Soto, Hernando. *The Other Path: The Invisible Revolution in the Third World.* New York: Harper & Row, 1989.

Falcoff, Mark, and Robert Royal (eds.). *The Continuing Crisis: U.S. Policy in Central America and the Caribbean.* Washington, DC: Ethics and Public Policy Center, 1987.

Fuentes, Carlos. *The Buried Mirror: Reflections on Spain and the New World.* New York: Houghton Mifflin, 1992.

Gibson, Charles (ed.). *The Black Legend: Anti-Spanish Attitudes in the Old World and the New.* New York: Knopf, 1971.

———. *Spain in America.* New York: Harper & Row, 1966.

Grindle, Merilee S. *State and Countryside: Development Policy and Agrarian Polities in Latin America.* Baltimore, MD: Johns Hopkins University Press, 1986.

Halperin, Donghi. *The Aftermath of Revolution in Latin America.* New York: Harper & Row, 1973.

Haring, C. H. *The Spanish Empire in America*. New York: Harcourt, Brace and World, 1963.

Kicza, John E. *The Indian in Latin American History*. Wilmington, DE: Scholarly Resources, 1993.

Kryzanek, Michael J. *U.S.–Latin American Relations*, 2nd ed. New York: Praeger, 1990.

Levine, Daniel H. *Religion and Politics in Latin America*. Princeton, NJ: Princeton University Press, 1981.

Lowenthal, Abraham F. *Partners in Conflict: The United States and Latin America*. Baltimore, MD: Johns Hopkins University Press, 1987.

Mander, John. *The Unrevolutionary Society: The Power of Latin American Conservatism in a Changing World*. New York: Knopf, 1969.

McCoy, Terry (ed.). *The Dynamics of Population Policy in Latin America*. Cambridge, MA: Ballinger, 1974.

Mercier Vega, Luis. *Roads to Power in Latin America*. New York: Praeger, 1969.

Mörner, Magnus. *Race and Class in Latin America*. New York: Columbia University Press, 1970.

Pastor, Robert. *Integration with Mexico: Options for U.S. Policy*. New York: The Twentieth Century Fund Press, 1993.

Pescatello, Ann M. *Power and Pawn: The Female in Iberian Families, Societies, and Cultures*. Westport, CT: Greenwood Press, 1976.

Pike, Fredrick B. *Spanish America, 1900–1970: Tradition and Social Innovation*. New York: Norton, 1973.

Riding, Alan. *Distant Neighbors: A Portrait of the Mexicans*. New York: Knopf, 1985.

Rodó, Jose Enrique. *Ariel*. Austin: University of Texas Press, 1988.

Silvert, Kalman. *The Conflict Society: Reaction and Revolution in Latin America*. New York: American Universities Field Staff, 1966.

Stepan, Alfred. *Rethinking Military Politics*. Princeton, NJ: Princeton University Press, 1988.

———. *State and Society: Peru in Comparative Perspective*. Princeton, NJ: Princeton University Press, 1978.

Tannenbaum, Frank. *Ten Keys to Latin America*. New York: Vintage, 1962.

Veliz, Claudio. *The Centralist Tradition in Latin America*. Princeton, NJ: Princeton University Press, 1980.

——— (ed.). *The Politics of Conformity in Latin America*. London: Oxford University Press, 1967.

Wagley, Charles. *The Latin American Tradition*. New York: Columbia University Press, 1968.

Wiarda, Howard. *Corporatism and National Development in Latin America*. Boulder, CO: Westview Press, 1981.

———. The *Democratic Revolution in Latin America*. New York: A Twentieth Century Fund Book, Holmes and Meier, 1990.

Wiarda, Howard, and Harvey F. Kline (eds.). *Latin American Politics and Development*, 4th ed. Boulder, CO: Westview Press, 1995.

Worcester, Donald E., and Wendell G. Schaeffer. *The Growth and Culture of Latin America*. New York: Oxford University Press, 1970.

Wynia, Gary W. *The Politics of Latin American Development*. New York: Cambridge University Press, 1990.

Index